IMAGES
of America

LAUREL

I0806334

ON THE COVER: The affordability of mass-produced automobiles during the 1920s fueled a growing demand for petroleum products, namely gasoline, motor oil, and asphalt. A major oil strike in the Oregon Basin of northern Wyoming spurred investors to build an oil refinery at Laurel, Montana, in 1929. Construction and, later, operation of the refinery employed scores of local men during the Great Depression. Crews worked long hours, often under challenging conditions, to get the refinery up and running. In this photograph, laborers take a break next to the domed tanks that stored crude oil shipped by rail to the Laurel refinery from northern Wyoming. (Courtesy of the Cenex Harvest States Refinery.)

IMAGES
of America

LAUREL

Ann Kooistra-Manning

ARCADIA
PUBLISHING

ISBN 978-1-4671-3311-1

Published by Arcadia Publishing
Charleston, South Carolina

Printed in the United States of America

Library of Congress Control Number: 2014958616

For all general information, please contact Arcadia Publishing:
Telephone 843-853-2070
Fax 843-853-0044
E-mail sales@arcadiapublishing.com
For customer service and orders:
Toll-Free 1-888-313-2665

Visit us on the Internet at www.arcadiapublishing.com

I dedicate this book to Elsie Johnston and everyone who has called Laurel home.

Contents

ACKNOWLEDGMENTS

This book was truly a community effort. I would like to thank all those who contributed photographs, stories, contacts, and research during this project. Without you, this book would not have been possible. I would like to begin by thanking Cody Allen at the Billings Public Library, Maxine Allman, Sedly Barsness, Brianna Bauer at the Yellowstone County Museum, Don Brohaugh, Michelle Caron, Janie Duncan, Vance George, T.J. Gilles, Steve Jackson of the Museum of the Rockies, Lilly Kooistra-Manning, Kathy Manders at St. Anthony's Catholic Church, Laurel High School, the *Laurel Outlook*, Laurel Museum president Jim Nelson, Barbara Nicholas, Allison Nys, Penny Redli of the Museum of the Beartooths, Nancy Schmidt and Geralyn Stevens at the Laurel Public Library, Gerald Shay, Dorothy Sitzman, and the Yellowstone Historic Preservation Board (YHPB). I am especially grateful to Marcia Hafner and Carrie Preller, who shared their space and companionship with me at the Laurel Chamber of Commerce while I scanned photograph after photograph from the Laurel Museum collection. Kevin Kooistra, the community historian at the Western Heritage Center, has earned my heartfelt appreciation for providing photographs and obscure historical resources. Judy Watson helped spread the word about the project and introduced me to Laurelites with historical photographs. Hal Dantic, who works at the Cenex Harvest States (CHS) Refinery, contributed a stunning collection of historical photographs documenting the construction and growth of the Laurel refinery. Ryan Mead deserves a hearty round of applause for digitally preserving and sharing with the community hundreds of iconic images depicting Laurel's heritage. Without a doubt, my gratitude extends to the late Elsie Johnston and the book committee members who devoted 12 years to researching and writing *Laurel's Story: a Montana Heritage*. Finally, I would like to thank my family, friends, and colleagues for their support and encouragement while I obsessively delved into the depths of Laurel's past.

INTRODUCTION

The town of Laurel sits in a valley framed by sandstone rimrocks to the north and the Beartooth and Pryor mountain ranges beyond the Yellowstone River to the south. The history of this Montana town is interlaced with the development of agriculture, railroads, tourism, and oil interests. It has seen prosperous times, when the city boomed, as well as economic challenges through the years.

Laurel's history began in 1882 when the Northern Pacific Railroad pushed through the Yellowstone Valley and established a station called Carlton. The next year, the railroad changed the name to Laurel to avoid confusion with another station along the rail line in Minnesota. By then, a small community of farmers, cattlemen, sheep growers, and horse breeders had settled along the Yellowstone near the mouth of the Clarks Fork River. A handful of businesses—two restaurants, a saloon, and a short-lived hotel—catered to the homesteaders, ranchers, and railroad workers in the vicinity. A ferry provided access to the homesteads and mining claims on lands ceded from the Crow Indian Reservation south of the Yellowstone River. Settlers established a school in 1885, and postal service was available at the section house that same year.

In 1889, the Rocky Fork and Cooke City Railroad hastily completed a line from the Northern Pacific Railroad south to the coal mines at Red Lodge with plans to continue into the mountains to the silver mines at Cooke City. That same year, the Rocky Fork Town and Electric Company platted the original townsite of Laurel south of the tracks about a mile west of the junction. The First Congregational Church and a parsonage were erected in 1891. Leon Rose built a two-story general store the following year. By 1899, the little community had grown to include two stores, a post office, a hotel, two saloons, a blacksmith shop, a livery stable, and a community hall. The railroad had also constructed a small depot on the north side of town.

Edgar Camp and his brother, Charles, opened a general store in Laurel in 1899. Soon after, Edgar's wife, Ida Camp, bought two parcels of land from the Minnesota and Montana Land and Improvement Company and platted a new townsite, called East Laurel, north of the Northern Pacific and Rocky Fork junction. By the end of the year, most of Laurel's residents and business owners had abandoned Old Laurel to set up shop in the new townsite. The new town prospered.

During the early 1900s, irrigated farming bolstered Laurel's growth as irrigation projects transformed the arid land around Laurel into prime farmland. A sugar beet processing plant opened in Billings in 1906, and the sugar company launched a two-fold campaign to develop the industry in the valley by enticing farmers to grow the lucrative but labor-intensive crop and recruiting farmworkers, primarily German-Russian immigrants, to work in the fields. Many of the immigrant farmworkers settled in neighborhoods south of the tracks in what came to be known as German Town.

Laurel grew so quickly that local contractors could not keep pace with the demand for homes and commercial buildings. Housing was in short supply, and a number of businesses operated from tent structures, some for a year or more, while waiting for wood-framed buildings to be erected. One contractor, Olaf Solso, constructed over 100 buildings in Laurel between 1906 and 1909, including a new brick high school that the community hoped would alleviate overcrowded conditions at Laurel's lone school.

Laurel incorporated in 1908 shortly before the Northern Pacific Railroad completed a major construction project to establish at Laurel a shipping and servicing center for the Northern Pacific, Burlington, and Great Northern railroads. The new facilities included a 40-stall roundhouse, shops, a new passenger depot, and the largest freight terminal yards between St. Paul and Seattle. With the transfer of the freighting terminal yards from Billings to Laurel in 1909, the city proclaimed a bright future.

Real estate development rapidly moved eastward toward the railroad facilities, fueled by investors such as Lucius Nutting, Walter Westbrook, Monroe Cramer, and William Allard. Building continued at a frenzied pace to accommodate the influx of railroad workers and their families and the new businesses attracted by Laurel's rosy prospects. Brick commercial blocks began to appear in the business district, and residential neighborhoods pushed northward. Laurel extended the city limits in 1919 to include the east-end neighborhoods, known as Railroad Town.

The Enlarged Homestead Acts of 1909 and 1912 brought a new wave of homesteaders to the valley seeking to establish dryland farms. Laurel's population continued to swell through the war years. Heavy rainfall produced bumper grain crops, and wheat fetched profitable prices. Farmers invested in new equipment, and local businesses expanded. The bottom fell out at the end of World War I. Grain prices collapsed while drought crippled production. By the early 1920s, Laurel was in the throes of economic depression with record numbers of farm foreclosures and bankruptcies and the failure of all three banks in the community.

The 1920s were bleak times in Laurel, its economy sustained primarily by the railroad, irrigated agriculture, and tourism. Laurel, on the Yellowstone Trail, had become a jumping off point for tourists bound for Yellowstone Park by rail and motorcar. As the rest of the nation plunged into the Great Depression, a major oil strike in northern Wyoming breathed new life into the community when investors began building an oil refinery south of town in 1929. The Laurel refinery contributed to Laurel's economic recovery and continued growth.

The next few decades brought new changes and challenges to the community. National chains moved into downtown Laurel, displacing local merchants. Technological innovations in the railroad industry reduced the need for the large crews of the past. The opening of the interstate shifted the commercial district from Main Street southward as new businesses sprang up between the tracks and the freeway. As Laurel's prosperity has ebbed and flowed, the people of Laurel have held tightly to pride of their community's history and heritage. The photographs and stories that follow retell the history of this small Montana town.

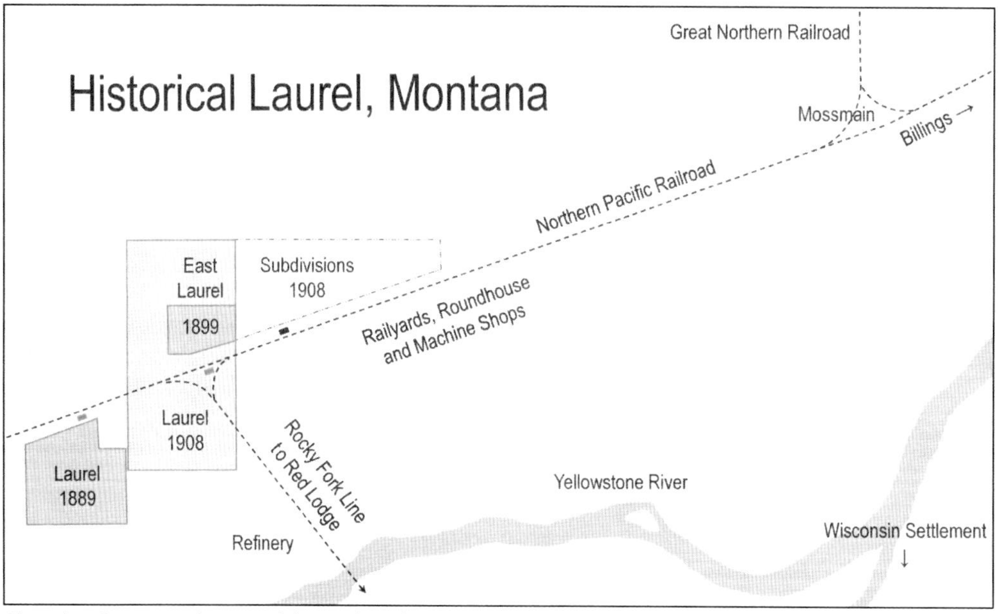

Shortly after completion of the railroad from Red Lodge to Laurel in 1889, the Rocky Fork Town and Electric Company platted the original townsite of Laurel. In 1899, Ida and Edgar B. Camp founded the present townsite, recorded as East Laurel, north of the tracks at the junction of the Northern Pacific and Rocky Fork lines. Within a decade, the fledgling community grew into a thriving railroad and agricultural center. (Courtesy of Ann Kooistra-Manning.)

One

Rivers, Rails, and Trails

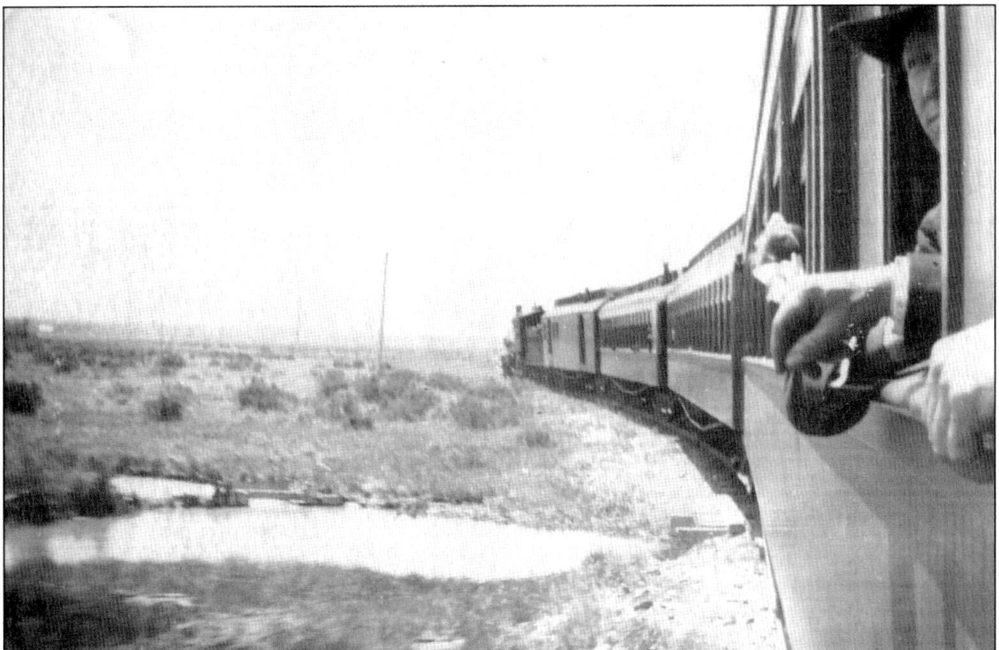

Arthur Frank Salsbury captured this scene of passengers leaving Laurel on a southbound train. This was a popular route for tourists bound for Yellowstone National Park by way of Cody, Wyoming. (Courtesy of the Western Heritage Center.)

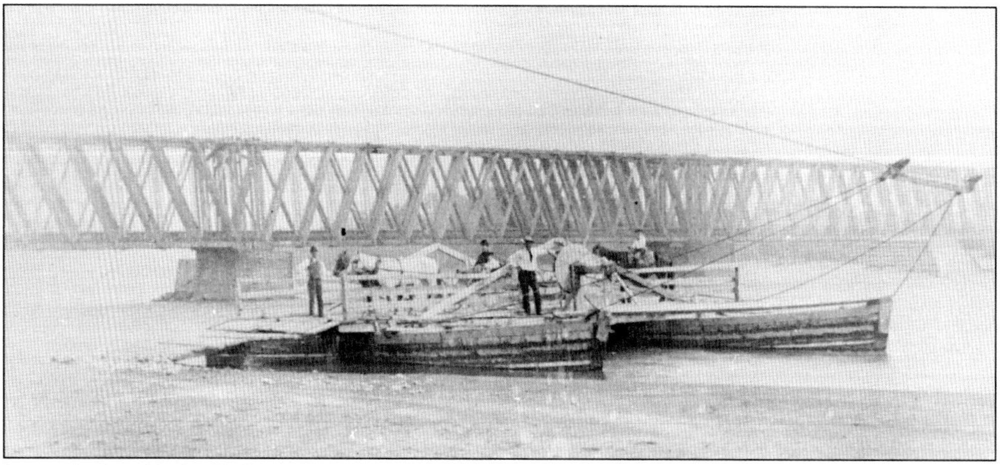

In 1883, the Clarks Fork Ferry Company installed a ferry across the Yellowstone River south of Laurel. Oliver Bundy bought the ferry in 1887. Bundy, pictured here at the helm, ferried horse-drawn wagons, farm machinery, and, at times, livestock from bank to bank a short distance upstream from the railroad bridge. (Courtesy of the Laurel Museum.)

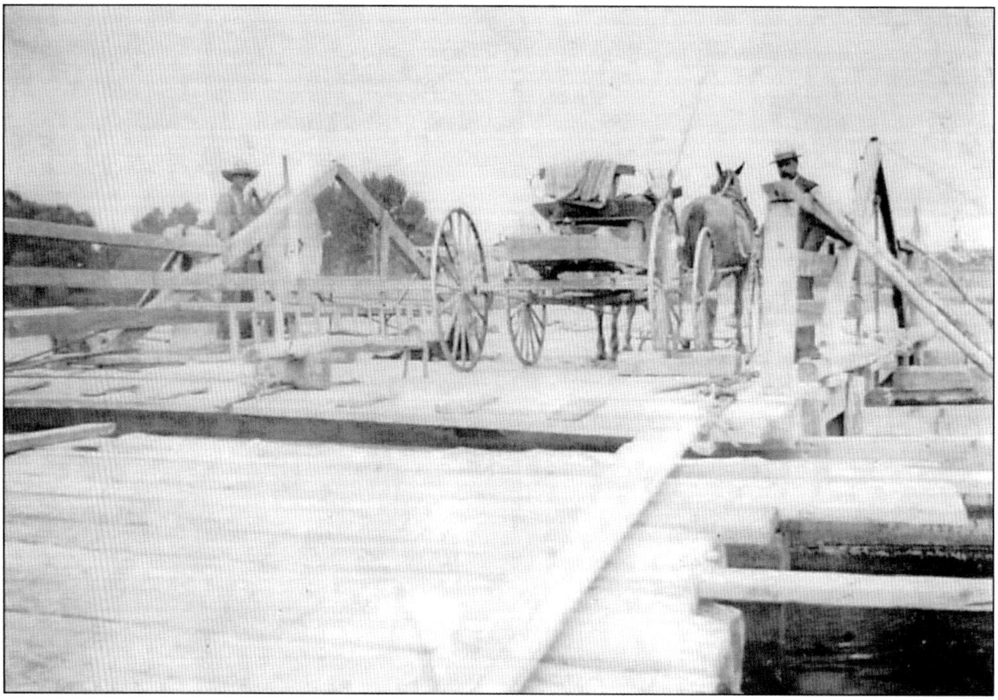

Before the Laurel wagon bridge opened in 1900, settlers south of the river faced up to a day's journey to cross by bridge at Columbus or Billings. The ferry, pictured here in 1898, was a lifeline to the north when the river was too high to ford. River crossings during spring runoff occasionally turned treacherous, overturning the ferry and dumping its cargo and passengers into the swift current. (Courtesy of the Yellowstone County Museum.)

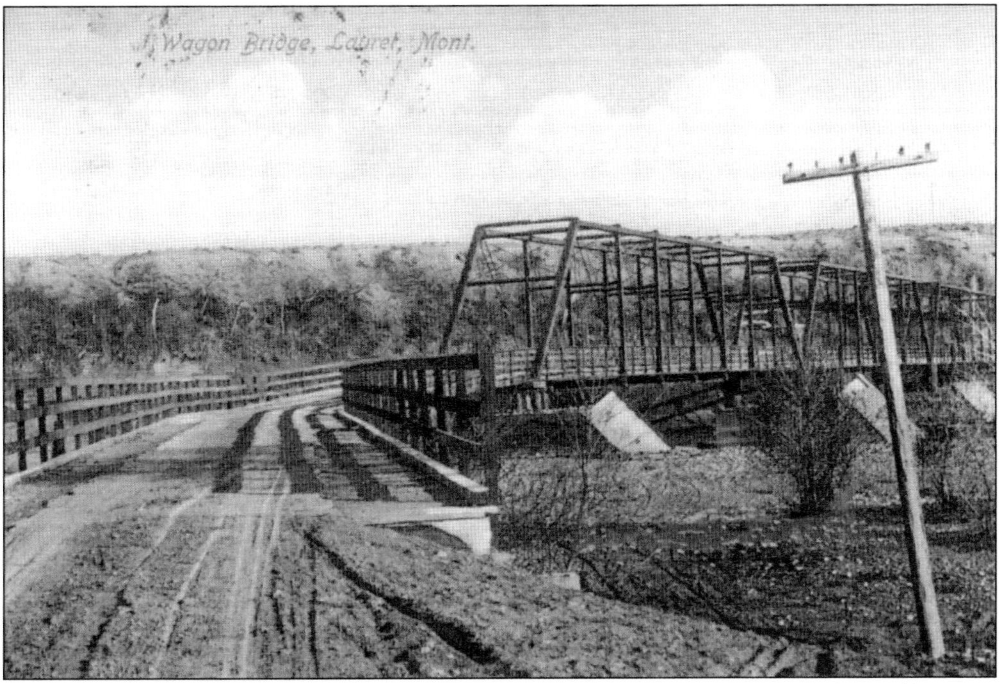

Laurel and communities south of the river in neighboring Carbon County rejoiced when Yellowstone County approved the building of a wagon bridge at Laurel in 1899. County commissioners awarded the contract to the lowest bidder, constrained to a $10,000 construction cost limit after Carbon County rebuffed a request to help finance the project. The Missouri Valley Iron and Bridge Company built the four-span Howe-truss bridge for $9,980. It spanned the river at a point midway between Laurel and Park City. The Old Red Bridge, as it was known to locals, opened to traffic in the spring of 1900 but, soon after, was badly damaged by ice, costing the county an additional $6,000 in repairs. Below, the Rutter, Kircheis, and Slater families pose along the bridge's railings around 1915. (Above, courtesy of Ryan Mead; below, courtesy of the Laurel Museum.)

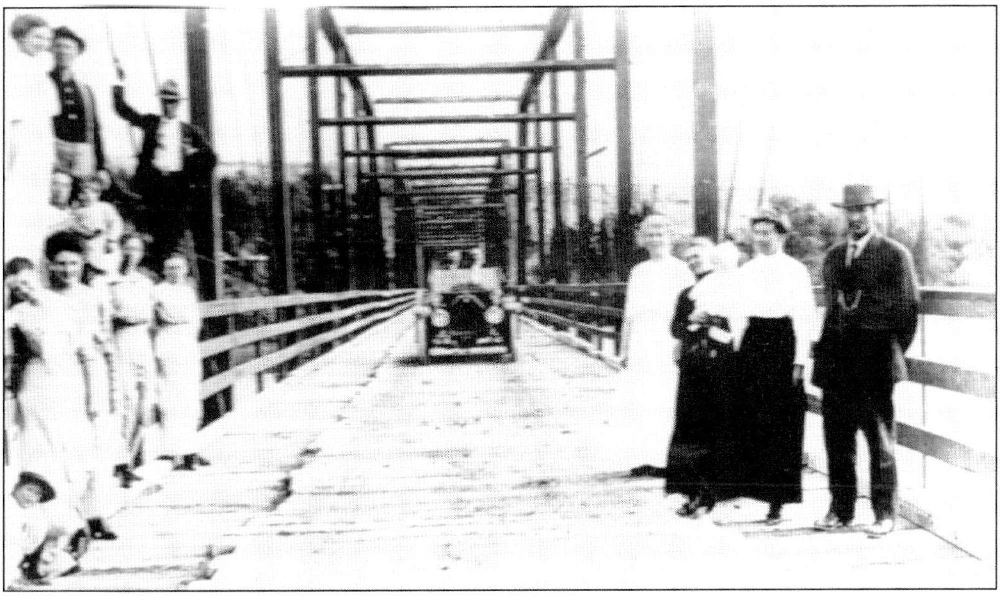

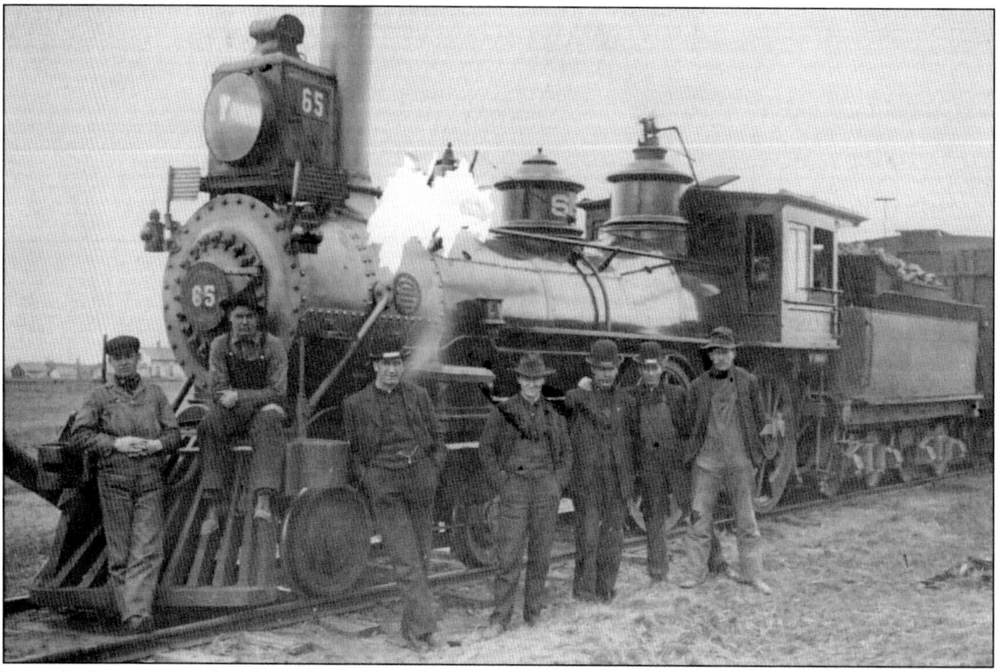

Laurel's heritage is closely tied to the railroads. Little more than a rail stop after the Northern Pacific Railroad pushed through the Yellowstone Valley in 1882, Laurel grew into a major shipping and servicing center for three major railroads with the completion of the roundhouse and railroad shops in 1908 and the relocation of the freight terminal yards from Billings to Laurel in 1909. (Courtesy of the Laurel Museum.)

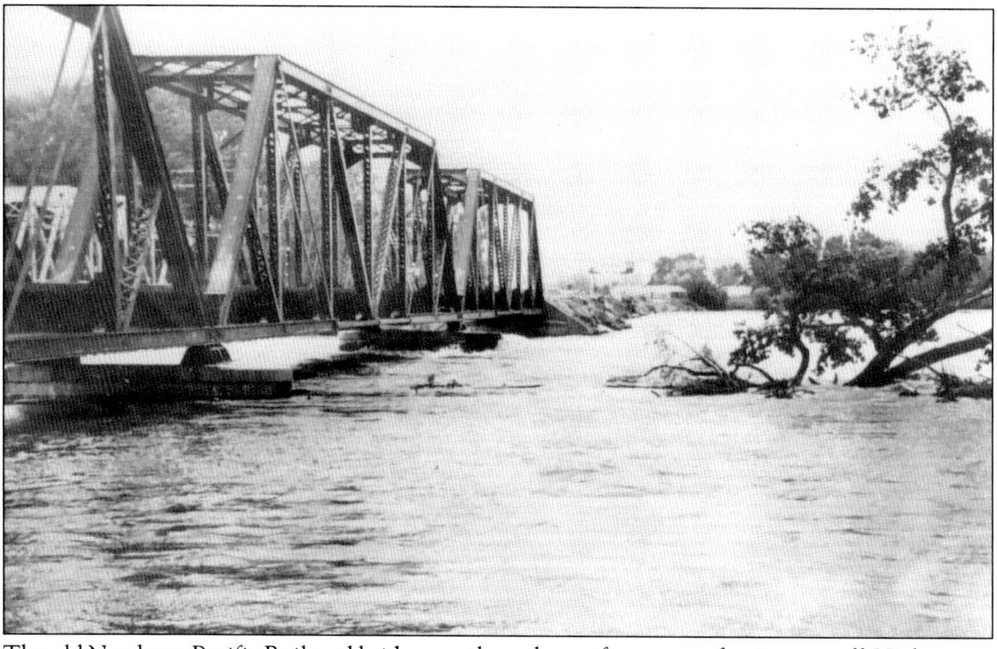

The old Northern Pacific Railroad bridge weathers the swift current of spring runoff. High water, drifting limbs, and ice jams wreaked havoc on early bridges over the Yellowstone and Clarks Fork Rivers. (Courtesy of the Laurel Museum.)

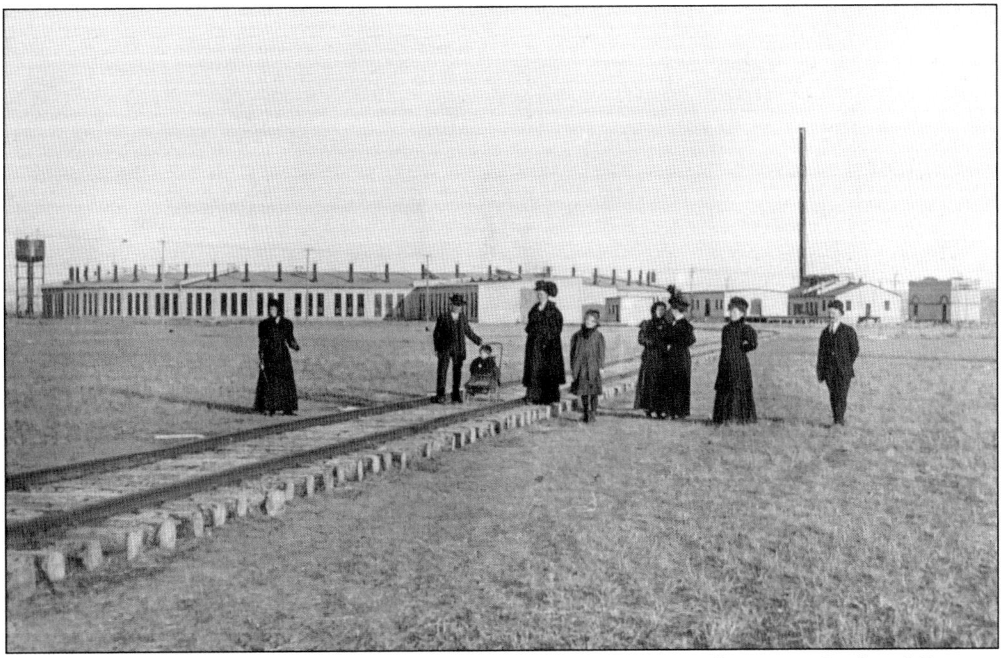

The families of Barber Atkins and Frank Valek tour the new roundhouse on Railroad Day, an elaborate event on July 4, 1909, celebrating the new Northern Pacific Railroad freight terminals at Laurel. The 40-stall roundhouse was completed the previous year, becoming the largest of its kind along the Northern Pacific line. (Courtesy of the Laurel Museum.)

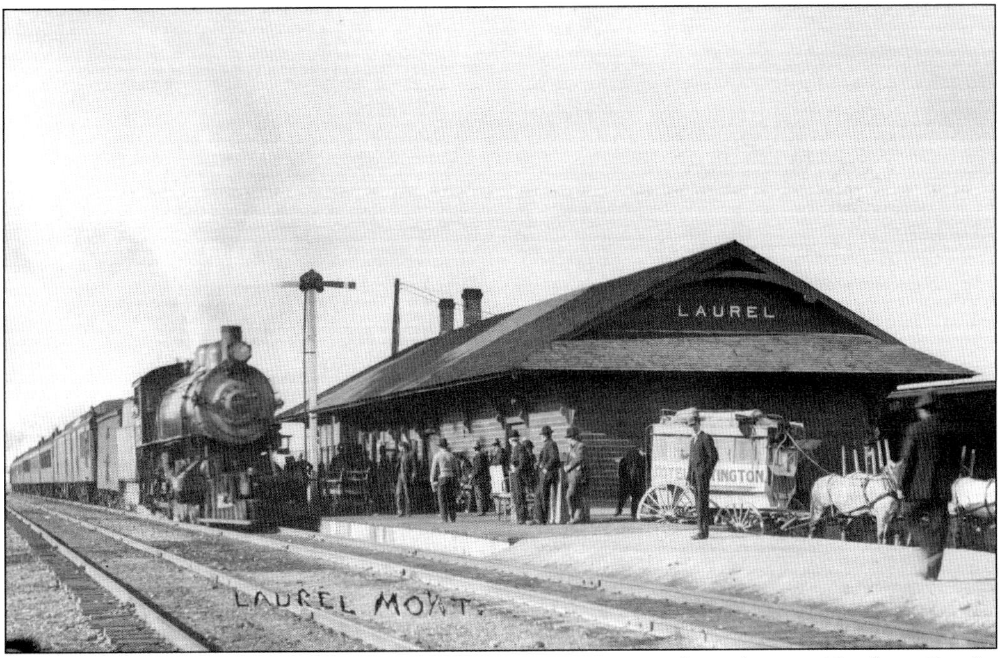

In 1909, a carriage stands ready to transport arriving passengers from the new Northern Pacific depot to the Hotel Boyington. The Hotel Boyington, better known as the Railroad Hotel, accommodated railroad employees as well as travelers. (Photograph by Slosson; courtesy of the Museum of the Rockies.)

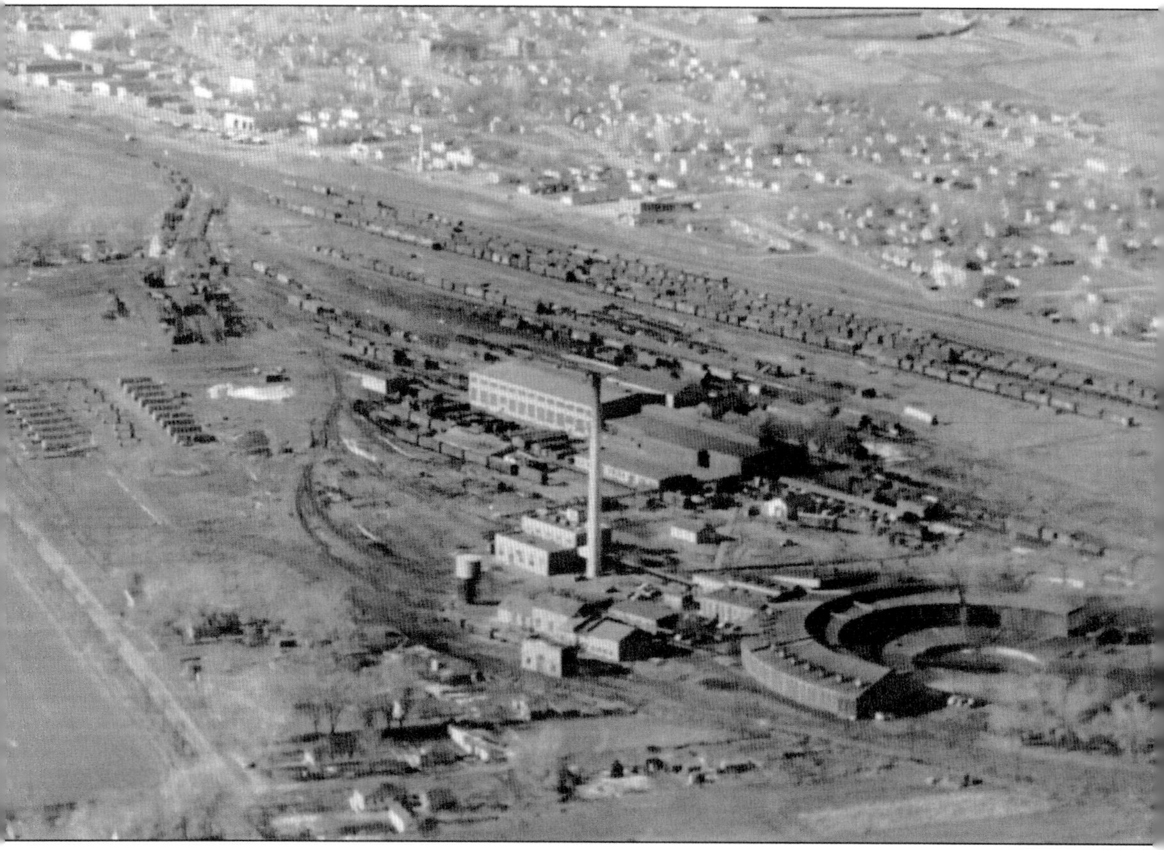

Laurel became a major freight transfer point for the Northern Pacific, Burlington, and Great Northern railroads. The expansive rail yards included a roundhouse, shops, an ice house, a freight depot, and loading docks. A water tower supplied water for powering the steam locomotives, and, eventually, a plant was built to make the 500-pound blocks of ice used to refrigerate boxcars. A passenger depot and beanery rounded out the facility. Newspapers lauded the railroad for transforming the fledgling community into a going concern. Such rapid growth did not come without a price. The newly incorporated city lacked water and sewer systems and struggled with a tight housing market and overcrowded schools. The 60-room hotel and 35 homes built in the Nutting Addition could not house all of the railroad employees and their families. Many made due by living in a boxcar village on the edge of the rail yards. (Courtesy of the Laurel Museum.)

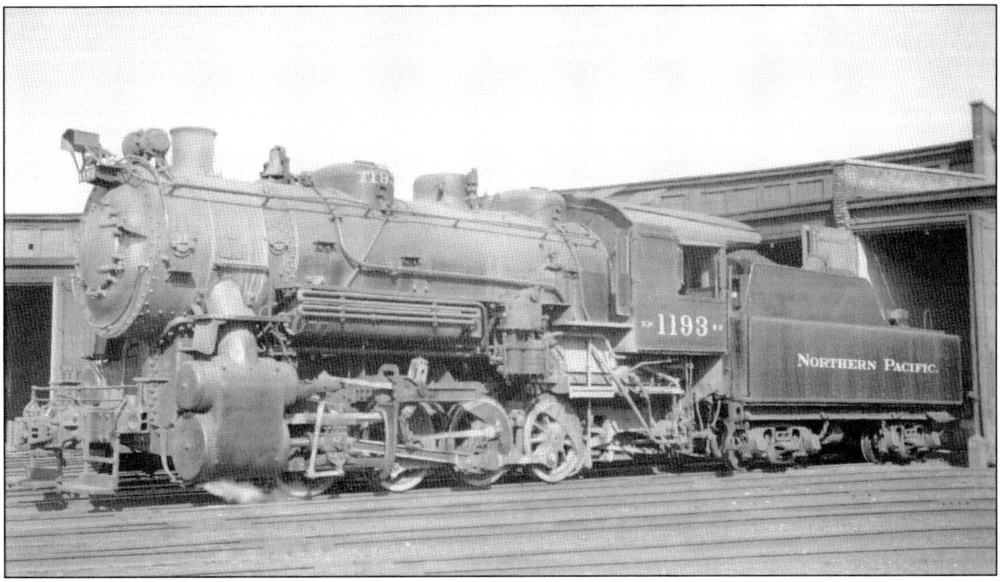

Northern Pacific Engine No. 1193 awaits repairs at the Laurel roundhouse in 1938. The Northern Pacific Railroad retired its fleet of steam engines by 1958, replacing them with faster and more efficient diesel locomotives. The shift to diesel engines and other industry innovations made the large crews that serviced and operated steam-powered locomotives a thing of the past. (Photograph by Warren R. McGee; courtesy of the Museum of the Rockies.)

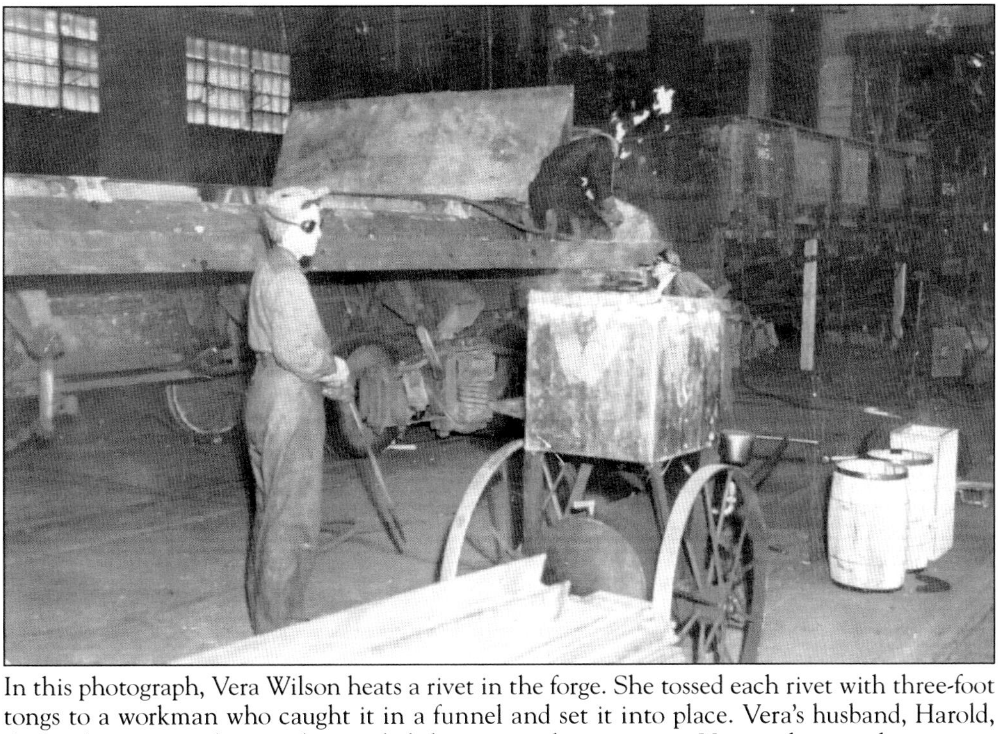
In this photograph, Vera Wilson heats a rivet in the forge. She tossed each rivet with three-foot tongs to a workman who caught it in a funnel and set it into place. Vera's husband, Harold, the workman atop the car, then sealed the rivet with an air gun. Vera and nine other women worked in the railroad shops during World War II while men served overseas. (Courtesy of the Laurel Museum.)

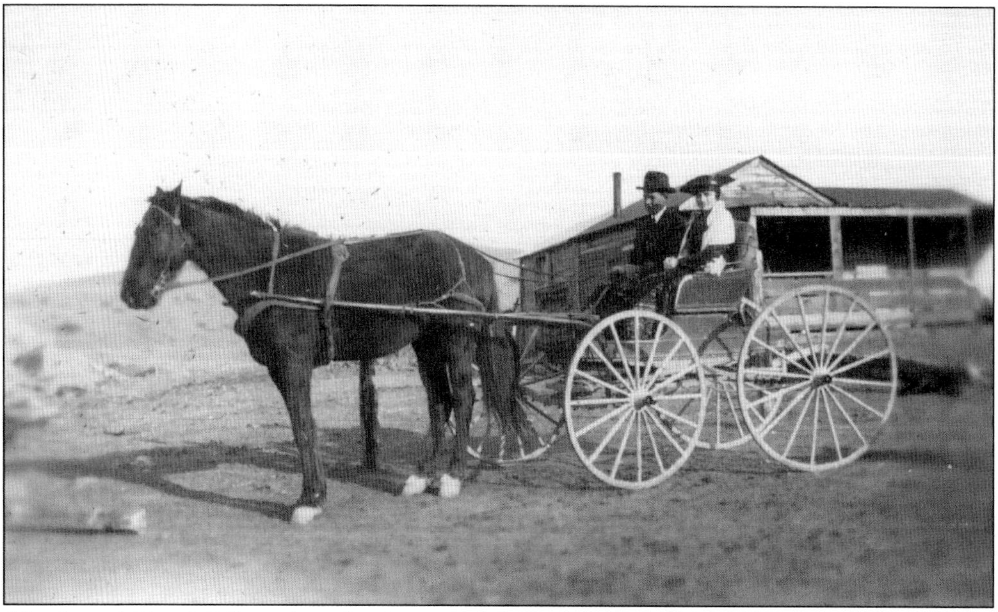

Claude and Hazel Gilbreath make the rounds by carriage, visiting family and friends in the Wisconsin Settlement in 1919. Hazel, the eldest daughter of James and Sarah Jordan, lived at the family homestead near Spring Creek before marrying and moving away. (Courtesy of the Laurel Public Library.)

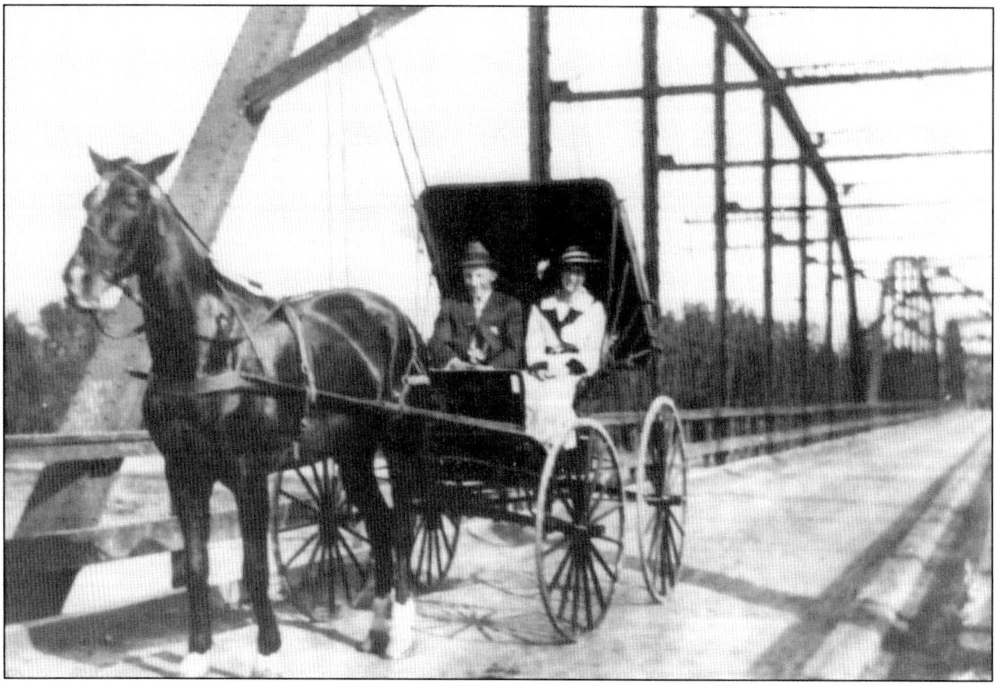

Roman Erb takes his cousin, Dorothy Young, for a carriage ride over the Yellowstone River during high water in 1915. (Courtesy of the Laurel Museum.)

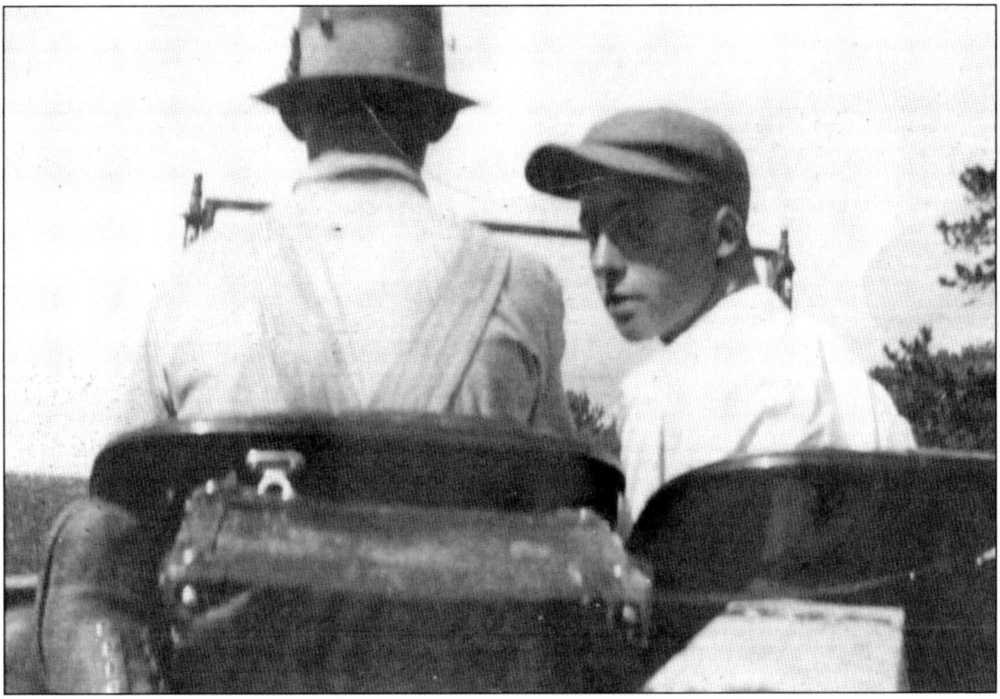

Motor touring gained popularity in the 1920s as many were drawn to leisurely explore America's scenic byways and national parks by car. Unfortunately, before the national Good Roads Movement gained momentum, motorists occasionally found themselves in the ditch or stuck in mud while traveling on country roads, often little more than rough, dirt tracks. (Above, courtesy of Gerald Shay; below, courtesy of the Laurel Museum.)

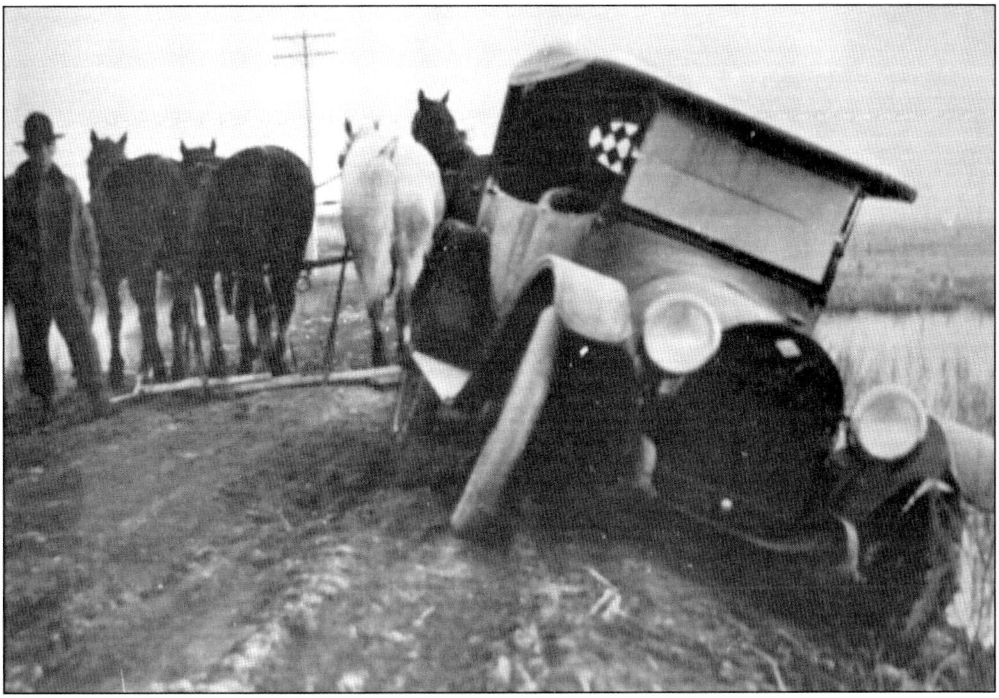

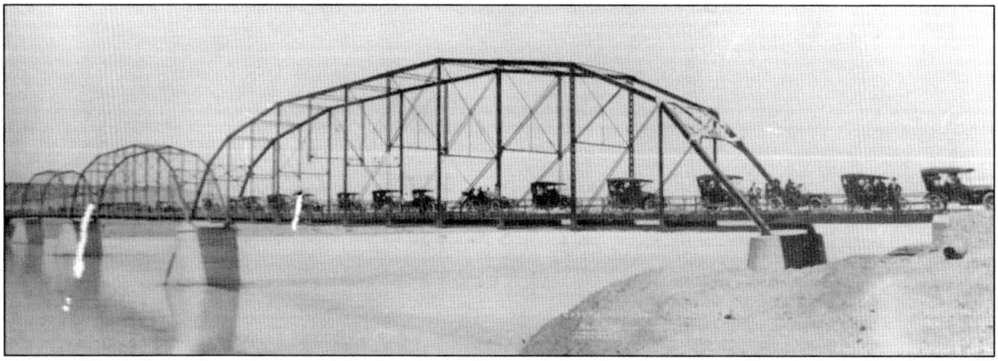

Automobiles span the new Laurel Bridge to celebrate the 1912 launch of the Yellowstone Trail. The Yellowstone Trail, an intercoastal highway with roadside tourist information tents and campsites, put Laurel on the map as a jumping off point for motorists headed to Yellowstone National Park's eastern gateway. The scenic Beartooth Highway opened in 1936, providing another route into the park by way of Red Lodge and Cooke City. (Courtesy of the Laurel Museum.)

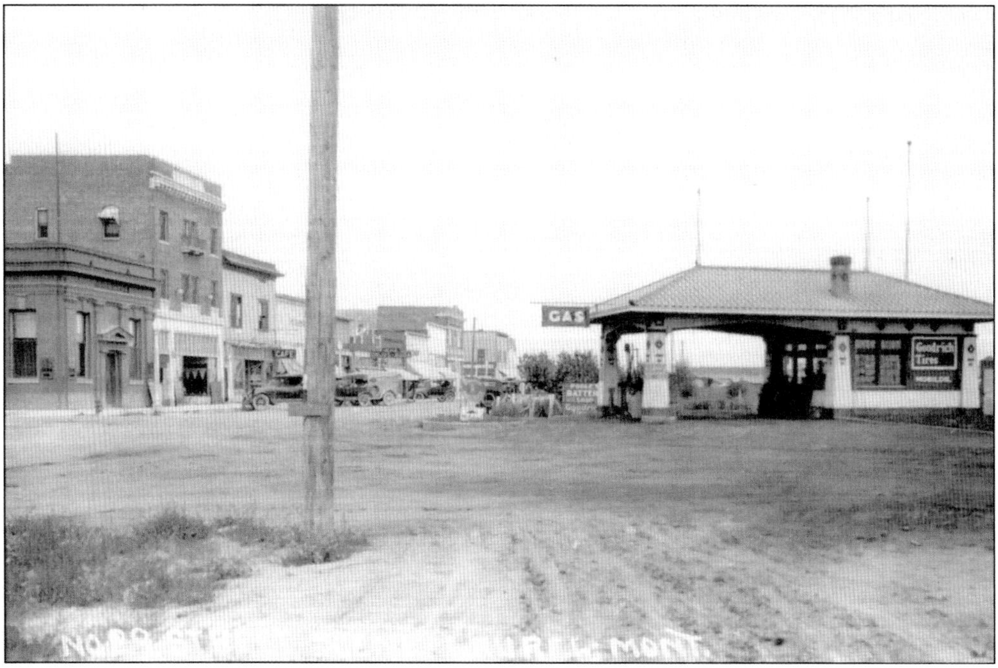

As more and more motorists took to the road, new gas stations and mechanic shops popped up in Laurel. This service station, conveniently located on the corner of First Avenue and Main Street, supplied motorists with gasoline, batteries, and tires. The service station moved a block west when the city widened the approach to the underpass in 1937. (Courtesy of Ryan Mead.)

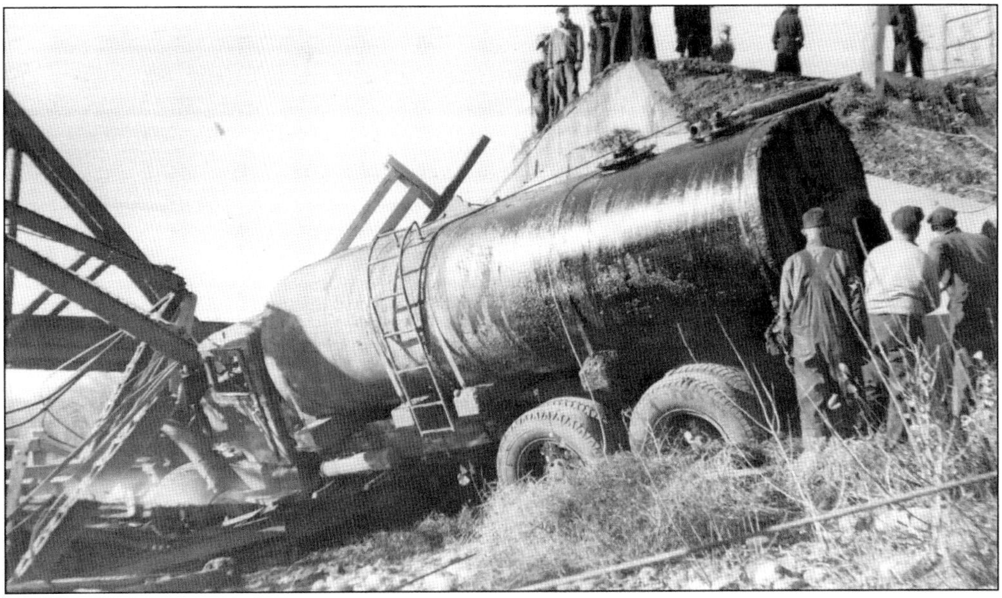

A span of the Laurel Bridge collapsed under the weight of a loaded oil tanker in 1935. The bridge, just east of the railroad bridge, was quickly repaired and continued in use until a federal project constructed a new steel-trussed bridge later that winter. (Both, courtesy of the Laurel Museum.)

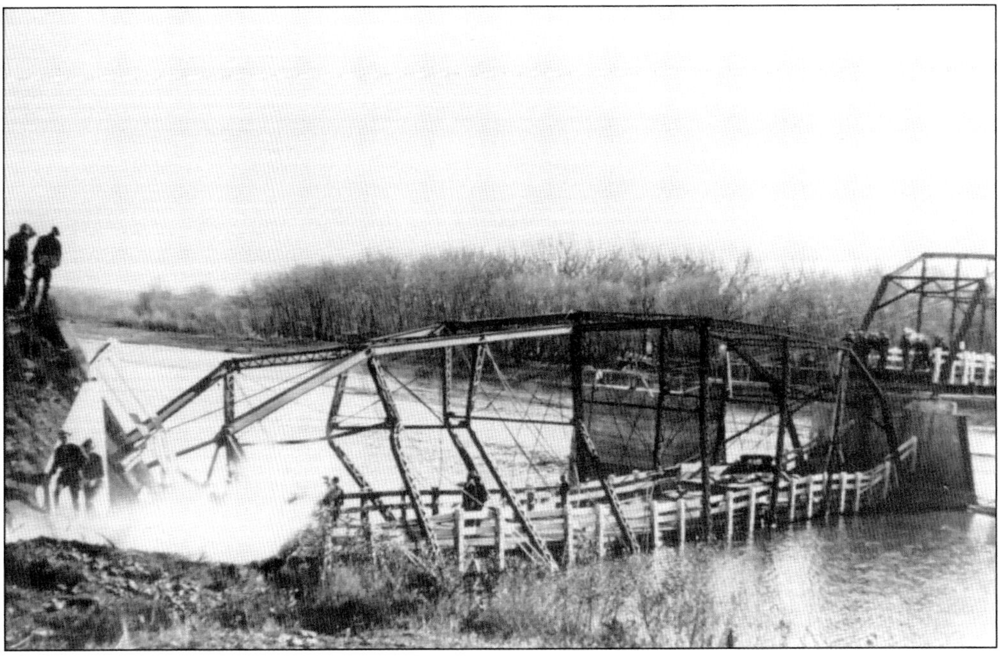

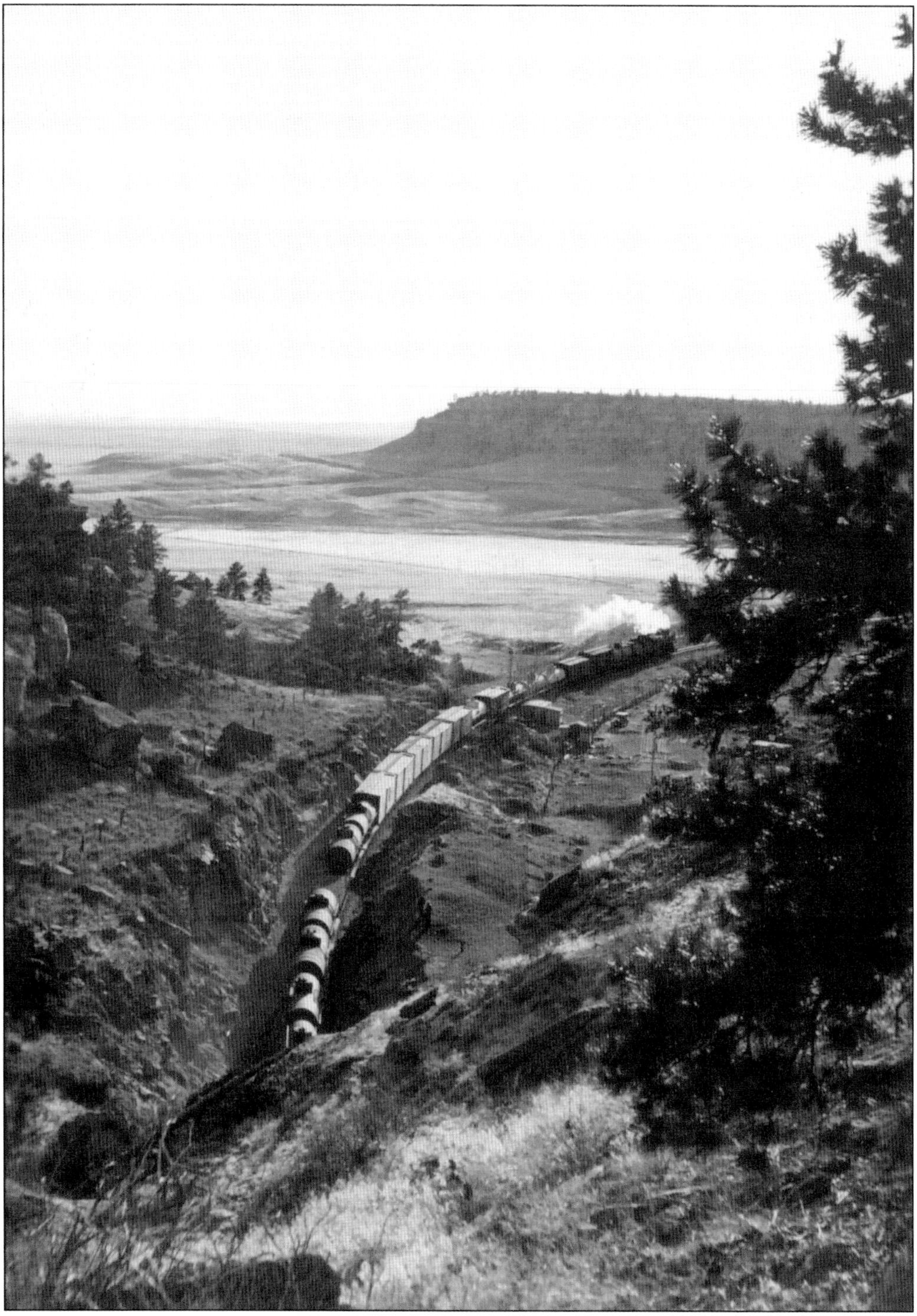

A Great Northern freight train passes through Echo Canyon on its way to Laurel. This branch line, originally chartered as the Billings and Northern Railroad, linked Great Northern's main line through northern Montana to the Northern Pacific Railway at Laurel in 1908. (Courtesy of the Western Heritage Center.)

Two

Carving a Living from the Land

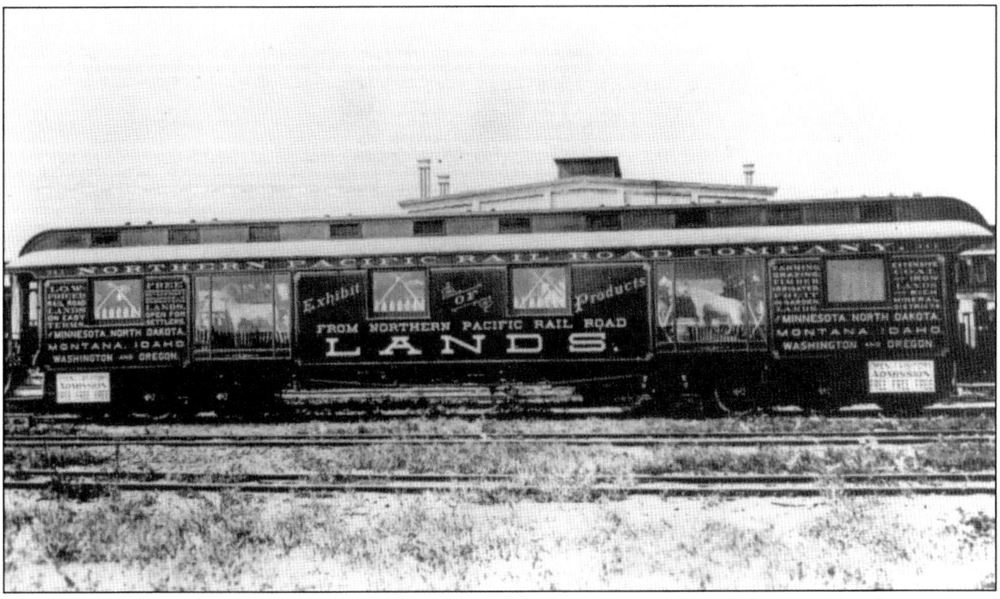

The Northern Pacific Railroad attracted American and European homeseekers and land speculators to the Yellowstone Valley through an aggressive advertising campaign. Illustrated brochures and traveling exhibits lauded the valley's rich agricultural and business prospects. The railroad further enticed settlement along its route by selling tracts of land for as little as $2.50 per acre through the Minnesota and Montana Land and Improvement Company. (Courtesy of the Western Heritage Center.)

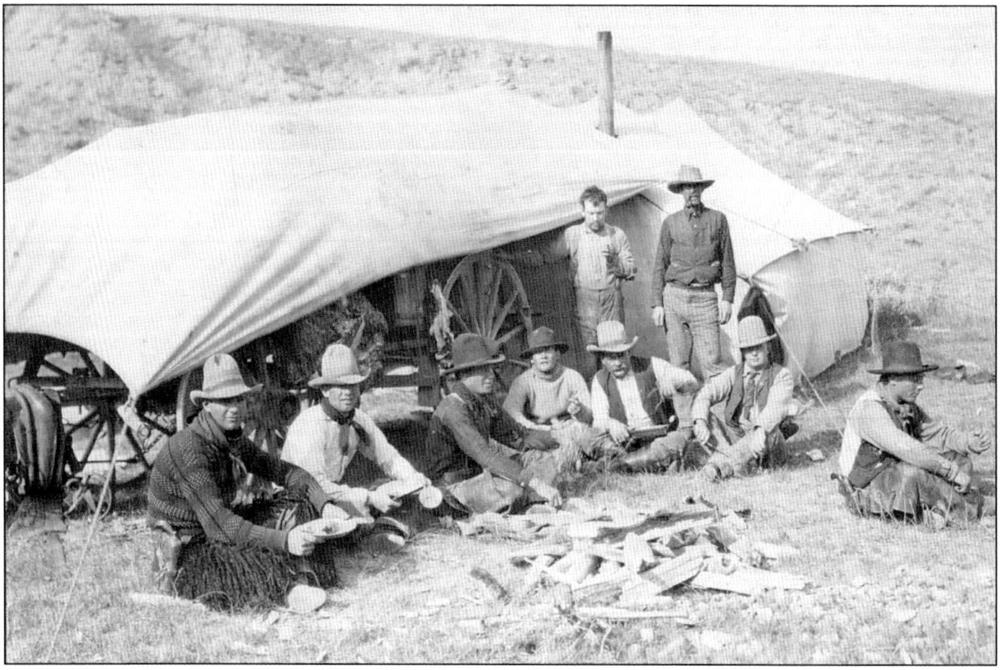

XIT cowboys take a break to eat while herding cattle in the Yellowstone Valley. The XIT Ranch, one of the largest cattle companies in the late 1800s, grazed herds on the open range from the Texas Panhandle into Montana. Smaller livestock operations, like the Montana Cattle Company, and family ranches occupied much of the rangeland around Laurel by the 1890s. (Courtesy of the Yellowstone County Museum.)

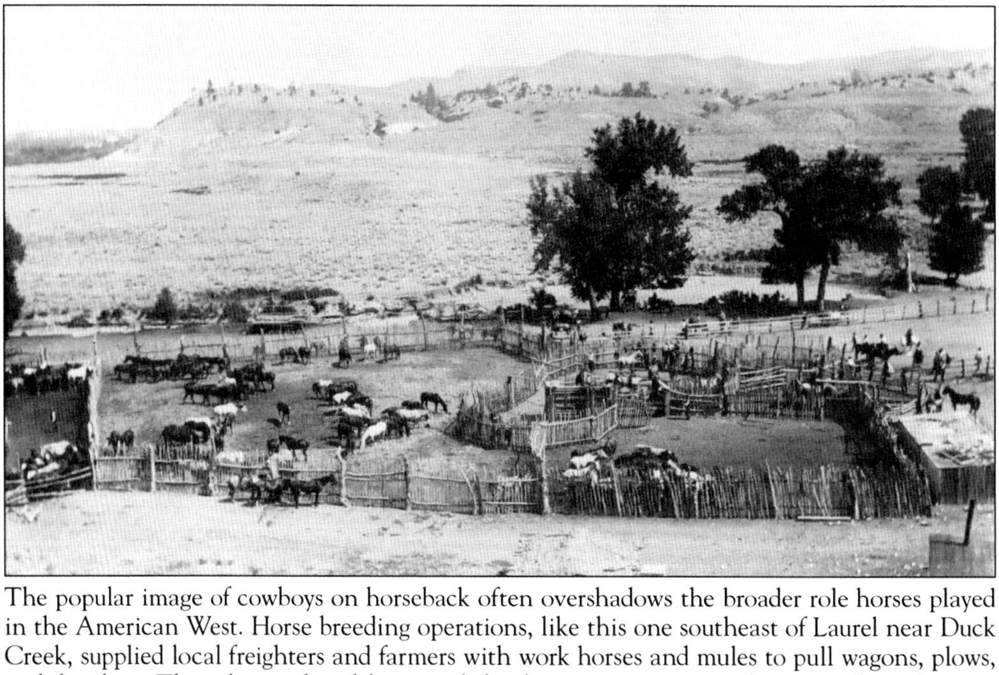

The popular image of cowboys on horseback often overshadows the broader role horses played in the American West. Horse breeding operations, like this one southeast of Laurel near Duck Creek, supplied local freighters and farmers with work horses and mules to pull wagons, plows, and threshers. They also produced finer stock for the carriages commonly seen on Laurel streets and county roads into the 1920s. (Courtesy of the Yellowstone County Museum.)

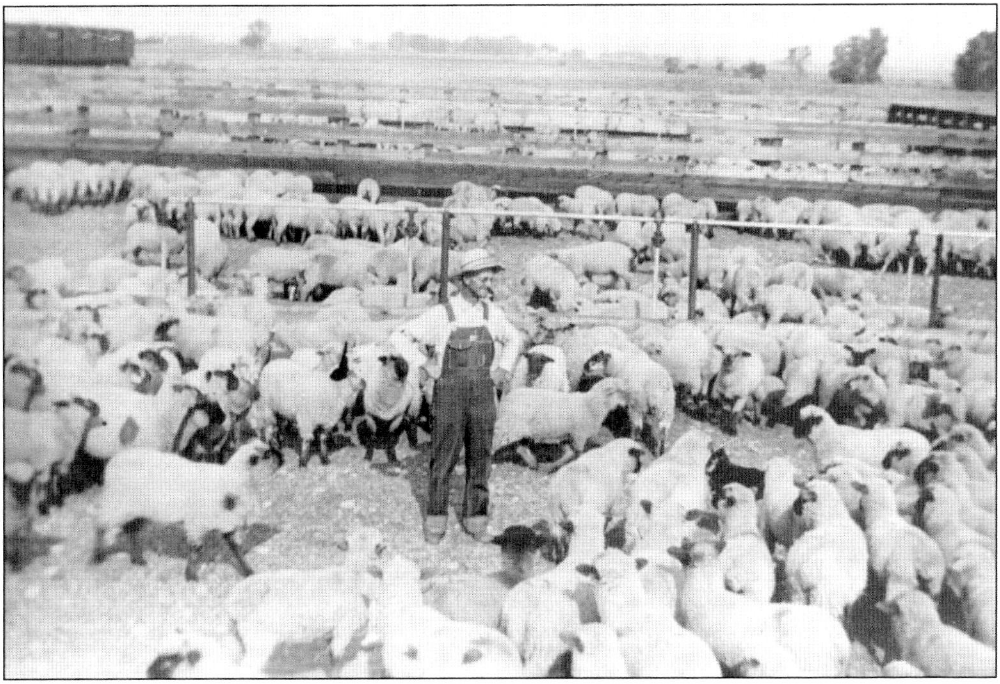

Northern Pacific stockyard foreman Earl Hoppel tends sheep being shipped by rail to eastern markets. Sheep, raised for mutton and wool, were once a livestock mainstay in the valley. William Allard, Frank Summers, and brothers Joseph and Oliver Bassett were among the early settlers who raised sheep on the grasslands and rimrock benches around Laurel. (Courtesy of the Laurel Museum.)

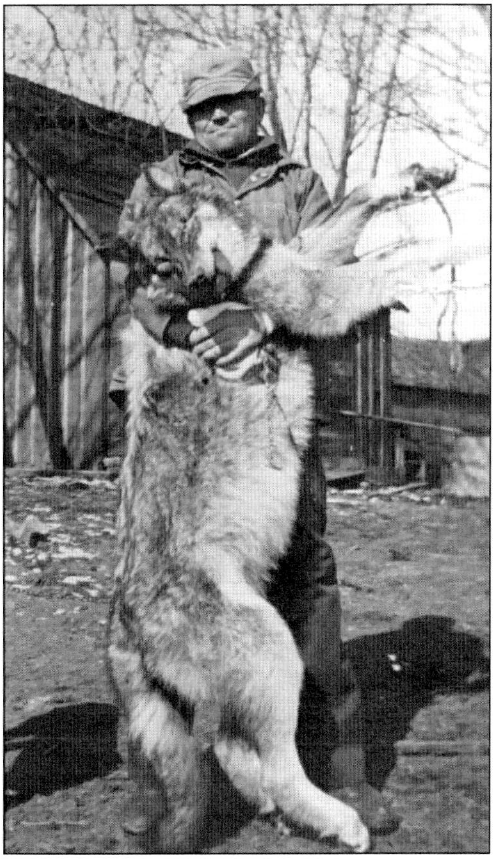

Roscoe Rutter displays a large wolf that he trapped. Wolf hunts were once common in the West. In the 1800s, hunters killed them for their pelts. As ranching took hold in the West, wolves that had historically fed on the dwindling herds of buffalo and wild game began to prey on livestock. Government-sponsored wolf extermination programs were implemented in the early 1900s to curb livestock predation. (Courtesy of the Laurel Museum.)

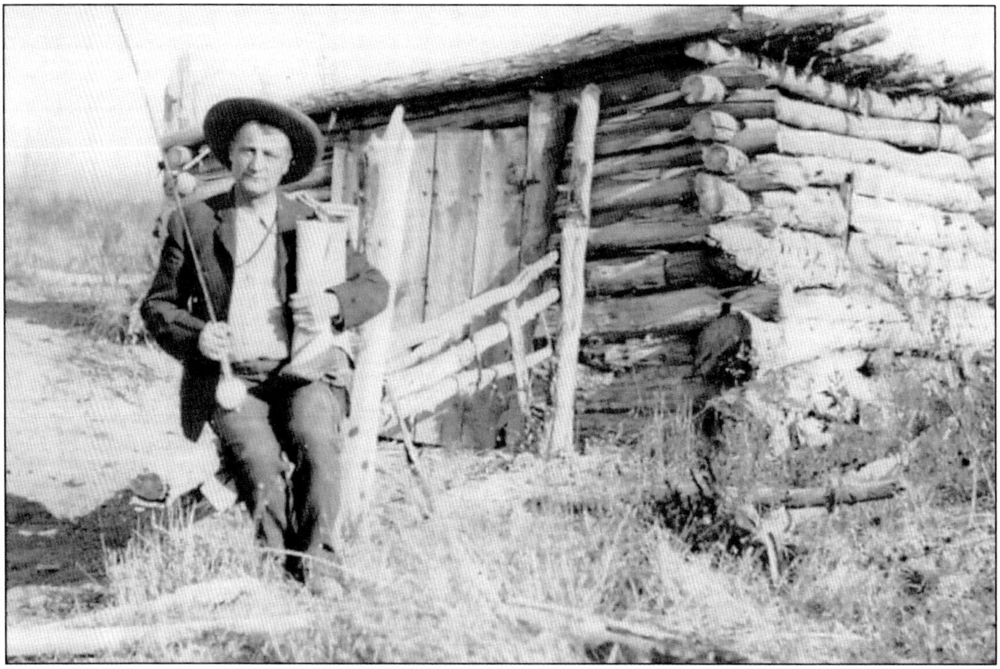

Bachelor Jean Diener poses with his fishing pole and tackle in front of his one-room cabin near Laurel in 1907. Many homesteaders in the Yellowstone Valley lived in rustic log cabins capped with a sod roof until they could build a more suitable home. (Courtesy of the Western Heritage Center.)

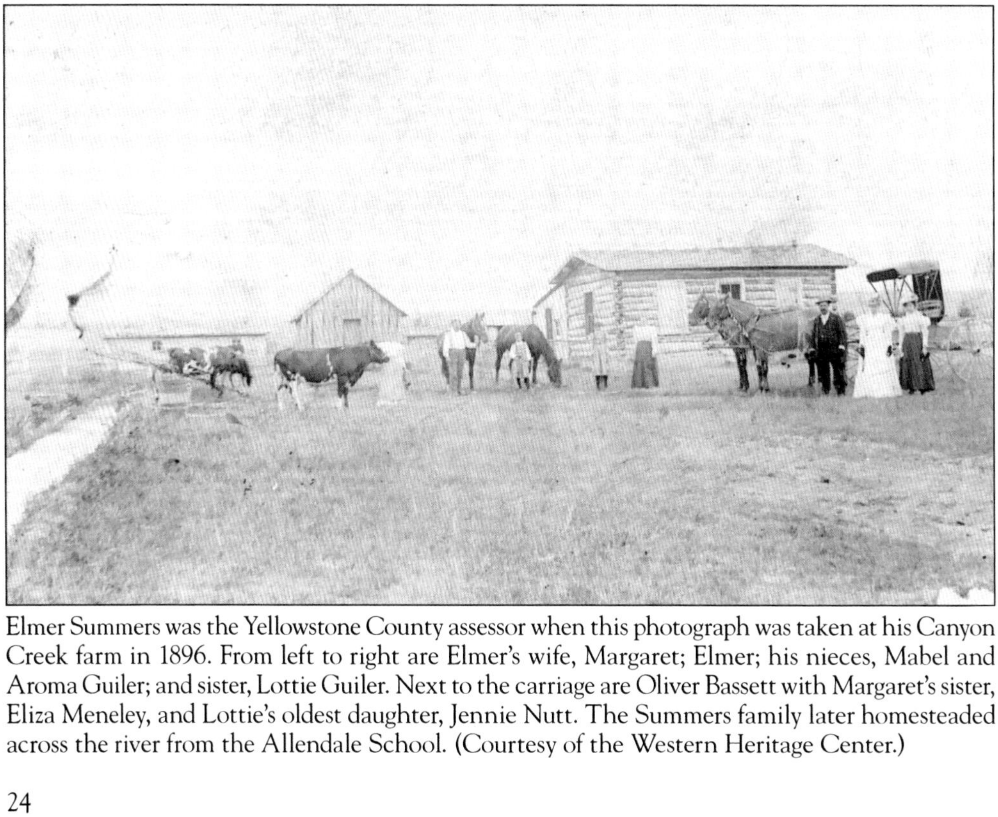

Elmer Summers was the Yellowstone County assessor when this photograph was taken at his Canyon Creek farm in 1896. From left to right are Elmer's wife, Margaret; Elmer; his nieces, Mabel and Aroma Guiler; and sister, Lottie Guiler. Next to the carriage are Oliver Bassett with Margaret's sister, Eliza Meneley, and Lottie's oldest daughter, Jennie Nutt. The Summers family later homesteaded across the river from the Allendale School. (Courtesy of the Western Heritage Center.)

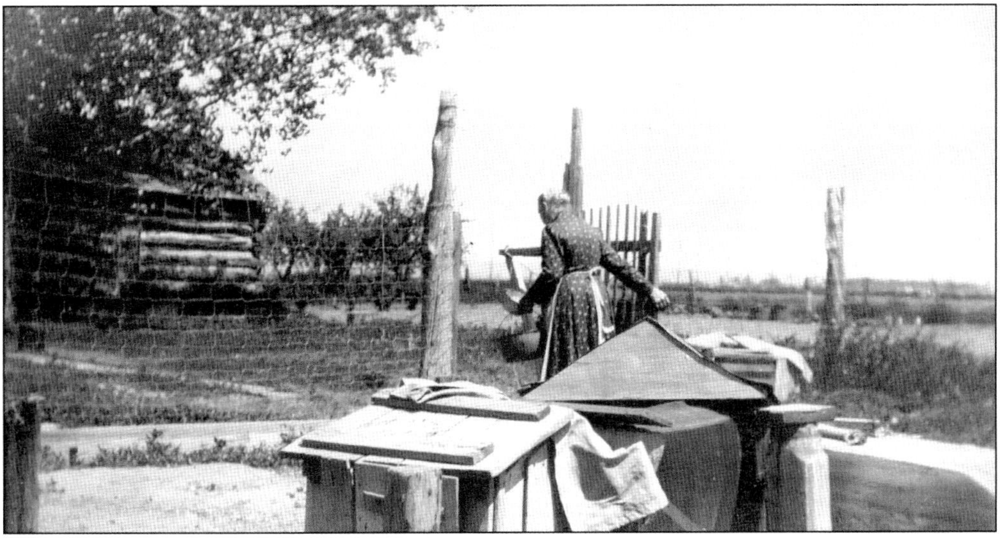

Pictured is Harriet Summers after feeding the chickens and gathering eggs at the family farm. Harriet and her husband, John Summers, moved with sons Elmer and Frank from Ohio to Montana in 1880, homesteading along Canyon Creek between Laurel and Billings. (Courtesy of the Western Heritage Center.)

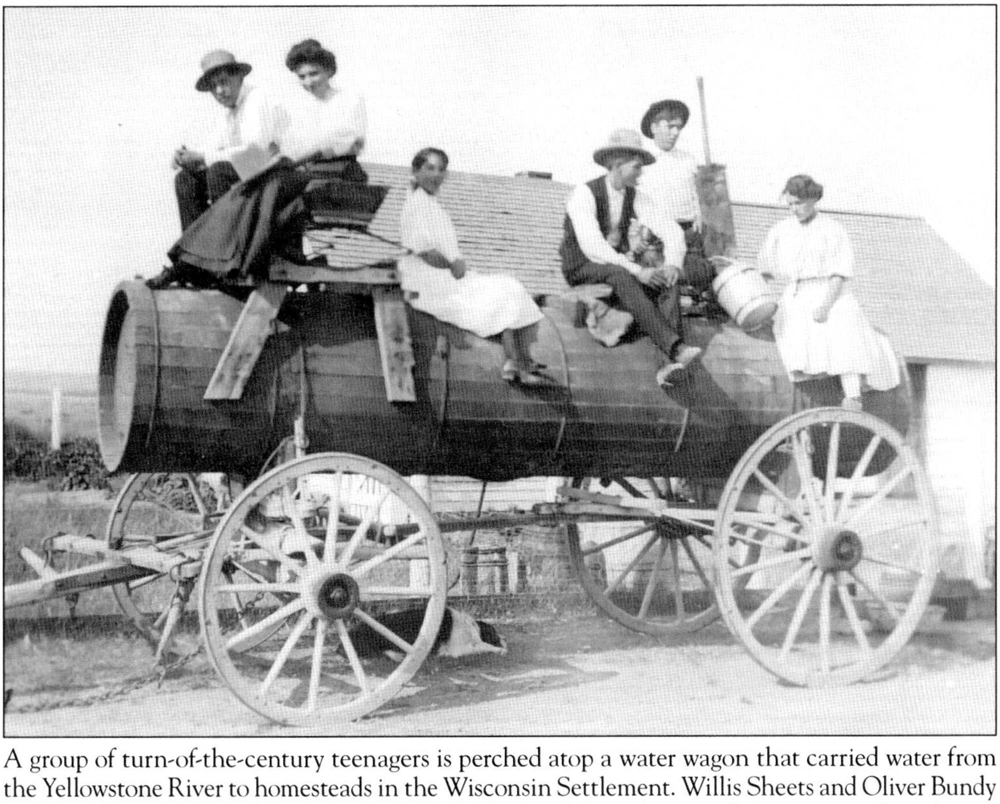

A group of turn-of-the-century teenagers is perched atop a water wagon that carried water from the Yellowstone River to homesteads in the Wisconsin Settlement. Willis Sheets and Oliver Bundy used similar wagons to deliver river water to city residents, who stored the water in barrels and cisterns before a municipal water system was installed. (Courtesy of the Laurel Public Library.)

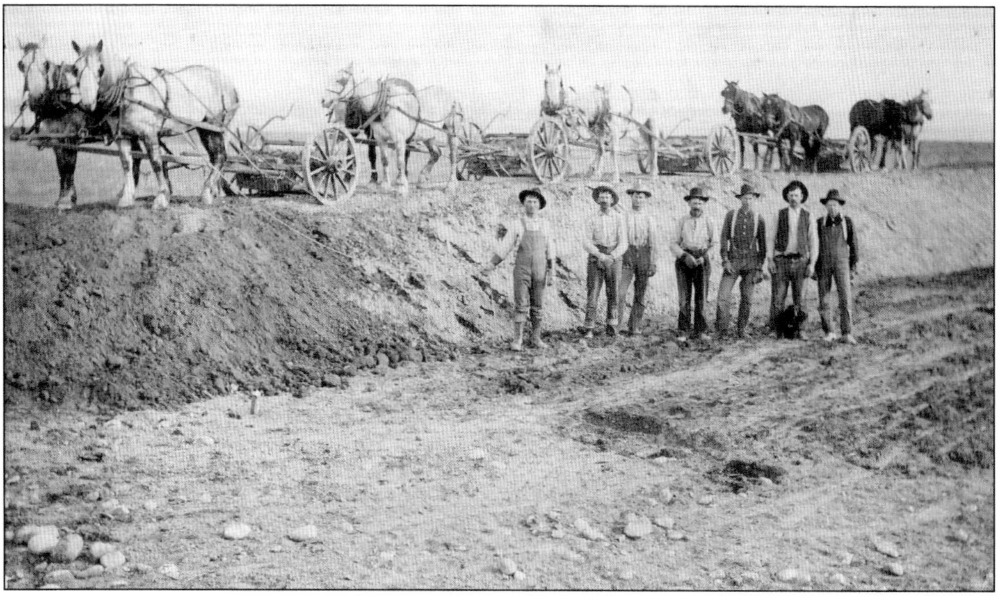

Laborers use shovels and horse-drawn scrapers and skids to trench out one of a dozen irrigation canals that fan eastward from the Yellowstone River near Laurel, diverting water from the river and channeling it by gravity to farms and communities throughout the valley in the Clarks Fork Bottom. (Courtesy of the Billings Public Library.)

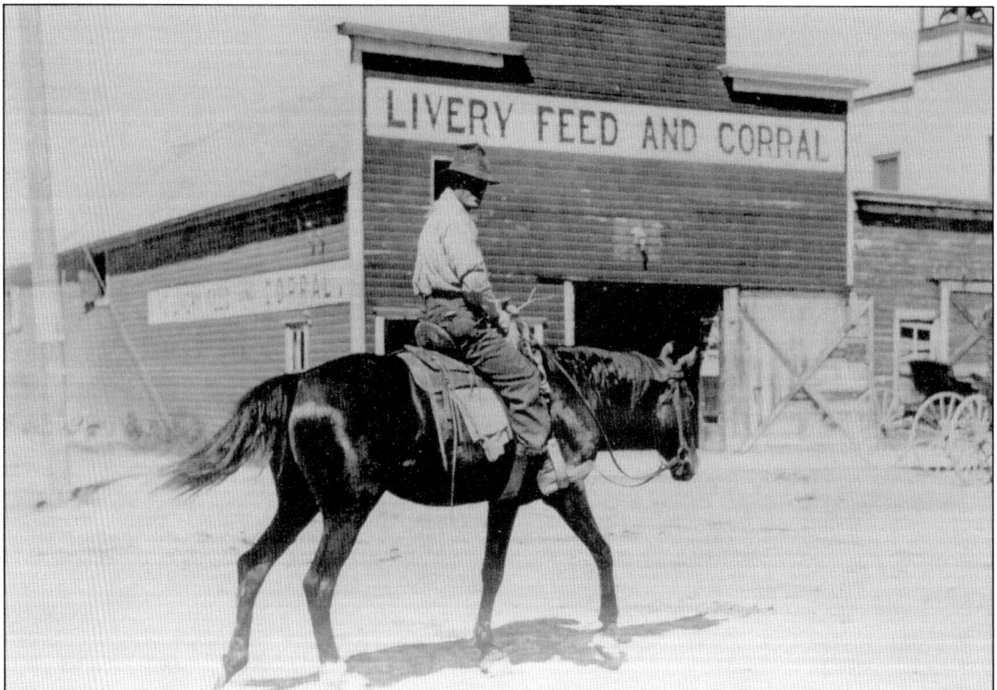

Ditch rider Daniel Foley rides out of Laurel to inspect the Big Ditch around 1911. The ditch rider controlled the head gates, monitored water levels flowing into lateral ditches and, when necessary, patched weakened canal banks with dirt-filled burlap sacks to prevent leaks and washouts. (Courtesy of the Laurel Museum.)

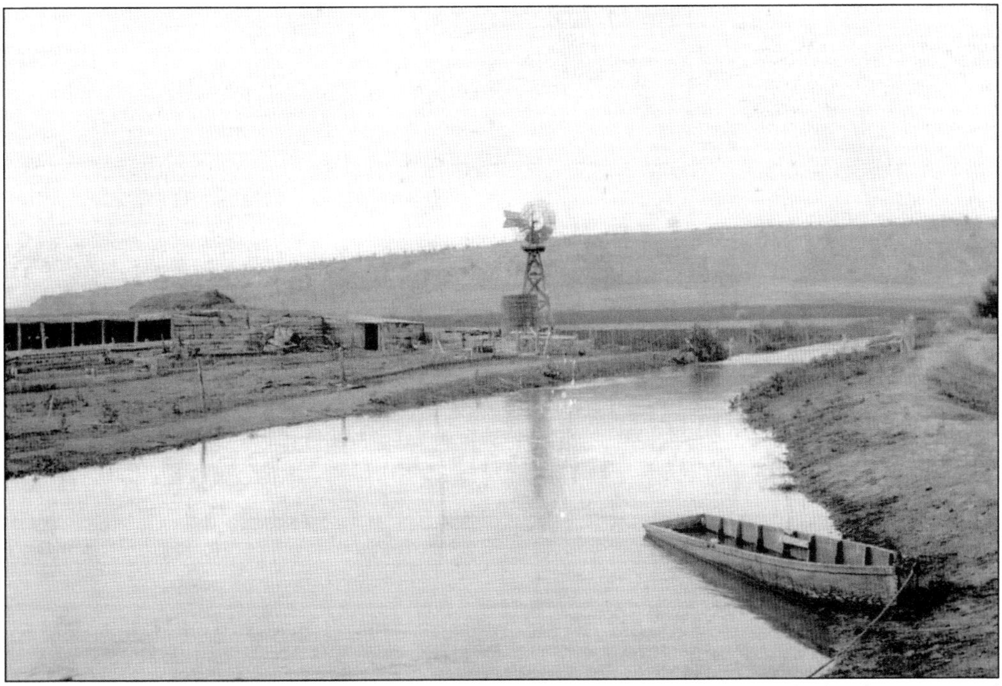

A network of canals and lateral ditches, built by companies and farmers, laces the landscape around Laurel. These early irrigation projects transformed the dry, arid prairie into prime agricultural land. (Courtesy of the Yellowstone County Museum.)

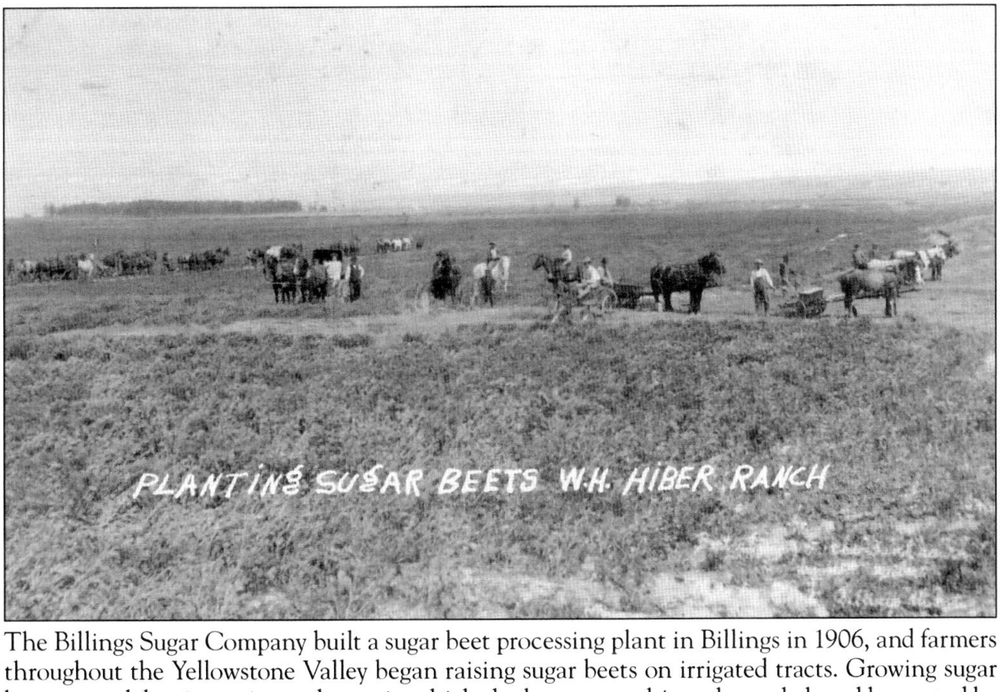

The Billings Sugar Company built a sugar beet processing plant in Billings in 1906, and farmers throughout the Yellowstone Valley began raising sugar beets on irrigated tracts. Growing sugar beets was a labor-intensive endeavor in which the beets were thinned, weeded, and harvested by hand, but the lucrative crop more than doubled farmers' returns per acre over alfalfa and grain crops. (Courtesy of the Billings Public Library.)

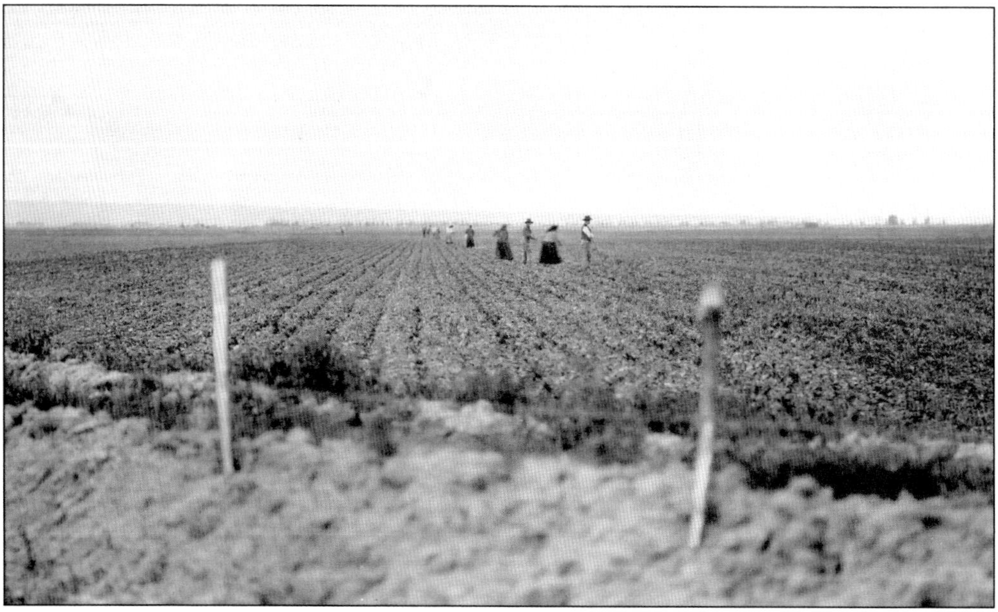

The sugar company began a campaign to recruit German settlers who had been successfully growing sugar beets for decades in the Volga region of Russia. The German-Russian immigrants who came to Laurel started as farm laborers until they were able to buy their own farms. A large community of German-Russian immigrants constructed homes south of the tracks in a neighborhood that came to be called German Town. (Courtesy of the Western Heritage Center.)

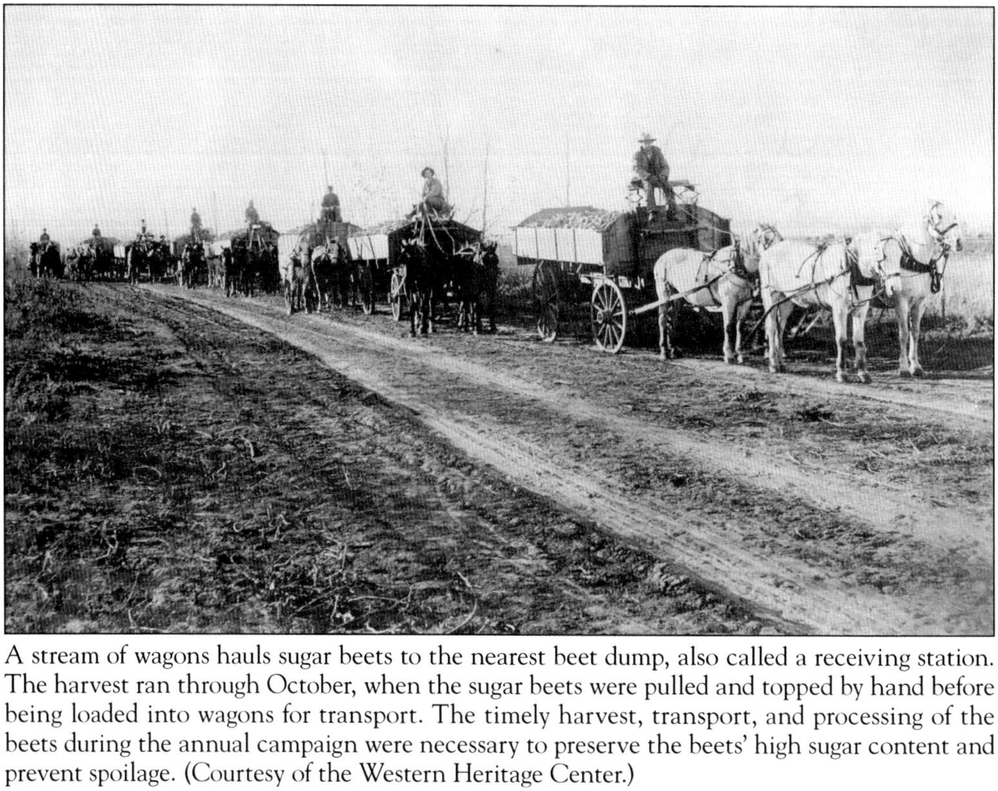

A stream of wagons hauls sugar beets to the nearest beet dump, also called a receiving station. The harvest ran through October, when the sugar beets were pulled and topped by hand before being loaded into wagons for transport. The timely harvest, transport, and processing of the beets during the annual campaign were necessary to preserve the beets' high sugar content and prevent spoilage. (Courtesy of the Western Heritage Center.)

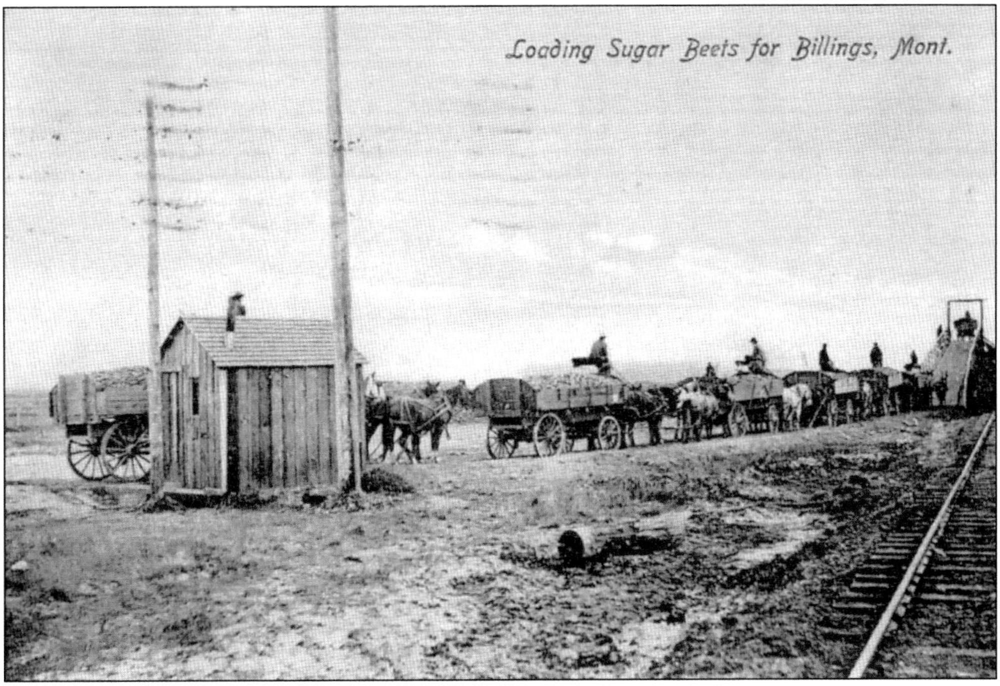

Sugar beet wagons line up to be weighed before emptying their loads. Beet receiving stations were conveniently located at rail sidings, where the beets could be loaded onto railcars and shipped to the sugar factory in Billings for processing. The Great Western Sugar Company bought the Billings sugar factory in 1910 and promoted larger-scale sugar beet production throughout the region. (Above, courtesy of the Yellowstone County Museum; below, courtesy of the Laurel Museum.)

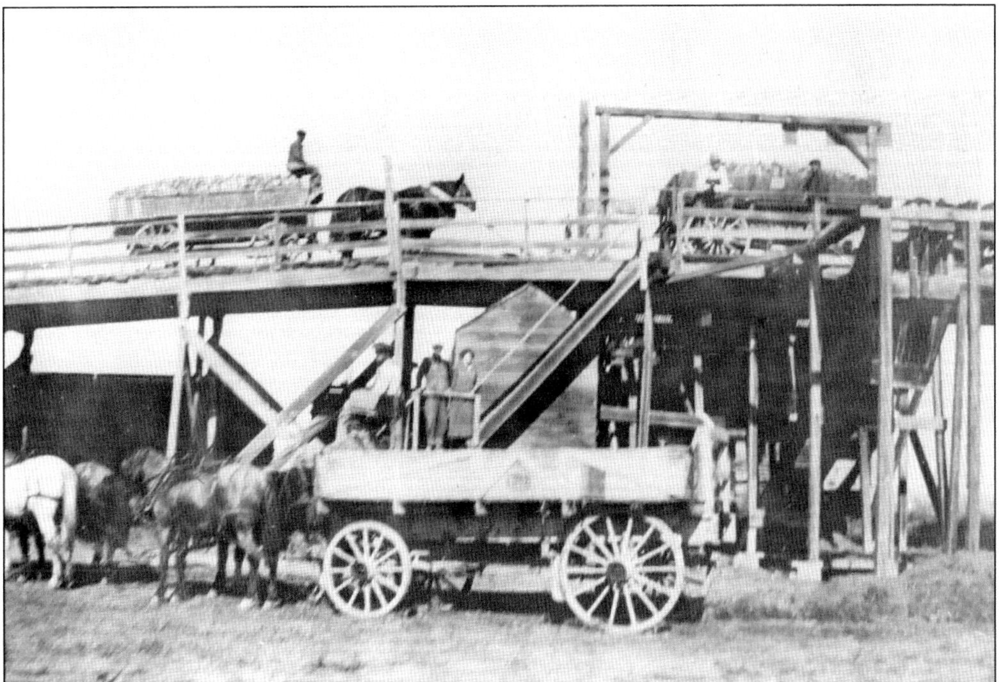

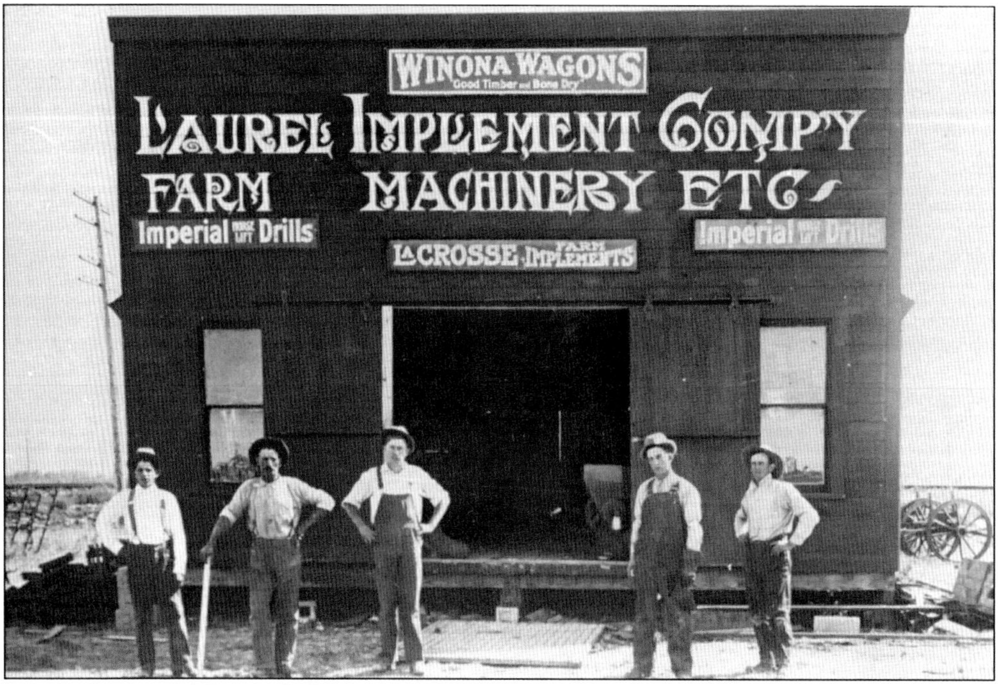

George Lonne and O.A. Solvik, proprietors of the Laurel Implement Company, carried a full line of harnesses, saddles, wagons, and farm equipment. Another implement store, the Erb-Harper-Rigney Company, also catered to local farmers and ranchers for several years before shutting its doors in 1915. (Courtesy of the Laurel Museum.)

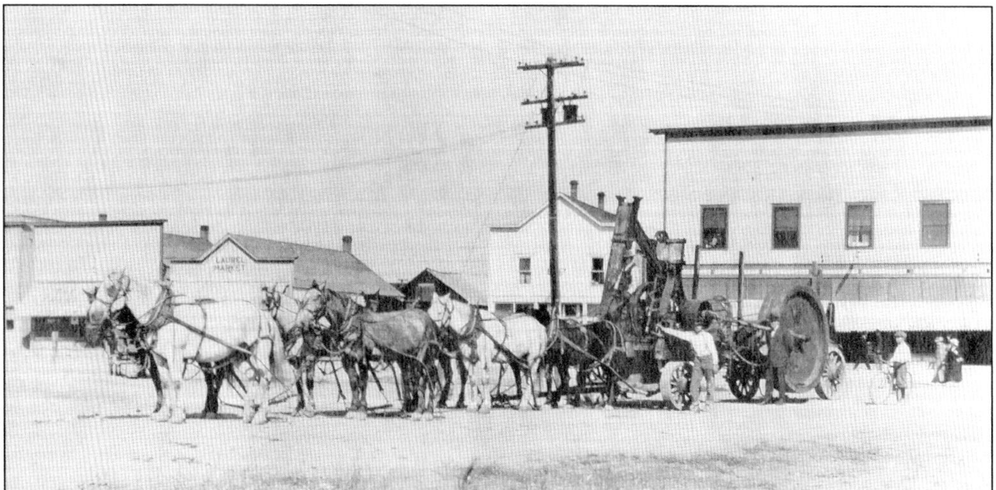

The Enlarged Homestead Act of 1909 attracted record numbers of homesteaders wanting to establish dryland farms. Growing wheat and barley required investment in large-scale farm machinery, such as the threshing separator pictured here. (Courtesy of the Laurel Museum.)

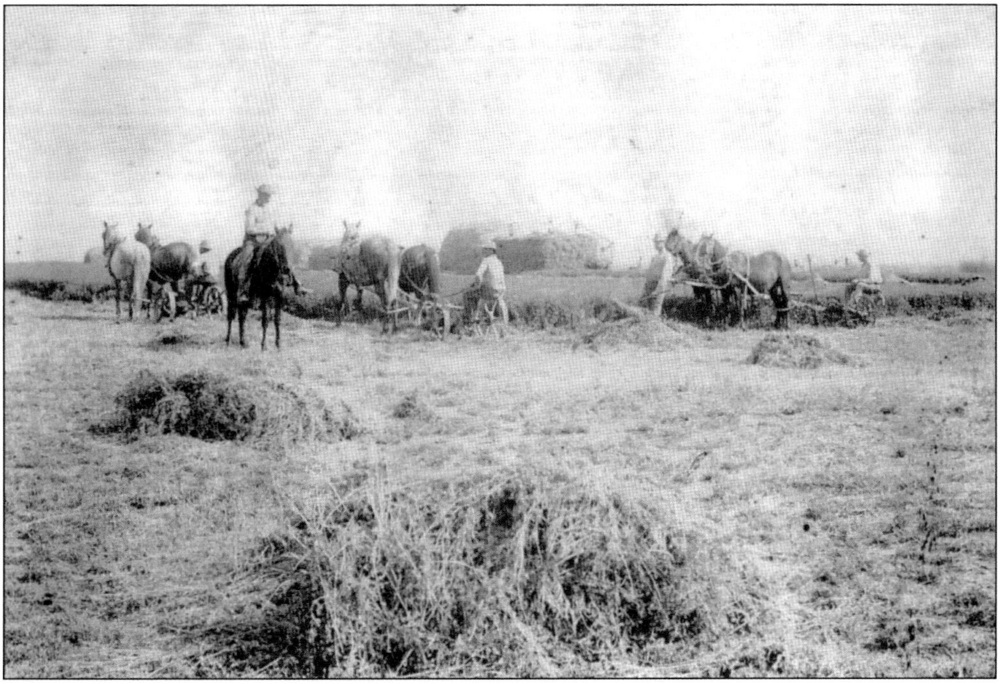

Irrigation produced bountiful alfalfa crops in the valley. Here, a crew mows and bails hay at the Hesper Farm north of Laurel. (Both, courtesy of the Yellowstone County Museum.)

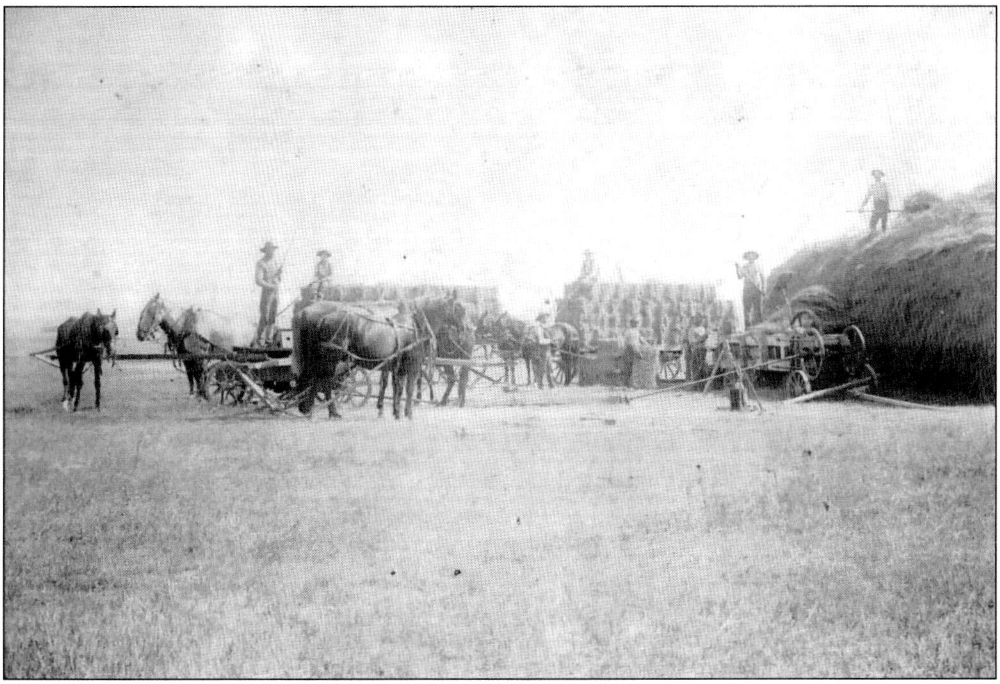

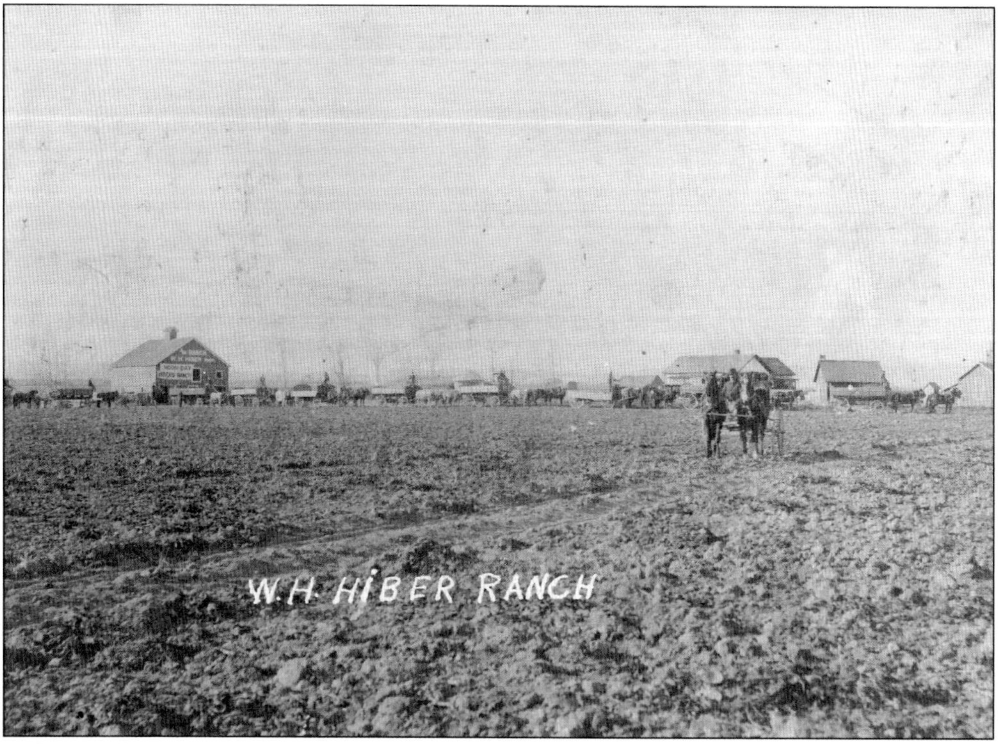

William Hiber, whose family settled east of Laurel in the 1890s, leads a line of wagons from his ranch to the fields where the crew will load sugar beets and haul them to the nearest railroad siding. (Courtesy of the Billings Public Library.)

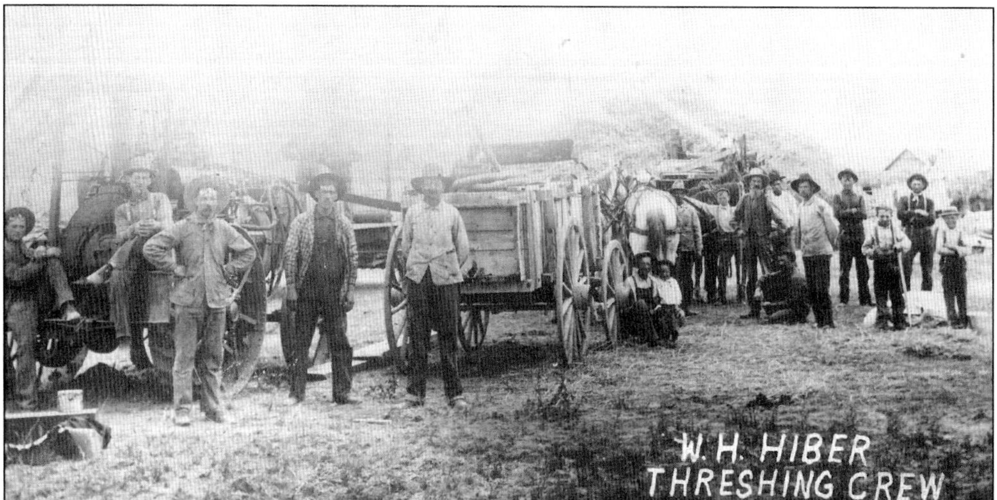

Pictured are William Hiber, center, and his threshing outfit in 1908. Hiber operated a steam threshing business that harvested and threshed wheat for other farmers in the valley. (Courtesy of the Billings Public Library.)

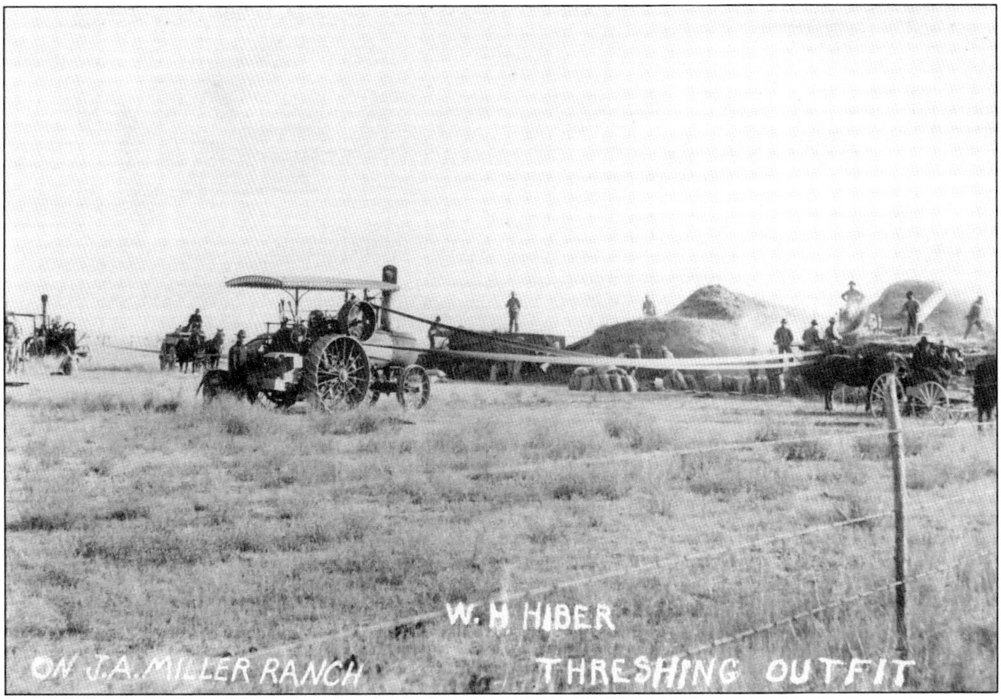

In the photograph above, William Hiber's crew threshes wheat on John Miller's ranch. Some farmers found it more economical to hire Hiber's threshing outfit than to invest in their own equipment and pay hired hands to bring in the harvest. (Above, courtesy of the Billings Public Library; below, courtesy of the Laurel Museum.)

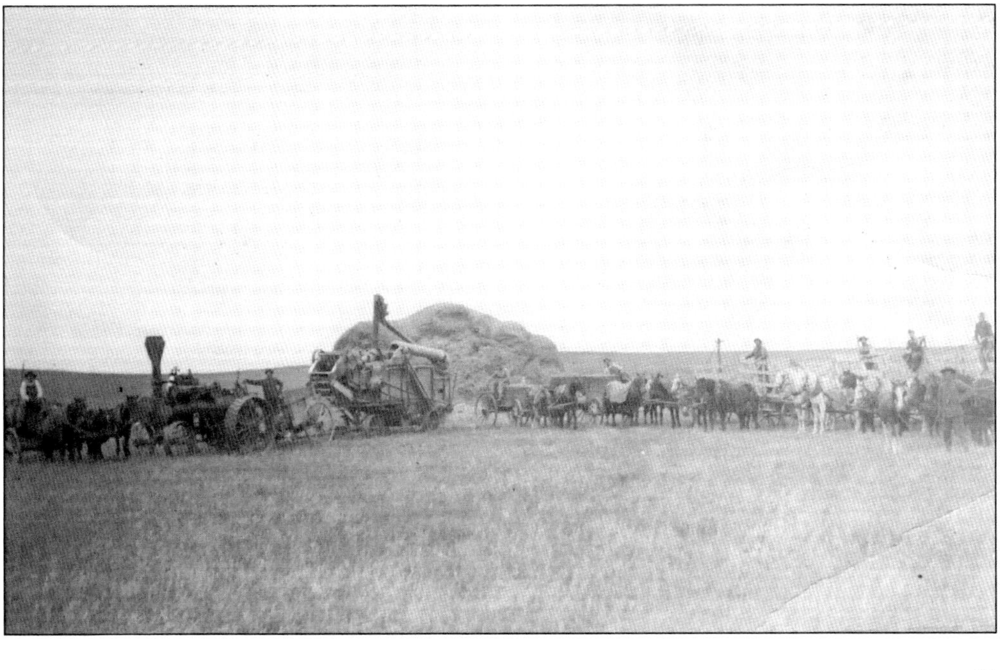

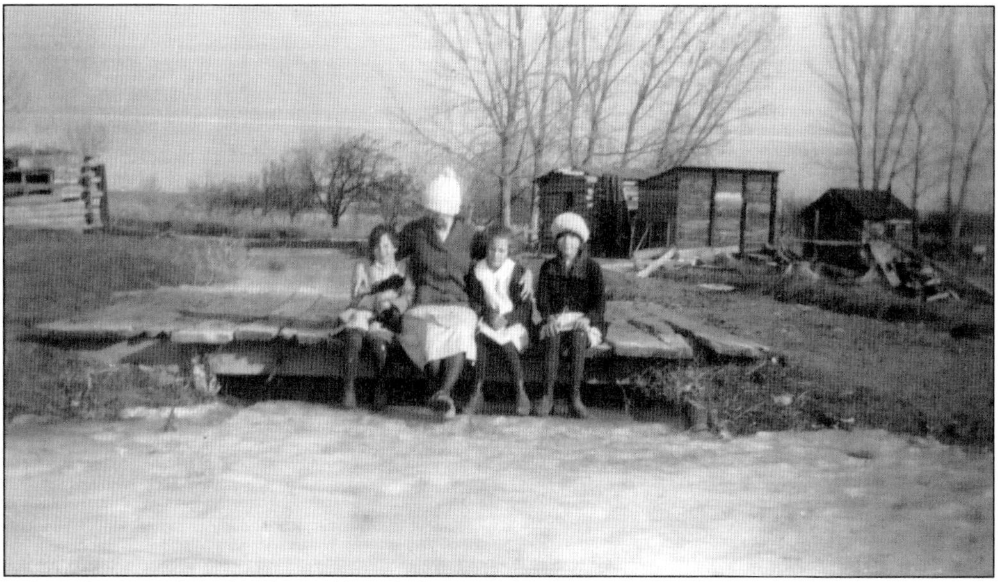

Ada Jackson and her daughters (from left to right), Doris, Marion, and Margaret, sit on a bridge over a frozen irrigation ditch that her husband, Charles, hand dug. Ada and Charles Jackson raised sugar beets, alfalfa, corn, and wheat on a farm south of Laurel on White Horse Bench Road. Their daughter, Marion, and her husband, Lisle Boyd, operated the farm after Ada was widowed. (Courtesy of Maxine Allman.)

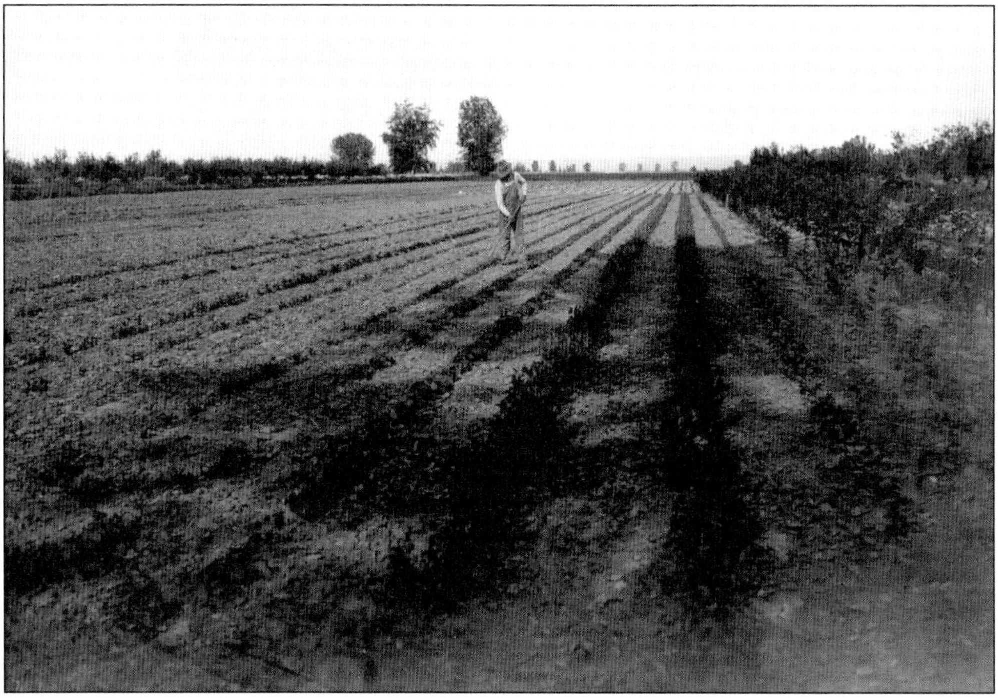

A farmer hoes sugar beets in a field at the Hesper Farm in 1907. The Hesper Farm, located six miles northeast of Laurel, began as an experimental sharecropping model for irrigated farming, raising primarily sugar beets, alfalfa, and corn as well as sheep. (Courtesy of the Western Heritage Center.)

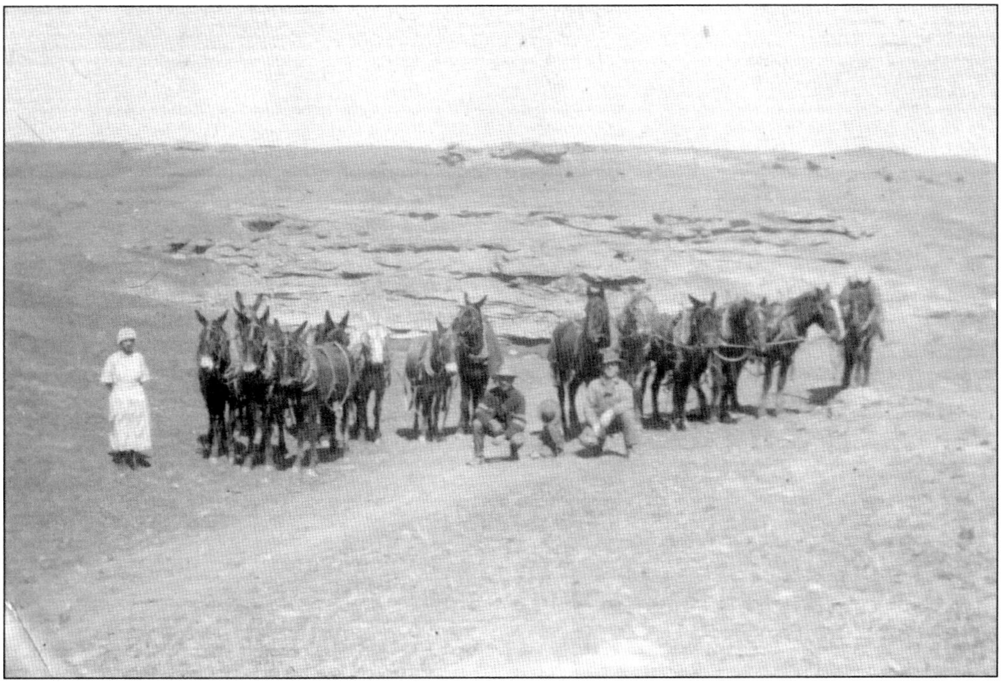

The Enlarged Homestead Act of 1909 allowed claims up to 320 acres. In 1912, the proving-up period dropped from five to three years. These changes sparked a record number of homestead entries in Yellowstone County. Prime agricultural land around Laurel had been claimed years before, and the new wave of homesteaders struggled to carve a living as dryland farmers on the arid, windswept prairie. (Courtesy of the Laurel Museum.)

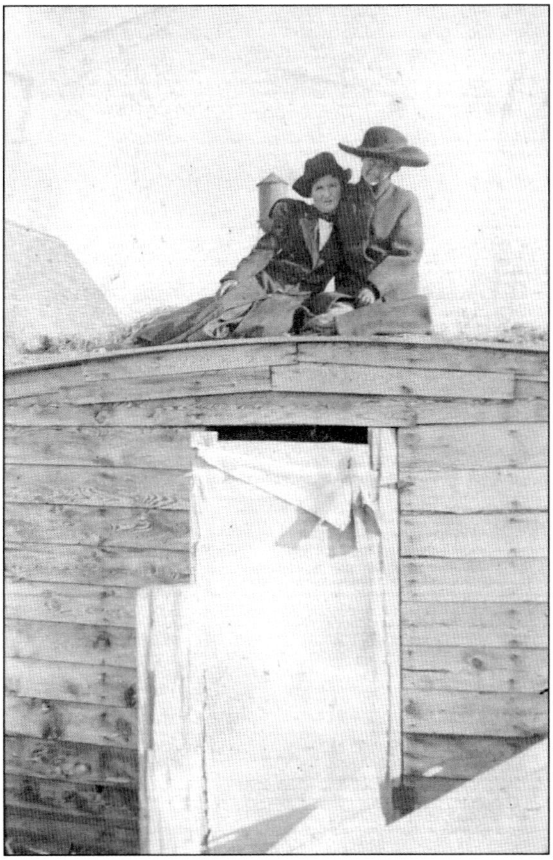

Esther Rutter, right, filed a homestead claim in 1910 near her sister, Emma Brickman, and brothers, Charles and Raynus Rutter, in the Wisconsin Settlement. She named her modest shack the "Lone Tree Homestead." Esther married Emil Kircheis in 1911, and they lived on the homestead for over a decade before moving into town, where Emil worked at the Northern Pacific yard office. (Courtesy of the Laurel Museum.)

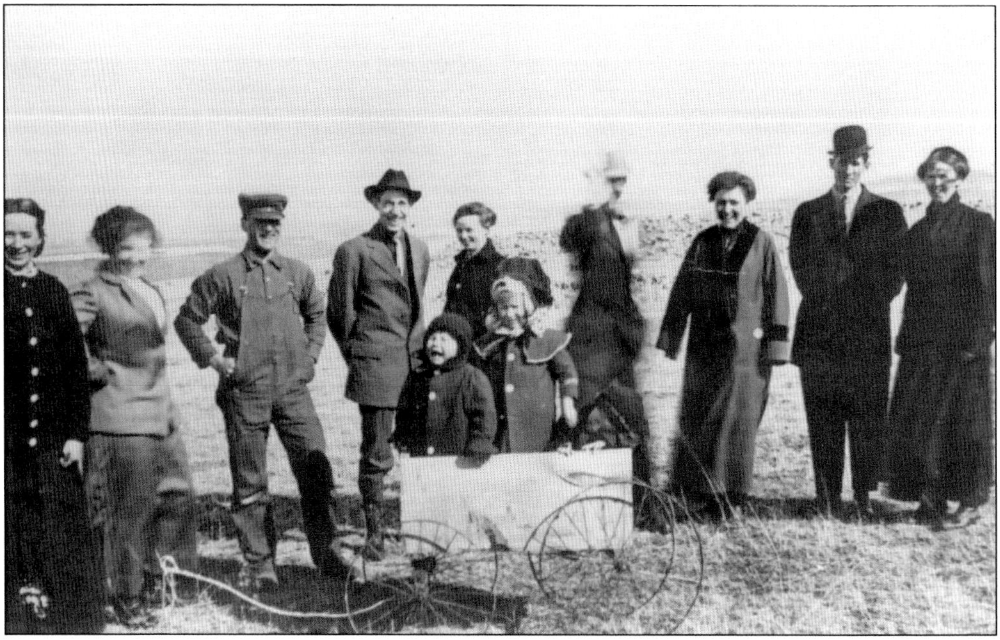

In 1909 and 1910, a group of young families left Wisconsin to homestead along Spring Creek, southeast of Laurel. Their cluster of homesteads came to be known as the Wisconsin Settlement. Pictured above are, from left to right, Emma (Rutter) Brickman, Mabel Rutter, Herman Brickman, Emil and Esther (Rutter) Kircheis, Claude and Hazel (Jordan) Gilbreath, Allen Rutter, and Nora (Bates) Rutter. Raymond and Alta Brickman are standing in the wagon. By 1925, many of these families had sold their homesteads, like the one below, to live and work in Laurel. (Above, courtesy of the Laurel Museum; below, courtesy of the Laurel Public Library.)

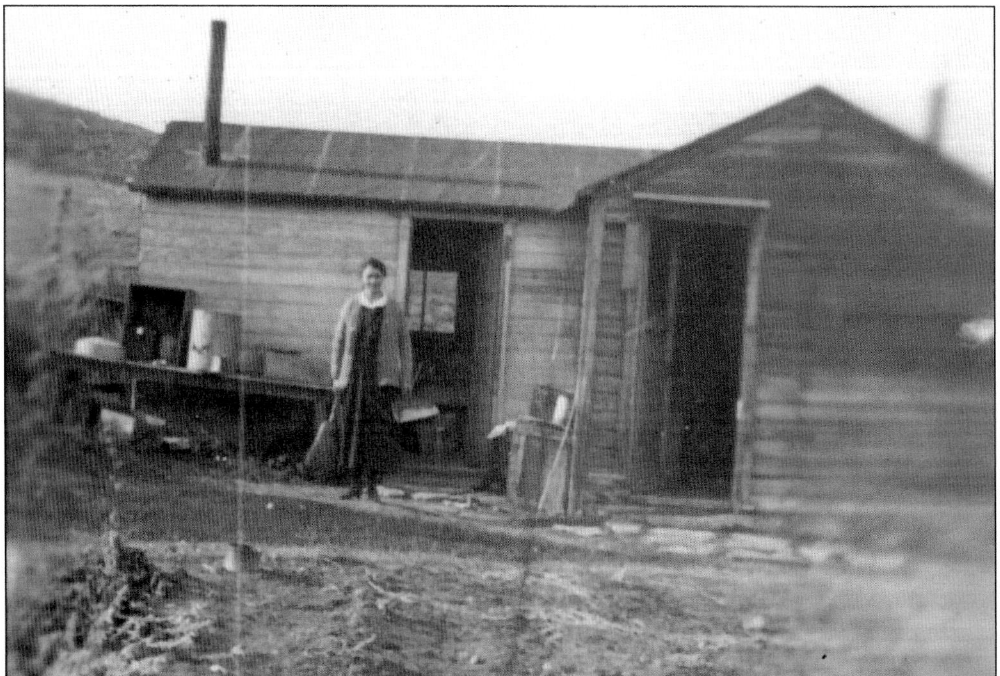

A couple, possibly Lottie and Roscoe Rutter, holds aloft a freshly plucked turkey to be roasted for a dinner party with their neighbors in the Wisconsin Settlement around 1915. (Courtesy of the Laurel Public Library.)

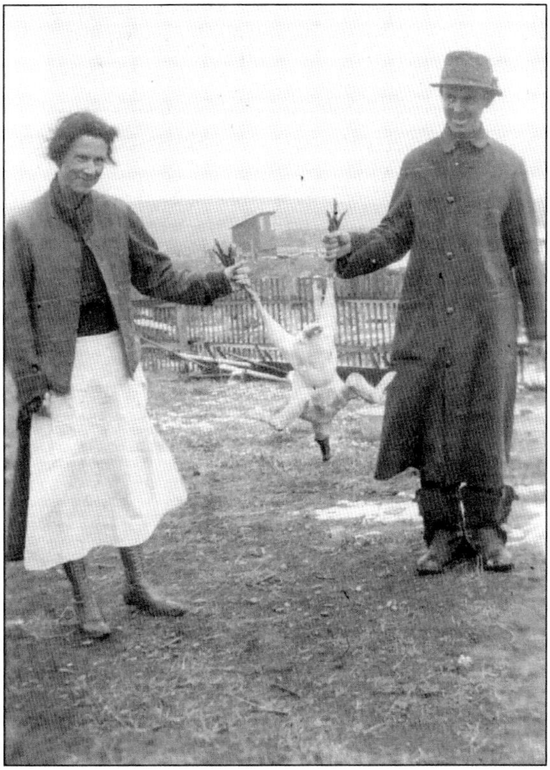

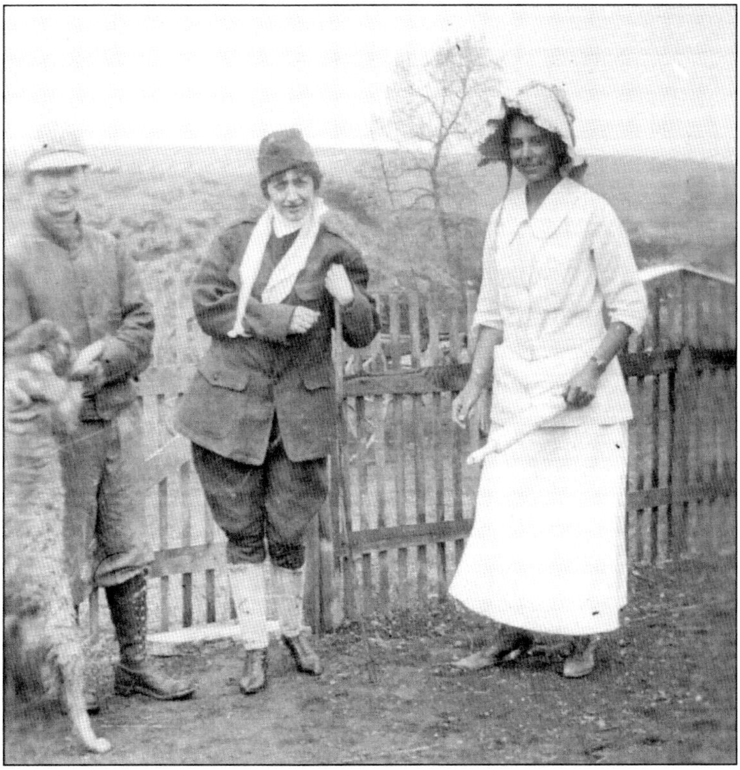

From left to right, Lynn Jordan and her sister, Ruby Winters, pay a visit to Emma Brickman, a neighbor in the Wisconsin Settlement. (Courtesy of the Laurel Public Library.)

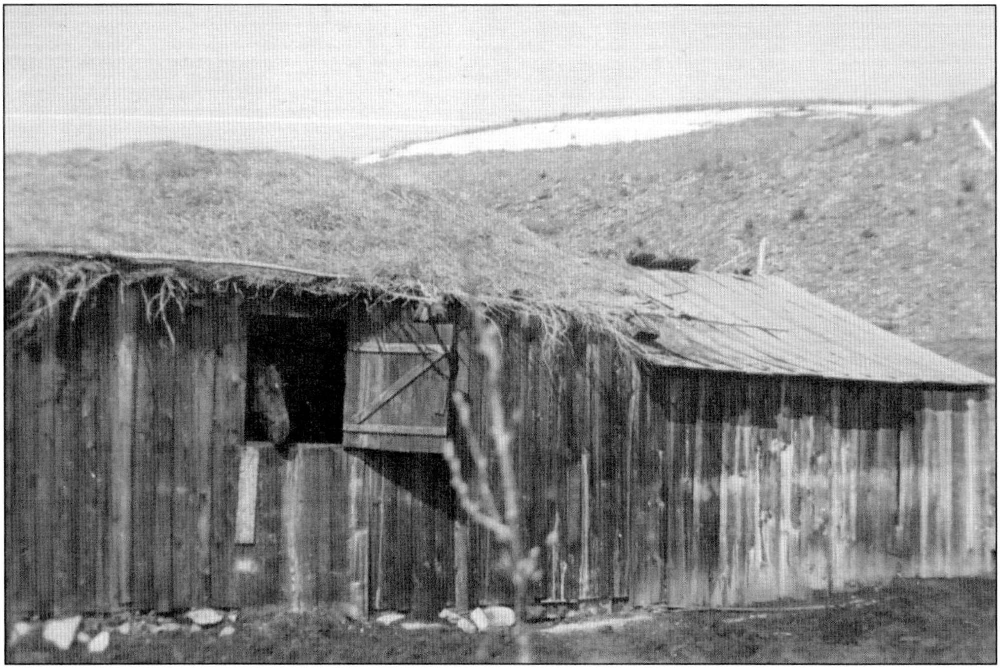

A horse peeks from the doorway of a rustic barn on a homestead southeast of Laurel. As settlers became more established, the traditional red wood-framed horse barns replaced crude outbuildings like this one. (Courtesy of the Laurel Public Library.)

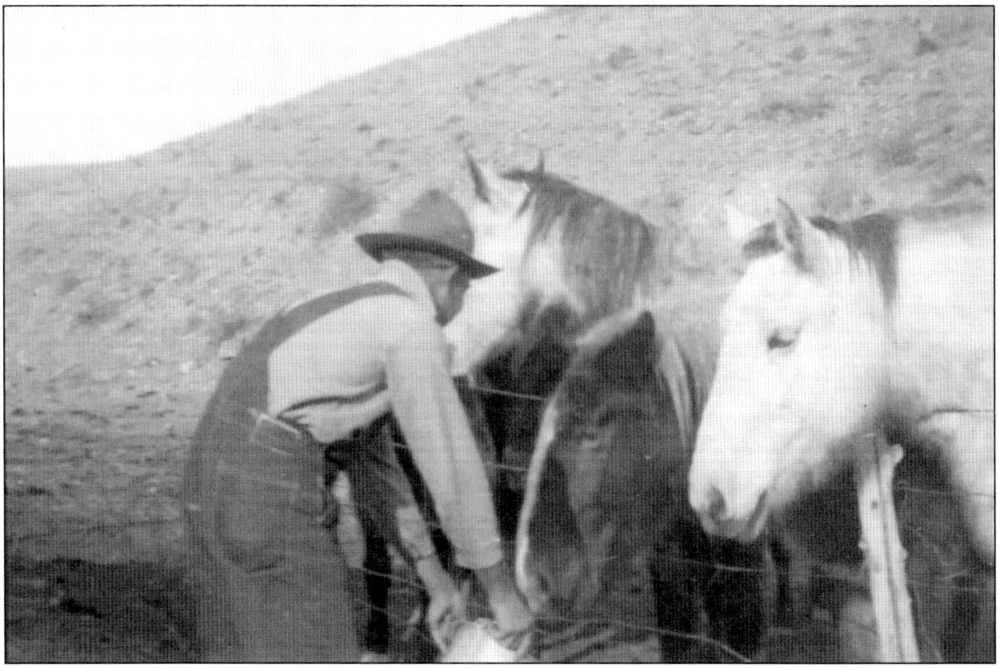

A farmer in the Wisconsin Settlement feeds his horses from a bucket of oats. (Courtesy of the Laurel Public Library.)

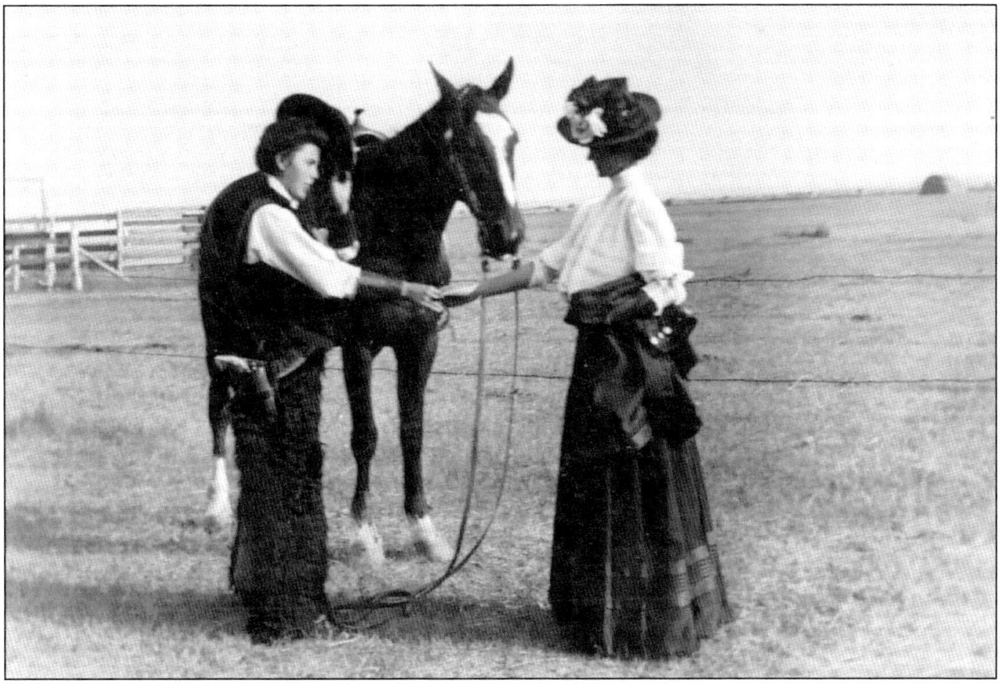

Courtesies are exchanged between a ranch hand and a young lady. (Courtesy of the Laurel Public Library.)

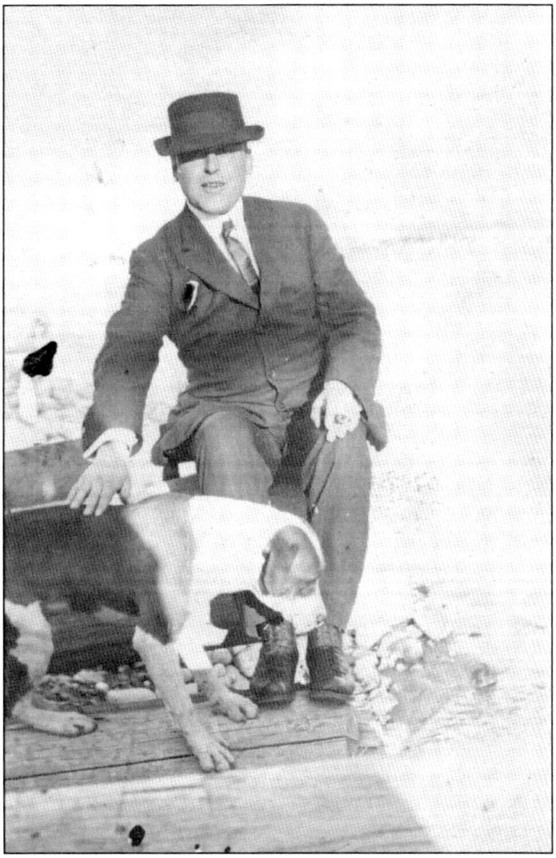

This photograph of Raynus Rutter and his dog was taken shortly after he came to Laurel in 1910. Raynus homesteaded in the Spring Creek area near his brother, Charles Rutter, and sisters, Emma Brickman and Esther Rutter. Soon after he arrived in the area, Raynus went into business with Howard Reeder as wholesale horse dealers. (Courtesy of the Laurel Museum.)

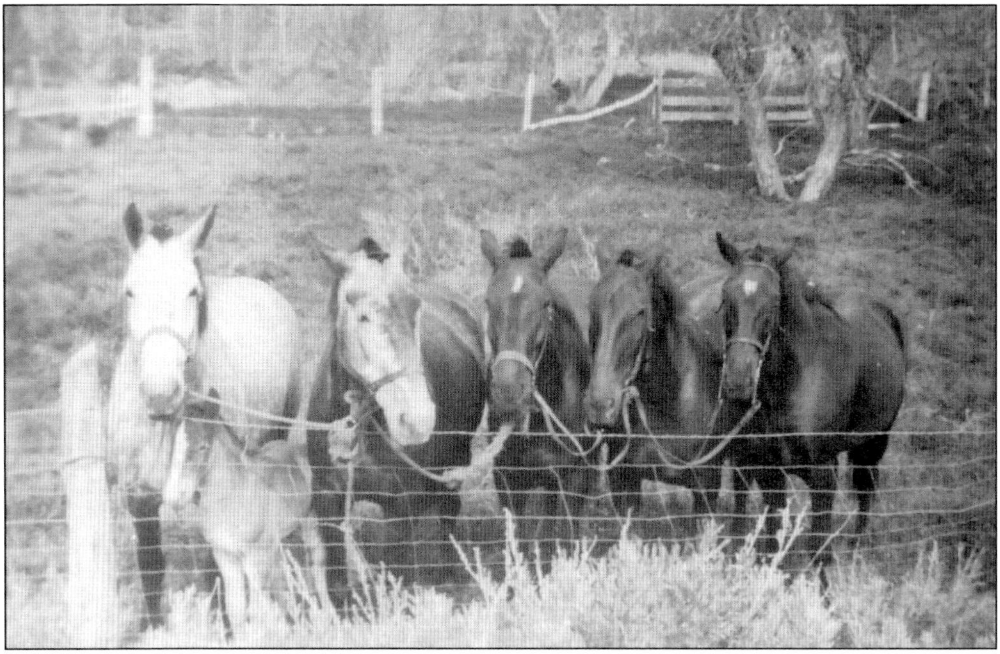

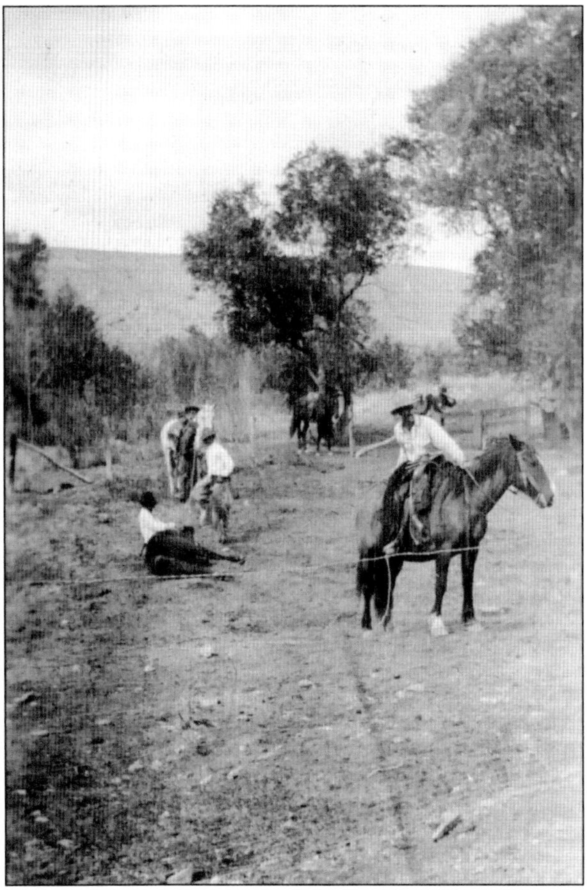

Tethered horses are pictured waiting for a day of cattle branding near Spring Creek. (Courtesy of the Laurel Public Library.)

Ranch hands rope and take down a calf during branding season. Branding ensures that ownership of cattle and horses can be easily determined. (Courtesy of the Laurel Public Library.)

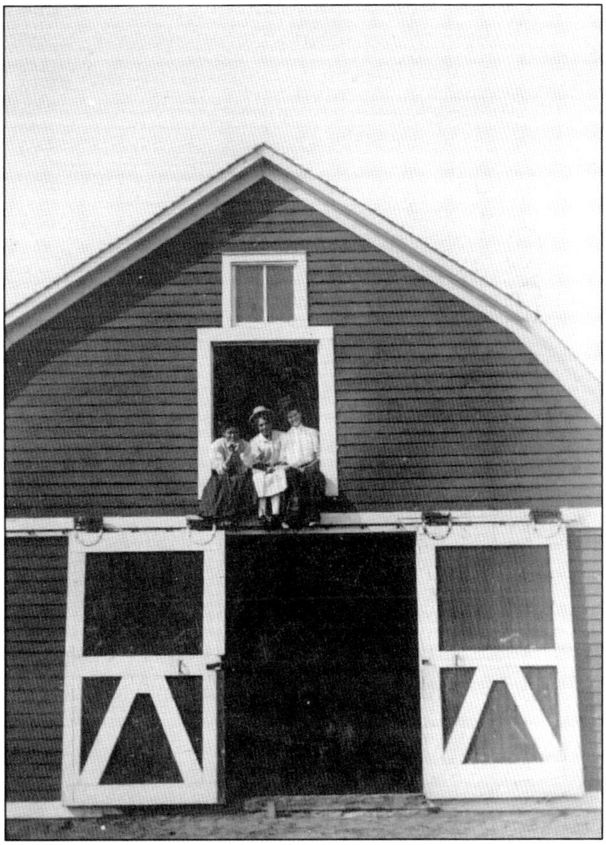

This horse barn set the stage for an afternoon of entertainment. Three young women are perched in the hayloft in the photograph at right. Below, a family, dressed in their Sunday best, lounges in the shade of the barn's doorway. (Both, courtesy of the Laurel Public Library.)

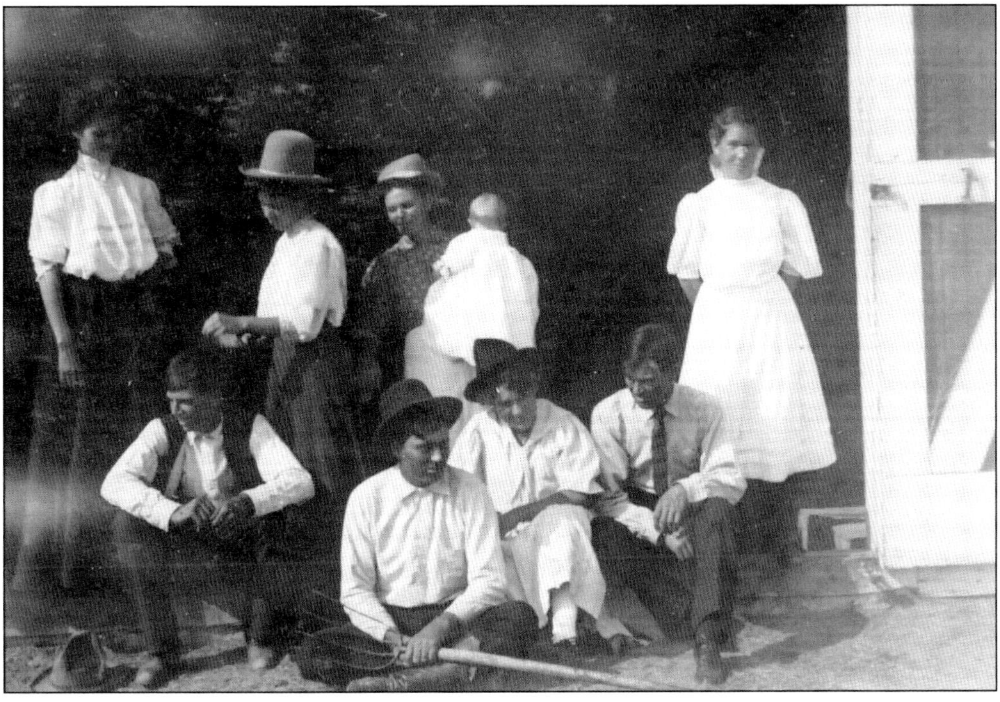

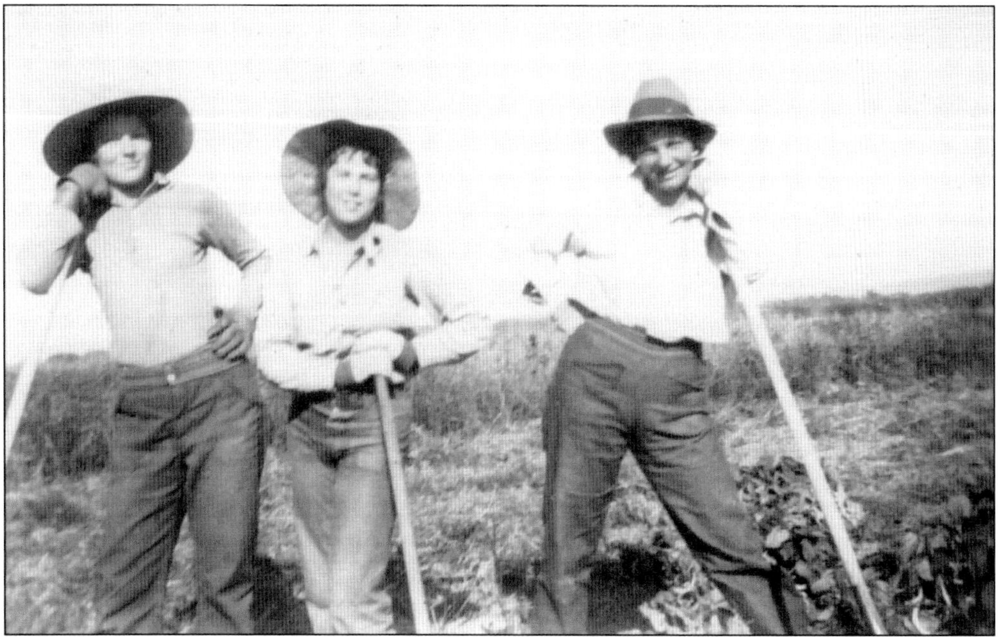

From left to right, sisters Marion, Doris, and Margaret Jackson thin sugar beets at their family farm south of Laurel. (Courtesy of Maxine Allman.)

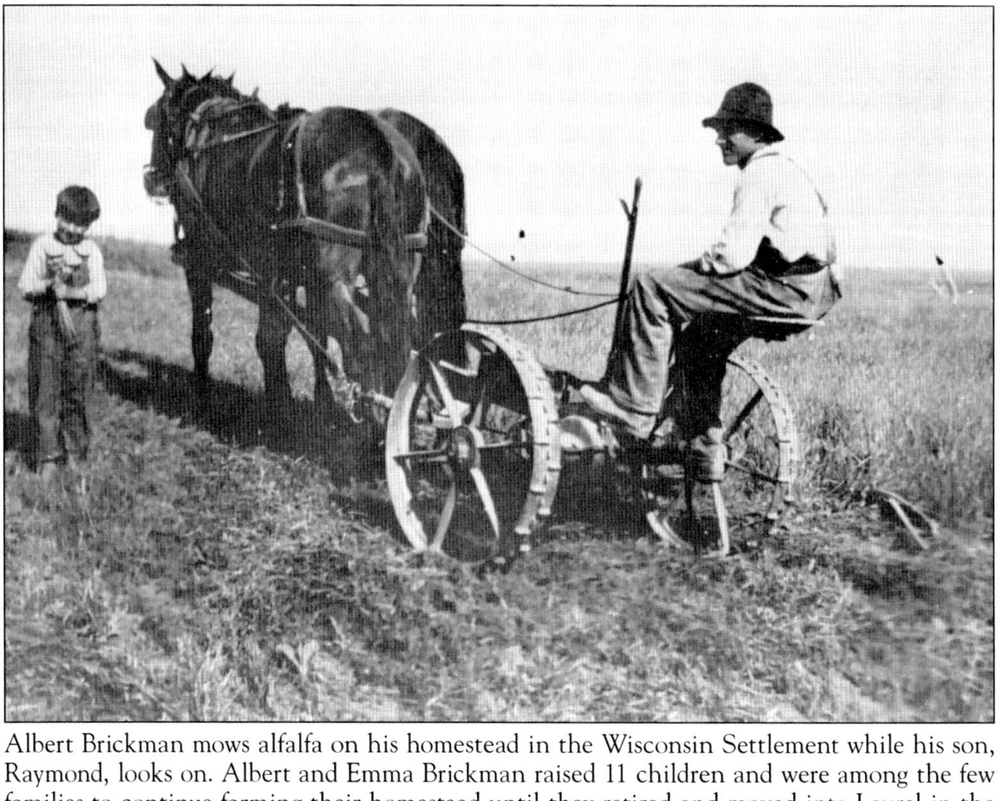

Albert Brickman mows alfalfa on his homestead in the Wisconsin Settlement while his son, Raymond, looks on. Albert and Emma Brickman raised 11 children and were among the few families to continue farming their homestead until they retired and moved into Laurel in the 1950s. (Courtesy of the Laurel Museum.)

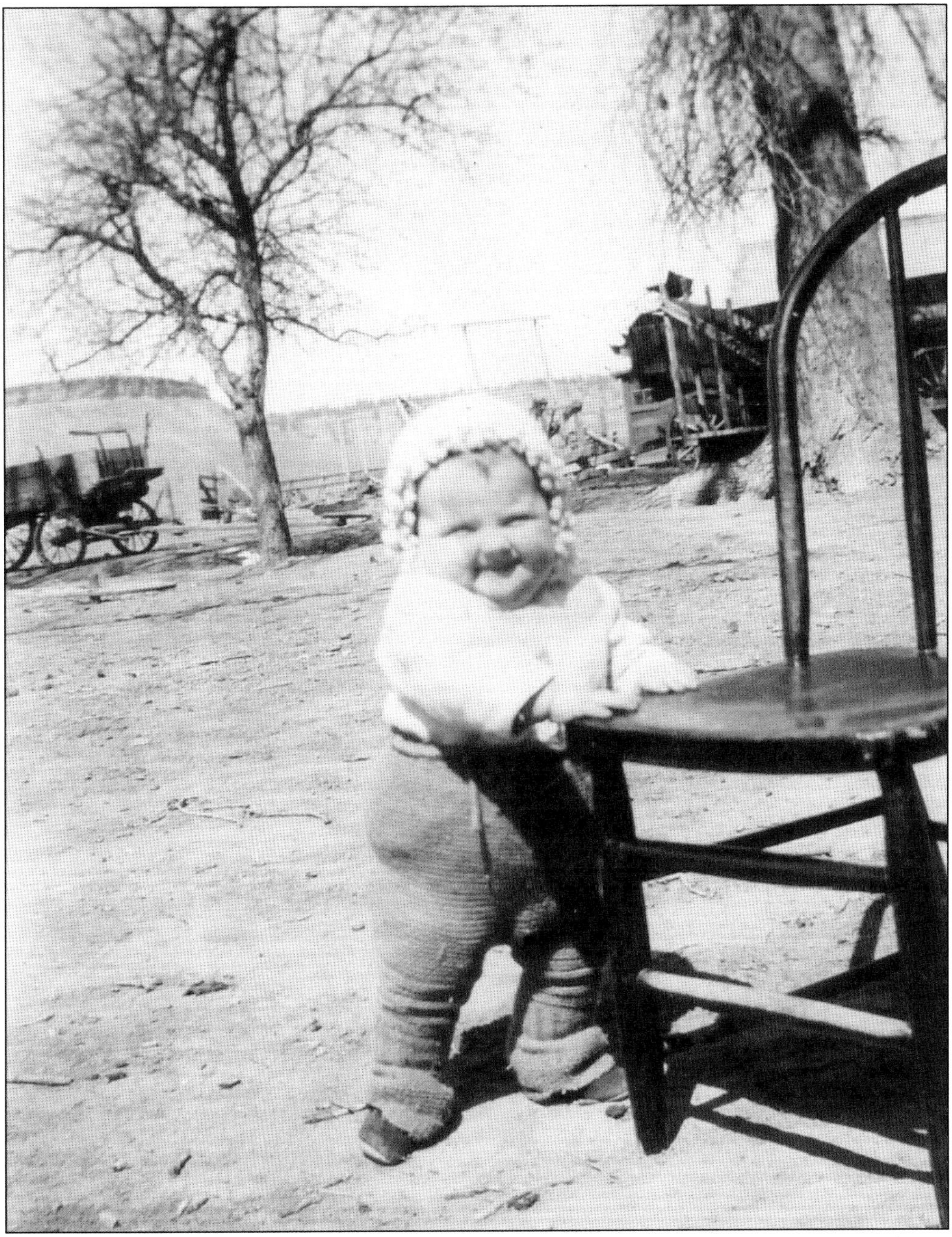

Little Rose Mary Fox steadies herself against a chair in the farmyard. Rose Mary was one of nine children born to Jacob and Elizabeth Fox, German-Russian immigrants who farmed near Square Butte. (Courtesy of the Western Heritage Center.)

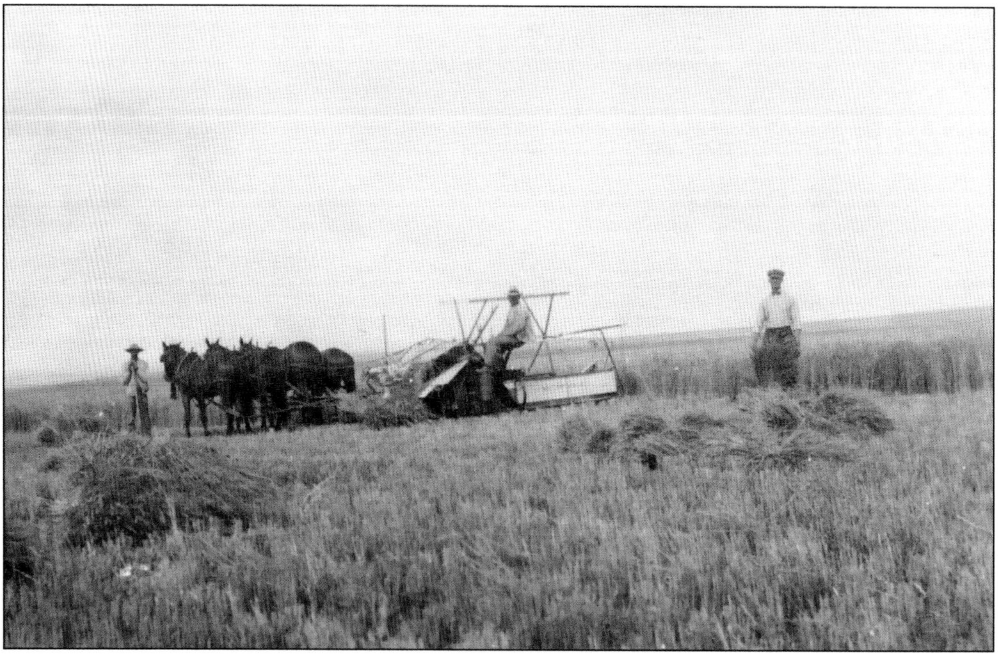

A farmer harvests wheat with a horse-drawn McCormick cutter. Farmhands then bundled the wheat into shocks. (Courtesy of the Laurel Museum.)

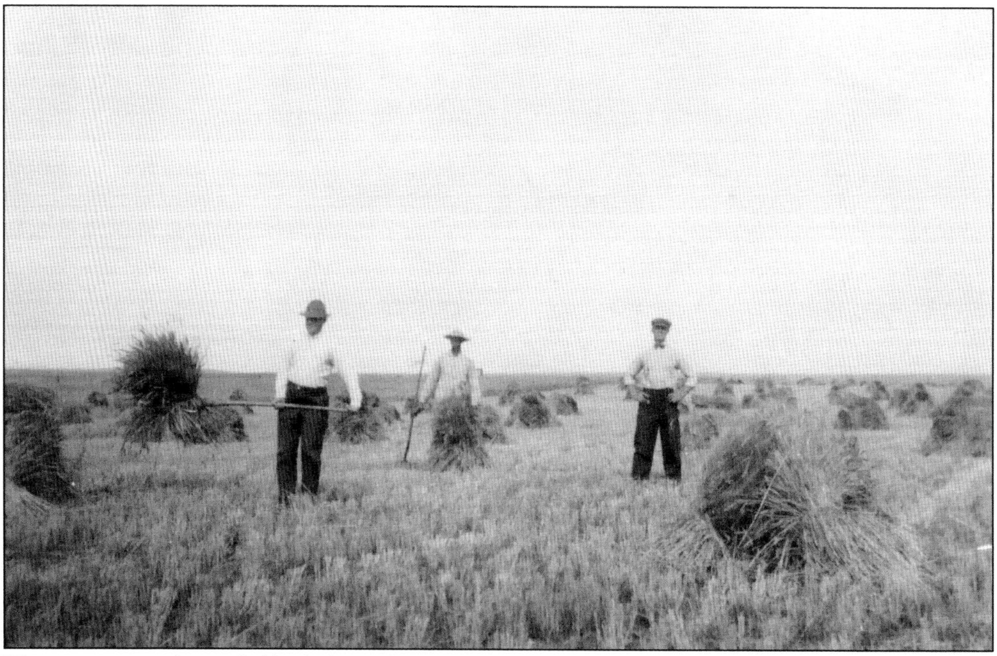

Three men stand in a field of wheat shocks. Plentiful rainfall produced bumper wheat crops for dryland farmers until a five-year drought began in 1917. The drought, coupled with a major drop in market prices after World War I, devastated the agricultural industry throughout the state. (Courtesy of the Laurel Museum.)

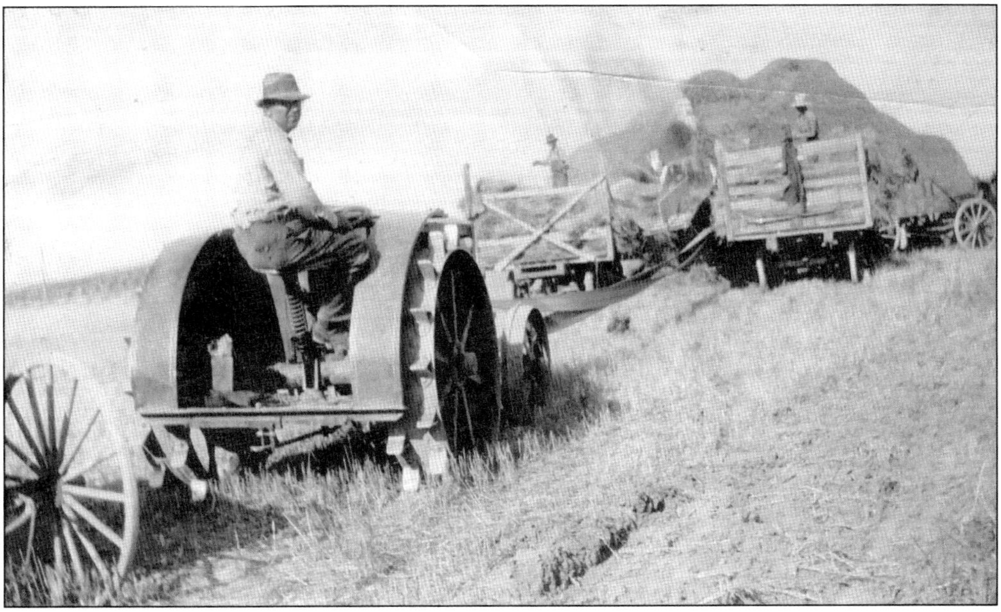

Although some farmers continued to use horse-drawn tractors and wagons into the 1940s, Henry Frank used a gas-powered tractor, seen here around 1930, to thresh wheat. Neighbors often helped each other during threshing season, moving from farm to farm and taking turns pitching wheat shocks into the threshing machine. The farmers' wives made sure the hungry crew was well-fed with a spread of roast beef or chicken and freshly baked cakes and pies. (Courtesy of the Laurel Museum.)

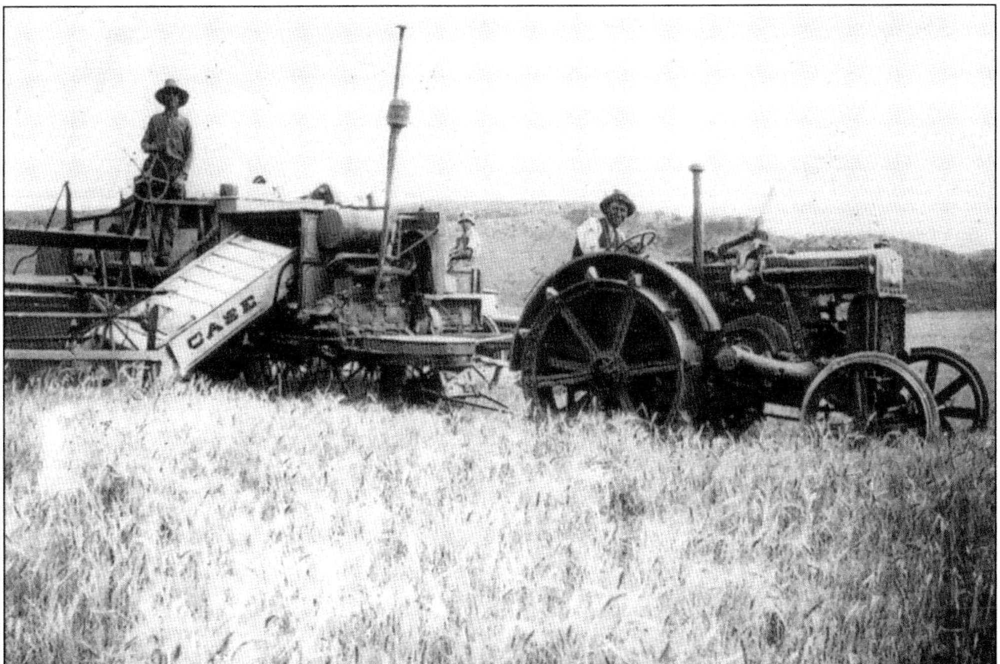

Henry Justiss harvests his wheat crop with an early model of the Case combine near Laurel. (Courtesy of Allison Nys.)

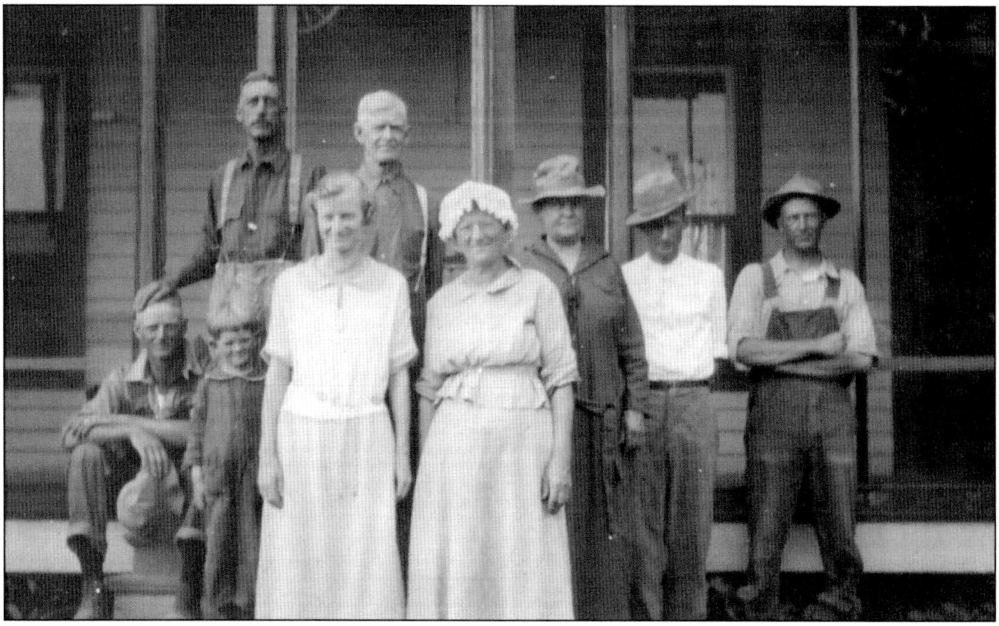

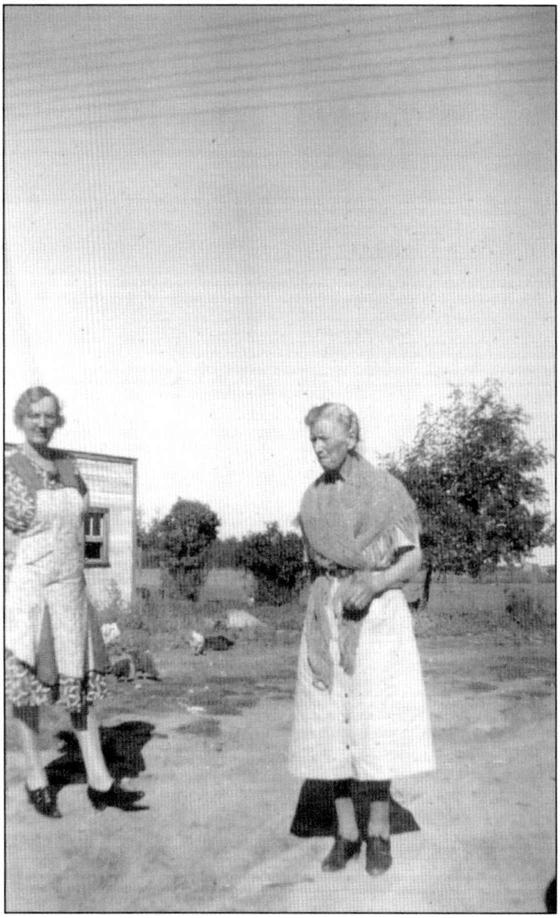

Melvin and Rachel Shay came to Laurel in 1909, leaving behind a proved-up homestead in Nebraska's Tornado Alley. They bought Fred Mitchell's farm three miles west of Laurel, where they raised their family. Pictured are, from left to right, (first row) son Vinton, an unidentified boy, daughter Valma, and Rachel; (second row) nephew Roscoe Shay, Melvin, Roscoe's wife Lela, an unidentified man, and son Norwood Shay. (Courtesy of Gerald Shay.)

Hens scrabble for feed in the farmyard behind Hazel Coombs (left) and Rachel Shay. Hazel and her husband, Edward, farmed near Square Butte, a short distance west of Melvin and Rachel Shay's place. (Courtesy of Gerald Shay.)

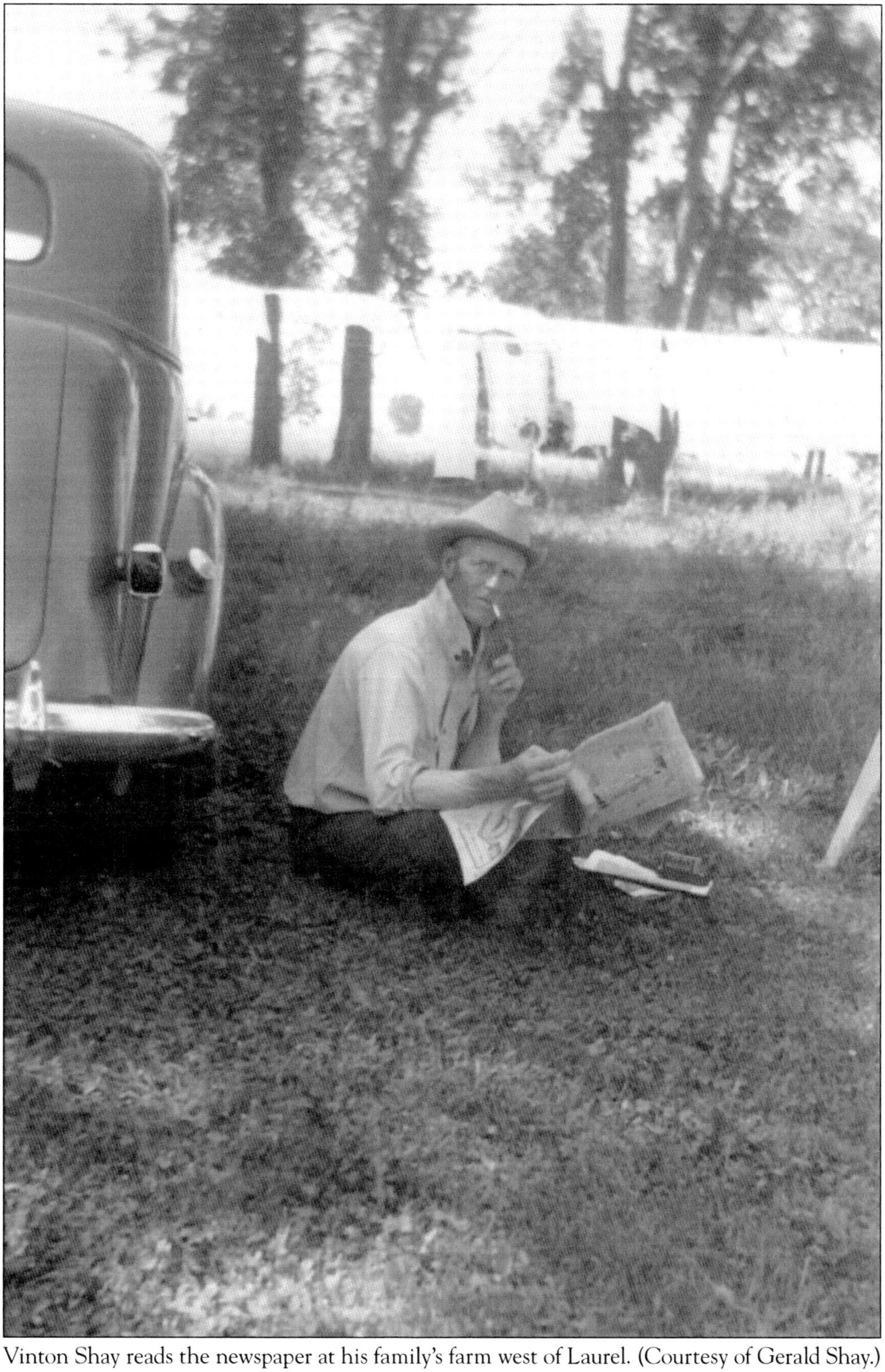

Vinton Shay reads the newspaper at his family's farm west of Laurel. (Courtesy of Gerald Shay.)

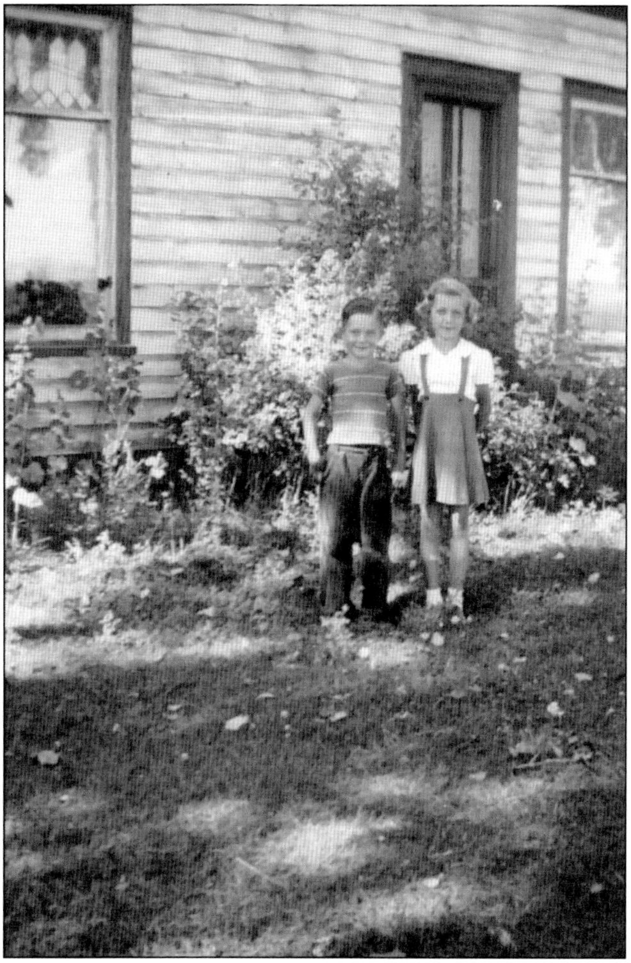

Robert and Maxine Boyd grew up on the family farm south of Laurel and attended the White Horse School through the eighth grade. The youngsters continued to call the homestead and assortment of log and plank outbuildings "the Ranch," a nickname that began with their grandmother Ada Jackson. (Both, courtesy of Maxine Allman.)

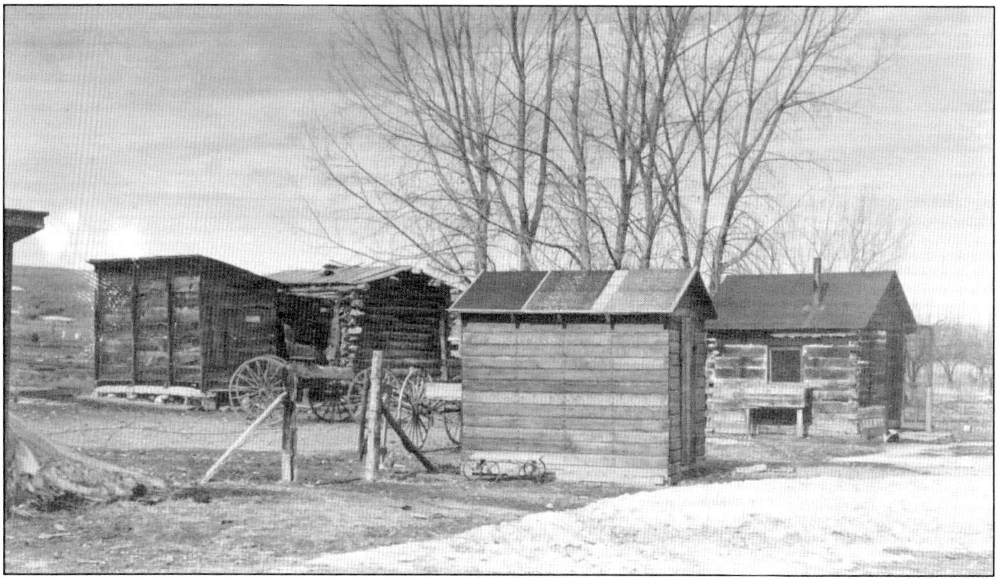

Three

A Growing Community

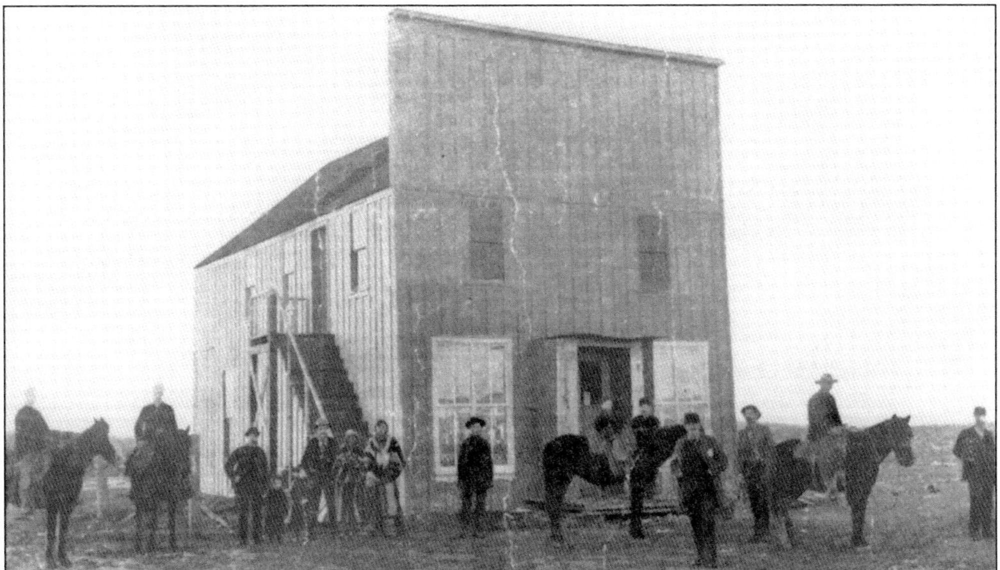

Leon Rose (at right center, with hands in pockets) built Laurel's first general store in 1892, shortly before W.A. Allen and Rev. John Guiler established a flour mill at nearby Allendale, a temperance-supporting community. Rose sold his Laurel store, which was directly south of the depot, to J.W. Gardner in 1895. Jacob Sanford (far right) began operating a pork packing house at Laurel around 1896. By 1899, the town of Laurel boasted two general stores, a post office, community hall, church, livery stable, blacksmith shop, and two saloons. A hotel, rooming house, and school rounded out the amenities of the growing community. (Courtesy of the Laurel Museum.)

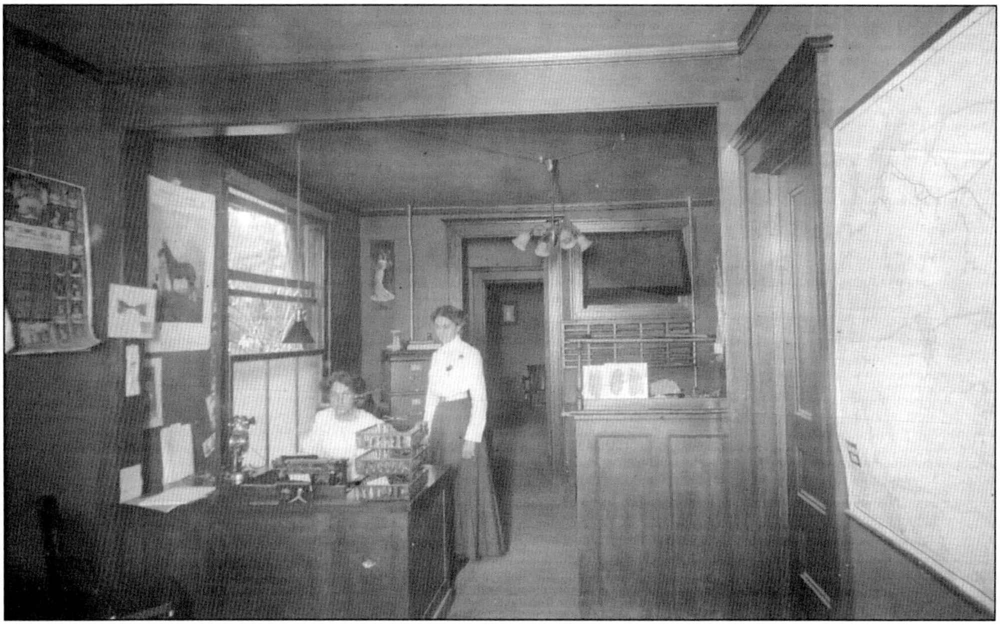

In 1899, Ida Camp bought two parcels of land north of the Northern Pacific and Rocky Fork railroad junction, about a mile east of Laurel. In July 1899, Ida and Edgar Camp platted a new townsite, called East Laurel. By the end of the year, the original townsite had been all but abandoned for East Laurel. Pictured is Edgar Camp's Billings real estate office around 1905. (Courtesy of the Laurel Public Library.)

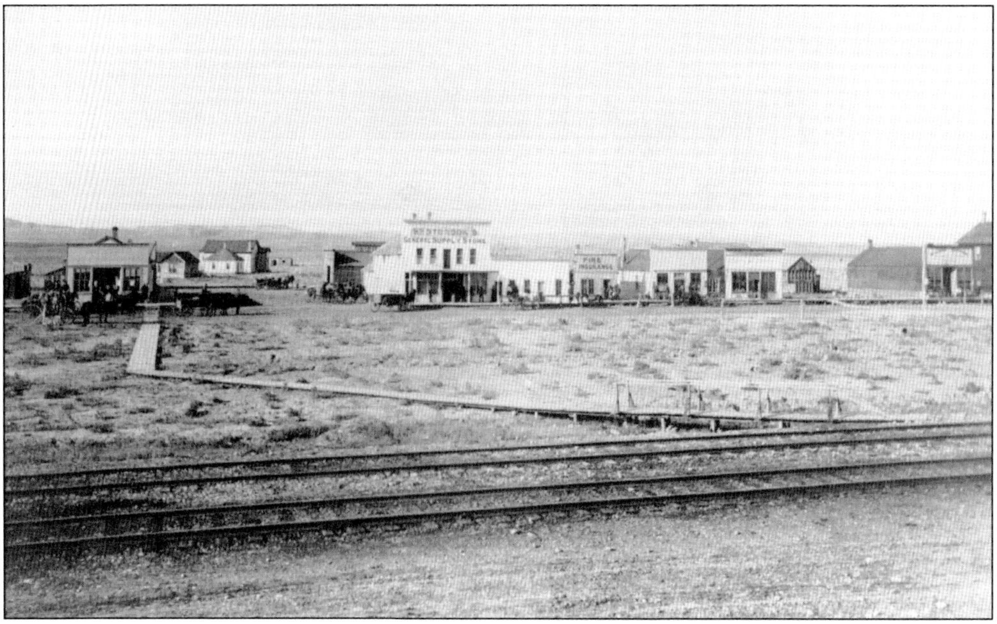

The boardwalk leads from the depot to Third Avenue and Main Street, the heart of East Laurel, in 1904. From left to right are the Camps' former mercantile, the Hohmann residence, the Congregational church and parsonage, Philip Hohmann's blacksmith shop, Walter Westbrook's store and warehouse, Edwin Fenton's fire insurance office, H.A. Noyes's saloon, R.O. Nore's general store, E.E. Lightfoot's saloon, and the Hotel Malcolm. (Courtesy of the Laurel Museum.)

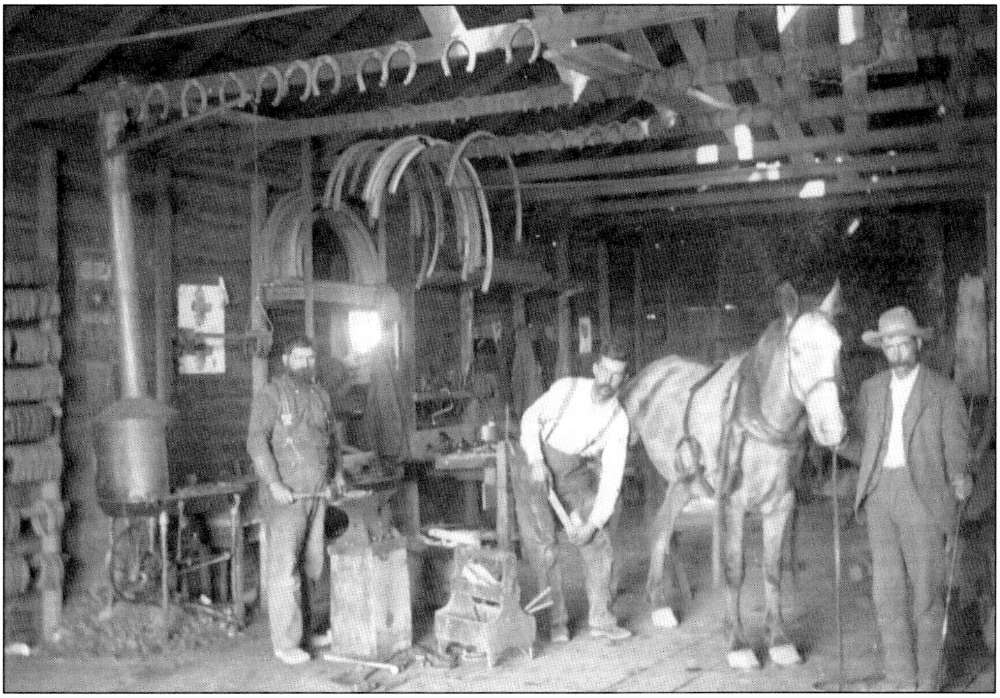

Charles Stout shoes Dick Mills's horse in Philip Hohmann's blacksmith shop in the new townsite around 1899. The following spring, Philip Hohmann moved his family from a two-room log cabin in Old Laurel to a newly built home across the street from his blacksmith shop in East Laurel. His wife, Louisa, was a nurse and midwife. (Courtesy of the Laurel Museum.)

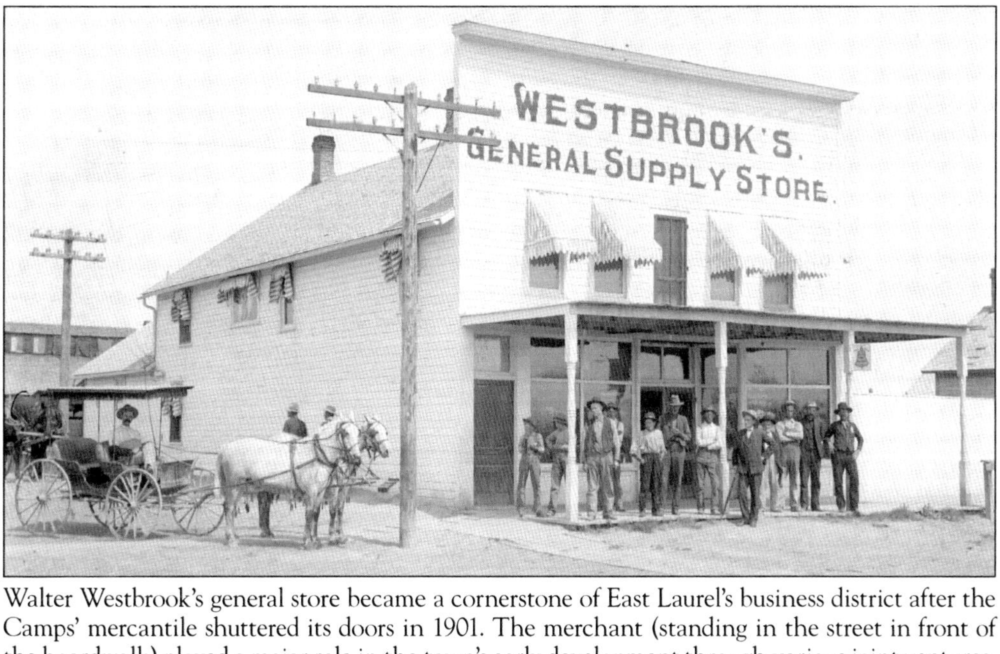

Walter Westbrook's general store became a cornerstone of East Laurel's business district after the Camps' mercantile shuttered its doors in 1901. The merchant (standing in the street in front of the boardwalk) played a major role in the town's early development through various joint ventures, including the Laurel Realty Company and the Laurel State Bank. He also served two terms as mayor, advocating for streetlights and a municipal water and sewer system. (Courtesy of Sedly Barsness.)

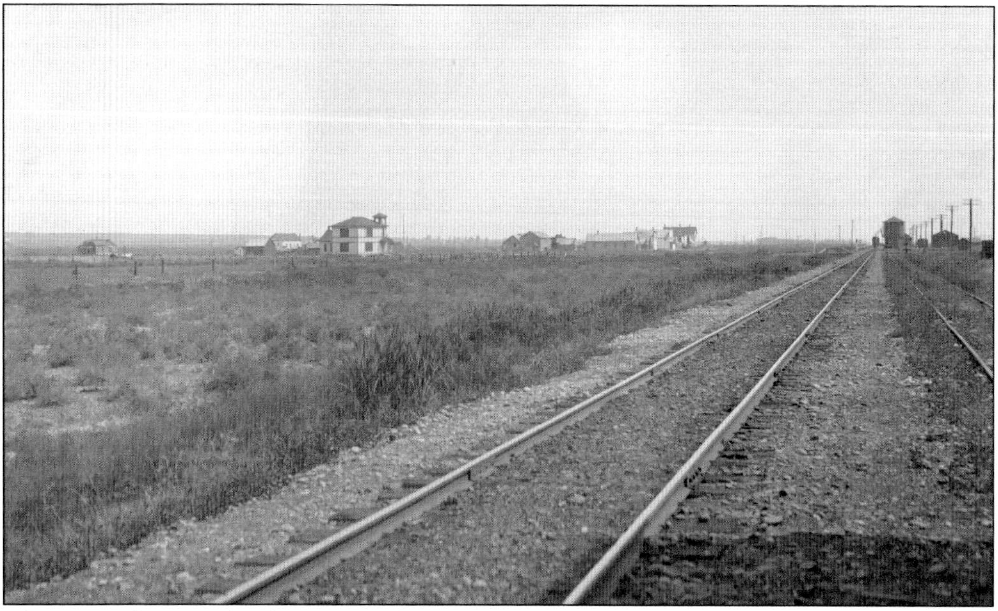

This 1904 photograph of East Laurel was taken west of town near Old Laurel. A two-story schoolhouse with a bell tower had been built north of the tracks, along with new shops, saloons, and homes. Other buildings in the new community, including the First Congregational Church, Laurel Hall, Edgar and Charles Camp's mercantile, Edwin Fenton's post office, and Susan Malcolm's hotel, had been moved on rolled logs from the original townsite. (Courtesy of Sedly Barsness.)

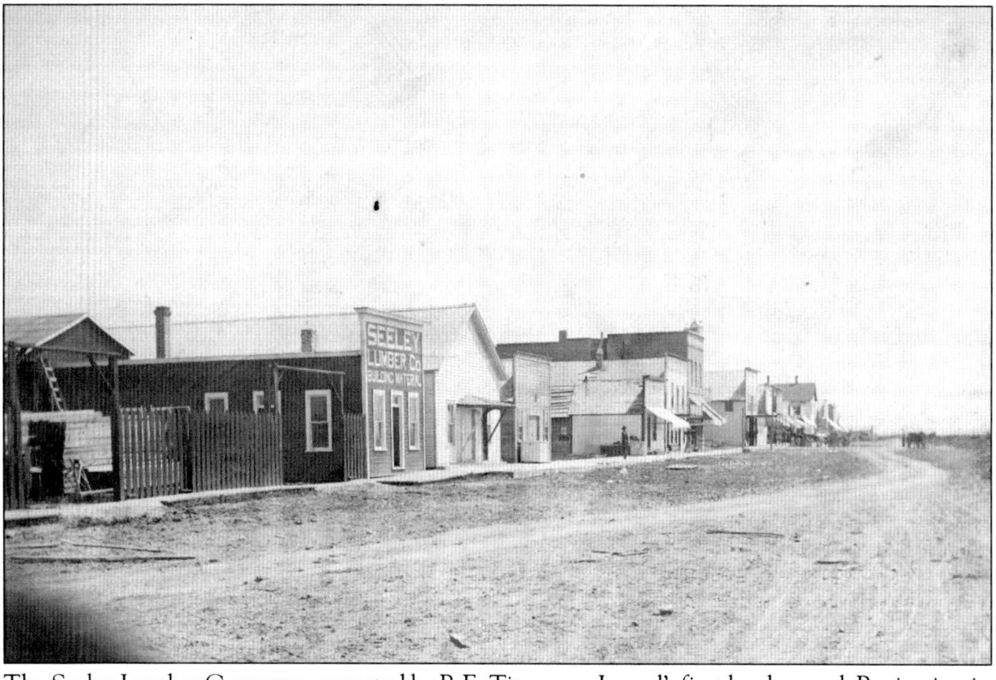

The Seeley Lumber Company, operated by R.E. Titus, was Laurel's first lumberyard. Beginning in 1906, builders and material suppliers could not keep up with Laurel's rapid growth. Laurel faced a housing shortage and many new businesses set up in temporary tent structures until wood-framed and brick buildings could be erected. (Courtesy of Sedly Barsness.)

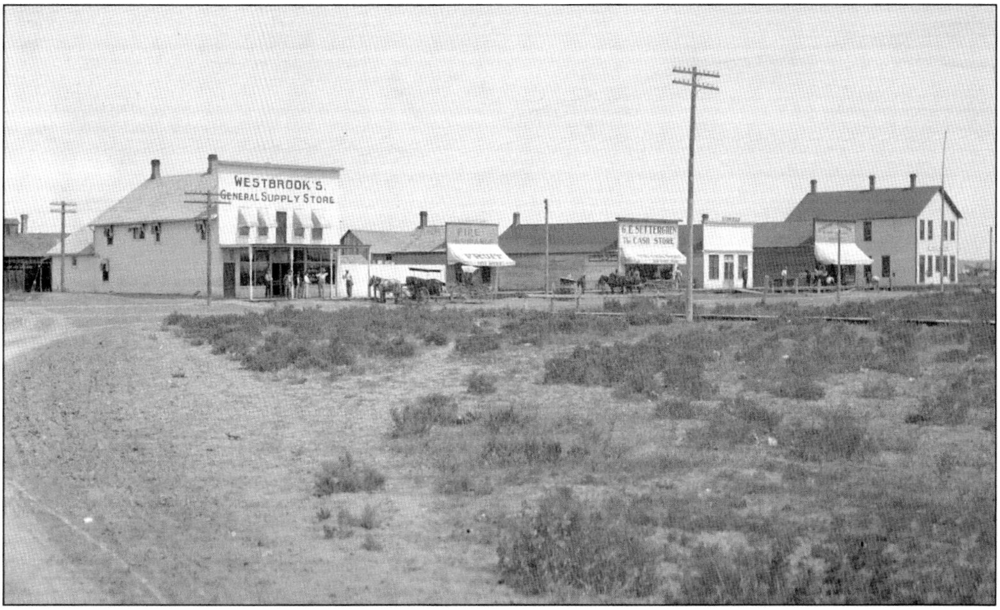

This view of West Main Street was taken about 1906. Four new businesses joined the block in 1907, including Lester Young's real estate office, Citizens National Bank, the Spencer-McIlrath general store in George Settergren's former location, and Ed Burla's saloon. In September 1907, all but the Hotel Malcolm (far right) were lost to a fire that started in a blacksmith shop near Westbrook's store. (Courtesy of Sedly Barsness.)

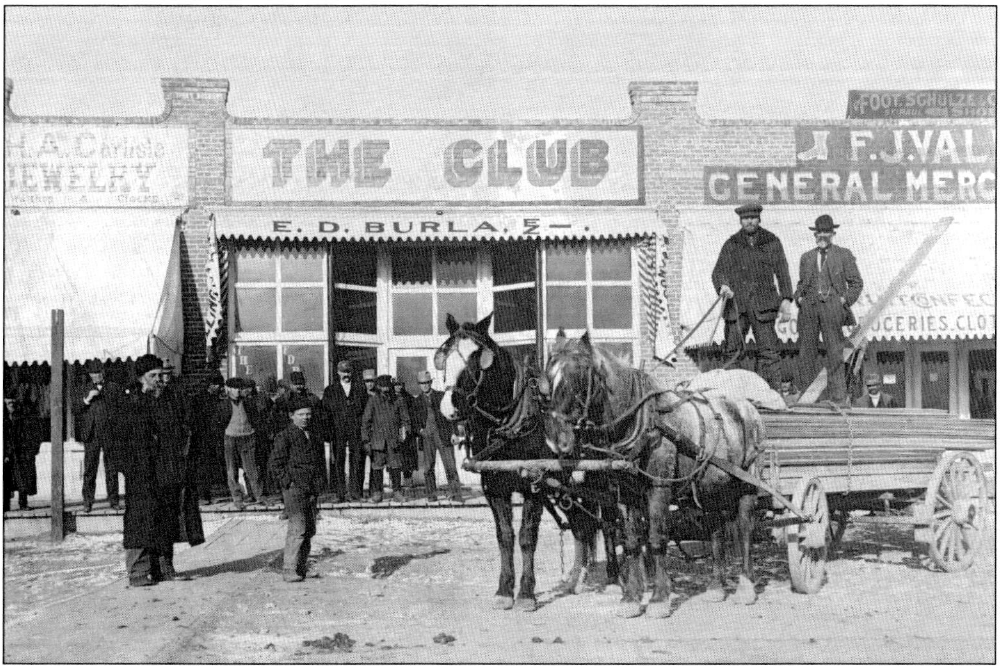

Laurel immediately began rebuilding in the wake of the devastating 1907 fire. This was the first of three large brick commercial blocks to be completed in 1908. The Club, Ed Burla's saloon, was flanked by two new establishments, Herb Carlisle's jewelry shop and Frank Valek's general mercantile. (Courtesy of the Laurel Museum.)

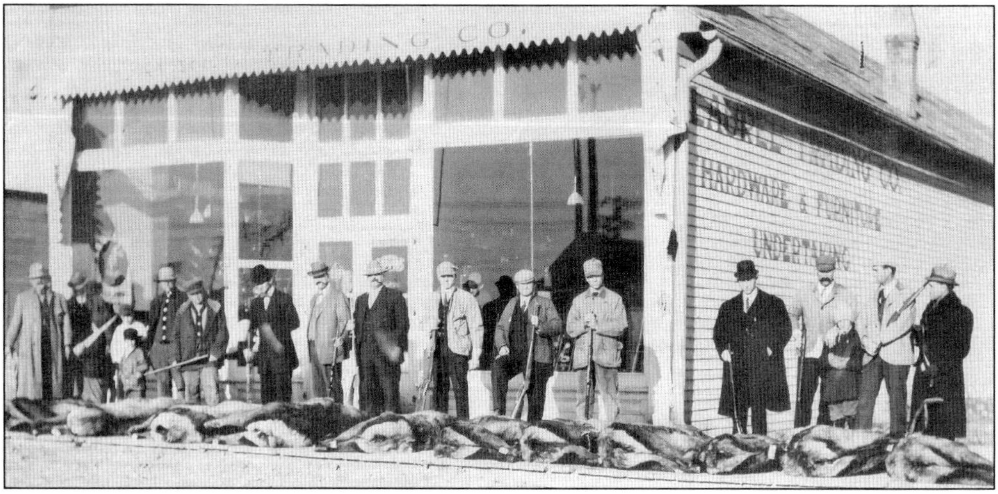

Elk hunters display their trophies on the boardwalk in front of the Laurel Trading Company. Bert Brockway, Charles Morris, and George Settergren established the company, a retail hardware and furniture store at 119 West Main Street, in 1906. (Courtesy of the Laurel Museum.)

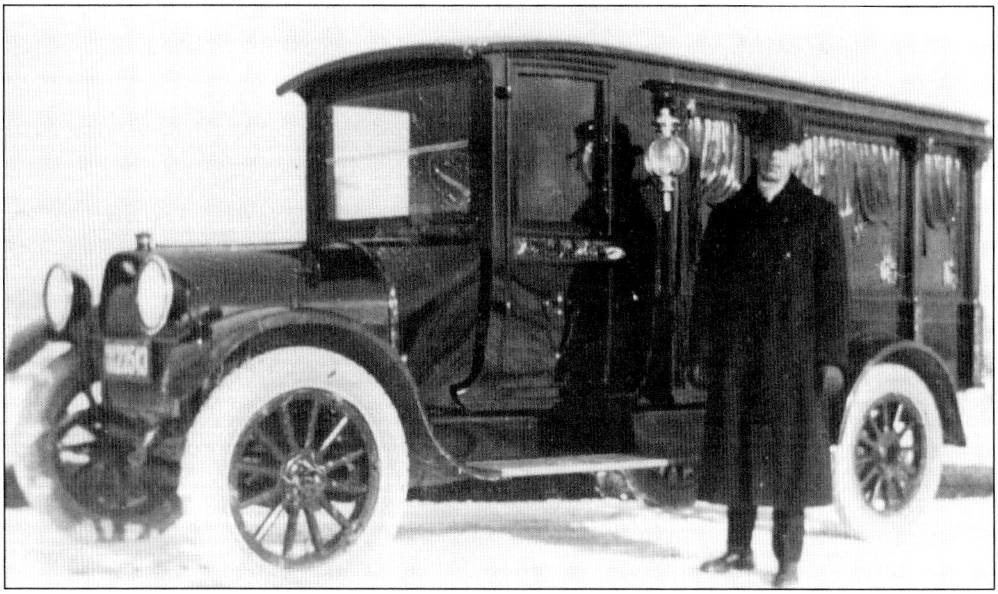

George Settergren stands next to his first motorized hearse. He ran his undertaking business behind the Laurel Trading Company before he built his own furniture store and funeral parlor at 20 First Avenue North in 1908. He moved his business to Billings in 1922. (Courtesy of the Laurel Museum.)

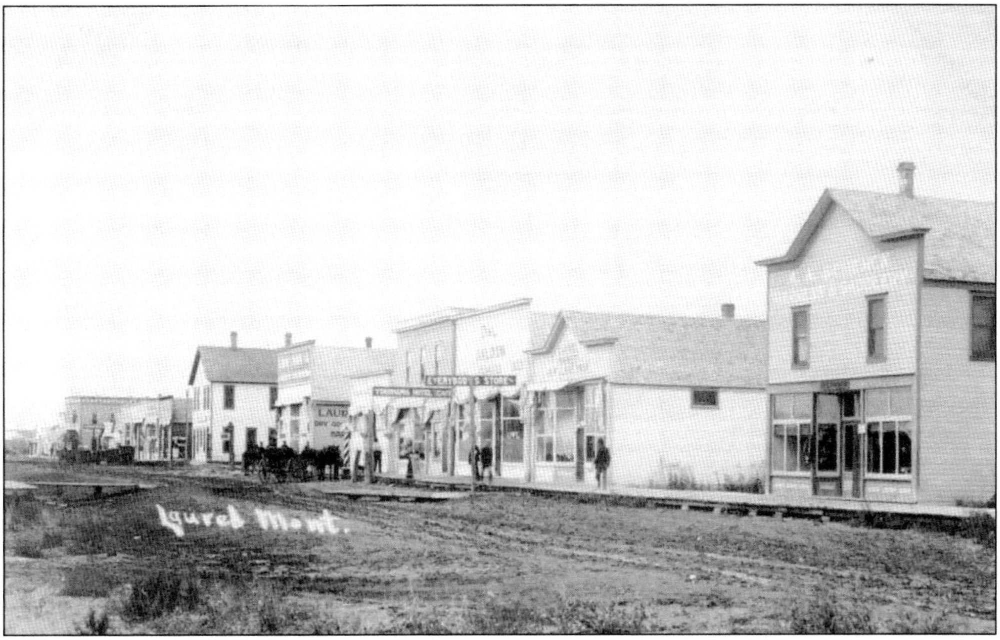

By 1908, a bank and new shops, eateries, and business houses lined West Main Street, reflecting the bustling community's rapid growth. Recruitment of farm laborers by the sugar company boosted the number of families living in Laurel from 14 in 1905 to 100 in 1907. Agricultural opportunities and the new railroad facilities at Laurel bumped the population to 806 residents by 1910 and 1,200 by 1912. (Courtesy of the Laurel Museum.)

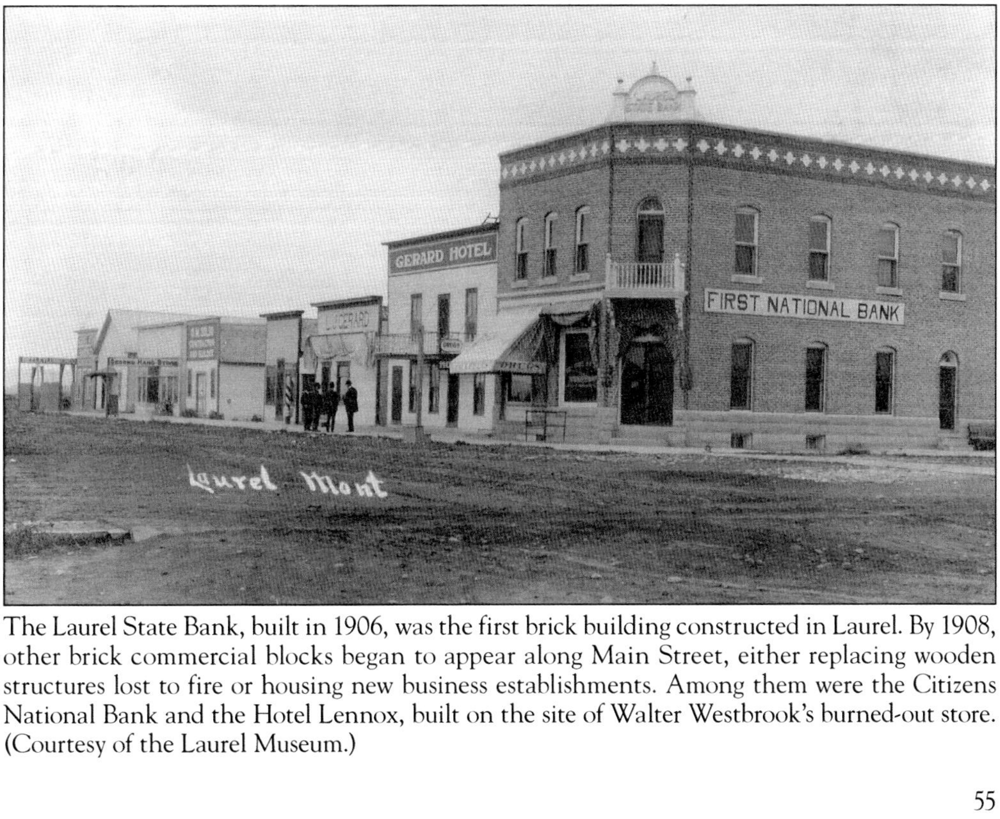

The Laurel State Bank, built in 1906, was the first brick building constructed in Laurel. By 1908, other brick commercial blocks began to appear along Main Street, either replacing wooden structures lost to fire or housing new business establishments. Among them were the Citizens National Bank and the Hotel Lennox, built on the site of Walter Westbrook's burned-out store. (Courtesy of the Laurel Museum.)

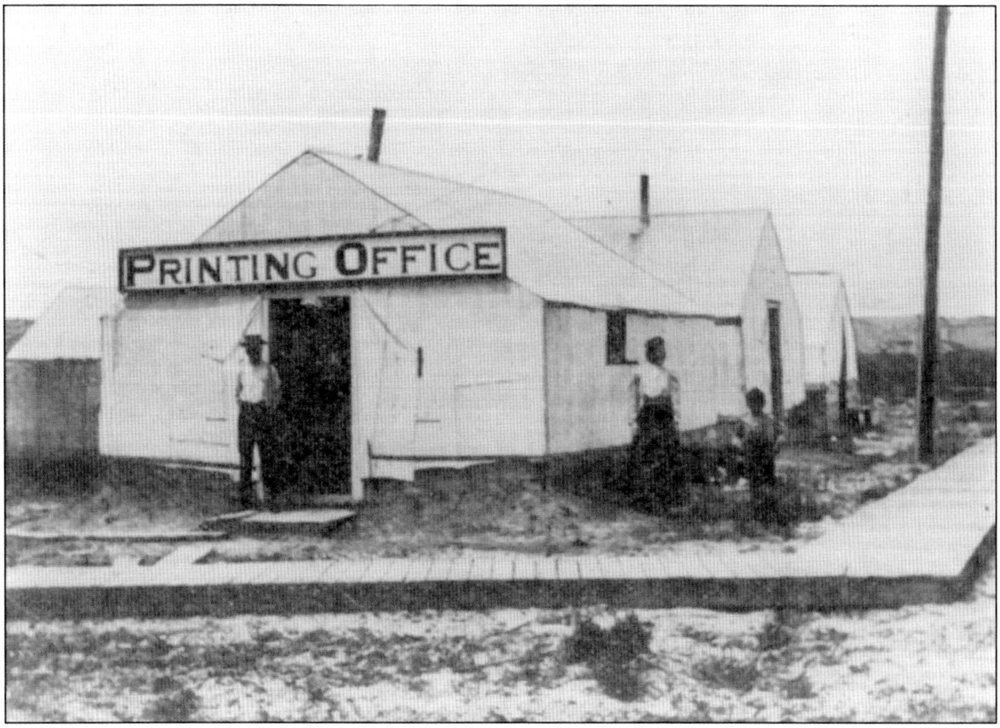

The *Laurel Sentinel*, the city's first weekly newspaper, kept townsfolk apprised of developments in the booming community. Daniel and Laura Watsabaugh published the *Laurel Sentinel* in a wooden-framed tent for nearly two years before their two-story building (below) was completed in 1908. (Both, courtesy of the Laurel Museum.)

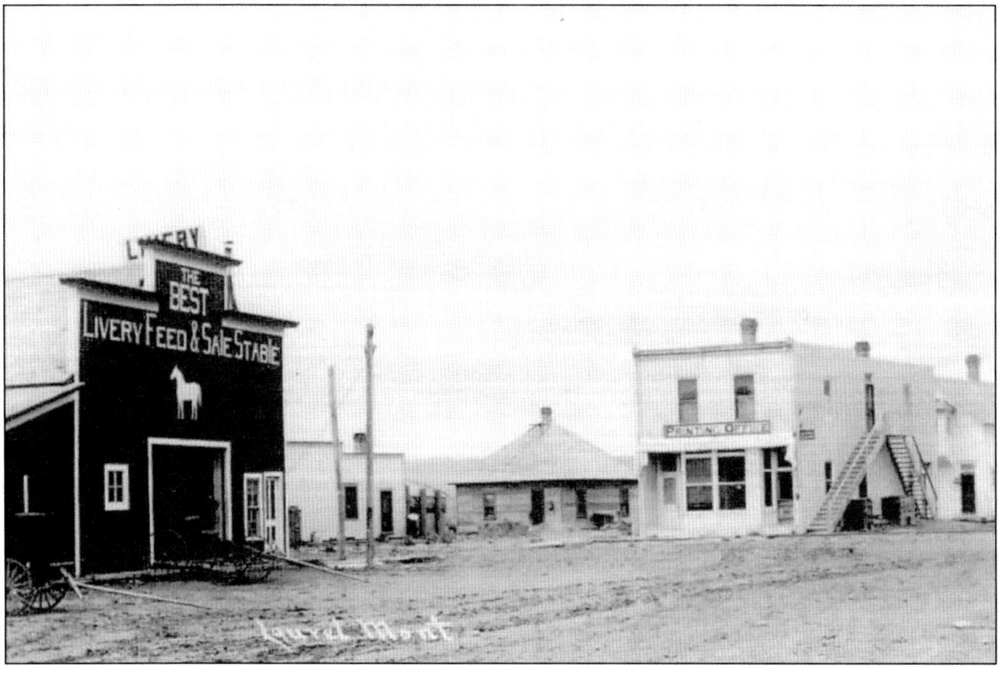

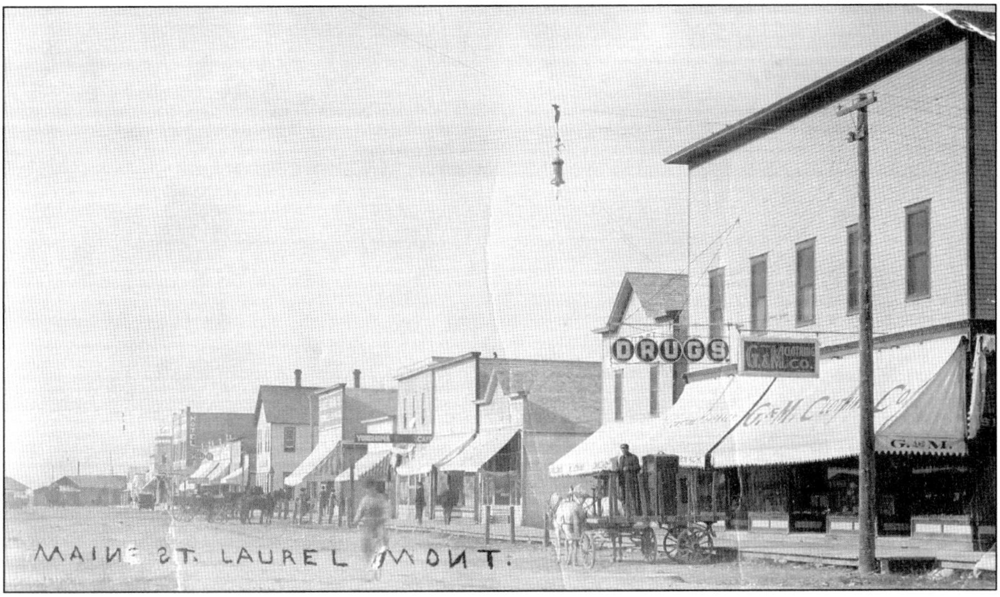

The city of Laurel incorporated in 1908. Elections soon followed, but not without a hitch. Postmaster Edwin Fenton tied with merchant Walter Westbrook in a bid for mayor. Responsibility then fell to the newly elected aldermen to select Laurel's first mayor. The decision went to Edwin Fenton. During his one-year term, Mayor Fenton and the city council established the first city charter and municipal bylaws, passed a business licensing ordinance, appointed a city engineer, organized and equipped a volunteer fire department, built a jail, and limited the number of saloons operating within city limits. Pictured below is Edwin Fenton, known to many locals as "Dad Fenton," at work in his insurance and realty office in the 1930s. (Above, courtesy of Ryan Mead; below, courtesy of Sedly Barsness.)

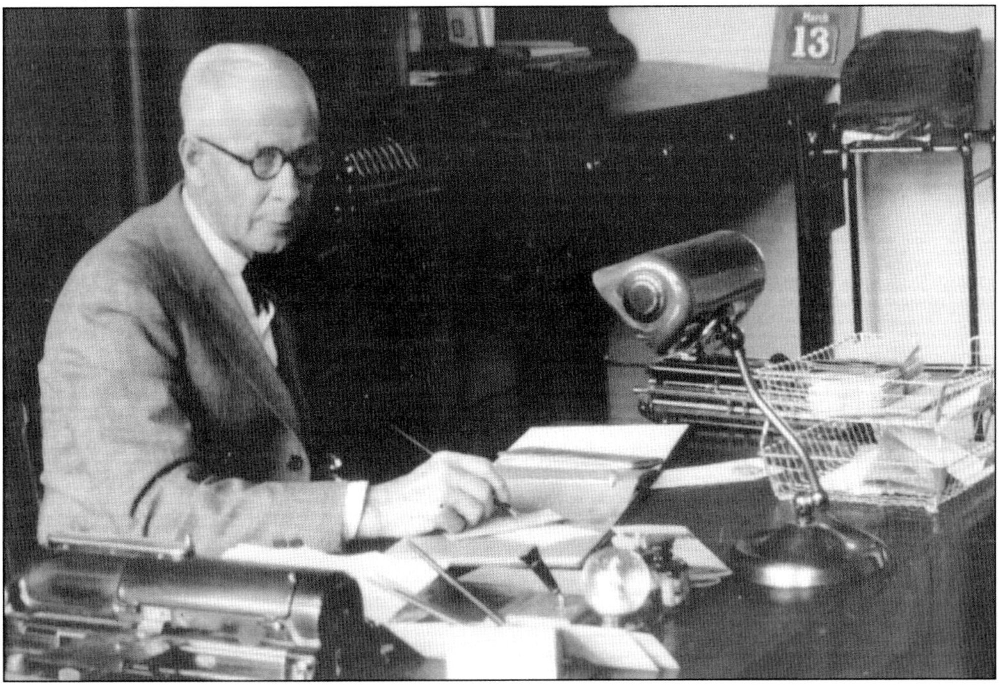

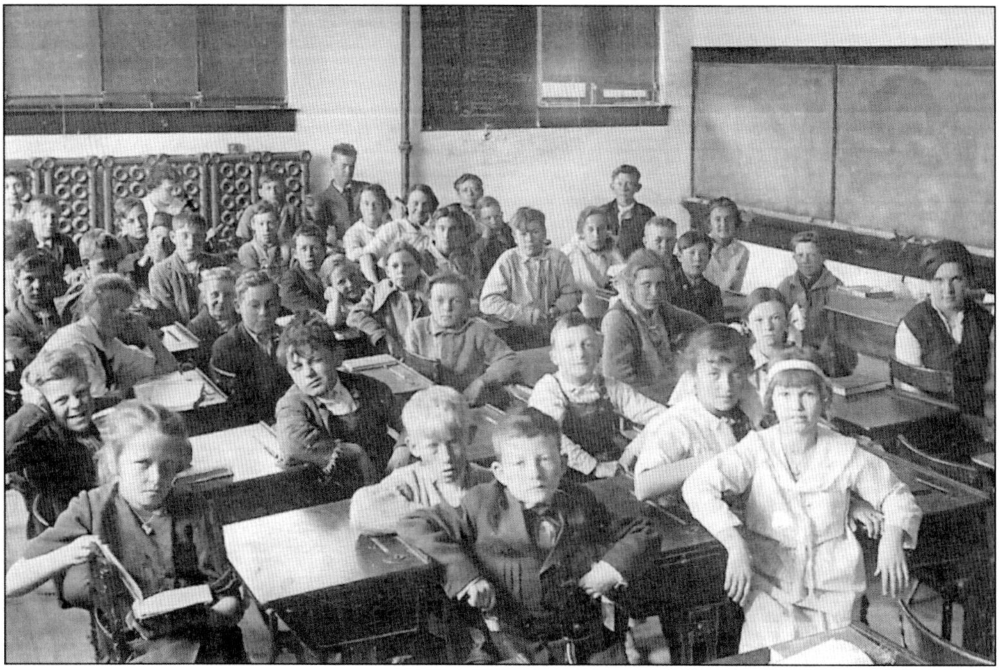

The swelling student population reflected Laurel's rapid growth between 1906 and 1920. Enrollment surged from 94 students at the end of the 1906–1907 term to 182 the following spring. A third classroom had been added to the two-room schoolhouse near the tracks, but student numbers soon overwhelmed the small school. Newly recruited teachers held classes in a nearby cottage and at the German Congregational Church until a new two-story high school was completed in 1909. Growth continued, and by 1921, Laurel boasted two new elementary schools on Cottonwood and Yellowstone Avenues as well as the high school and a gymnasium with classrooms. Plans were also underway to build a middle school. (Above, courtesy of Barbara Nicholas; below, courtesy of the Laurel Museum.)

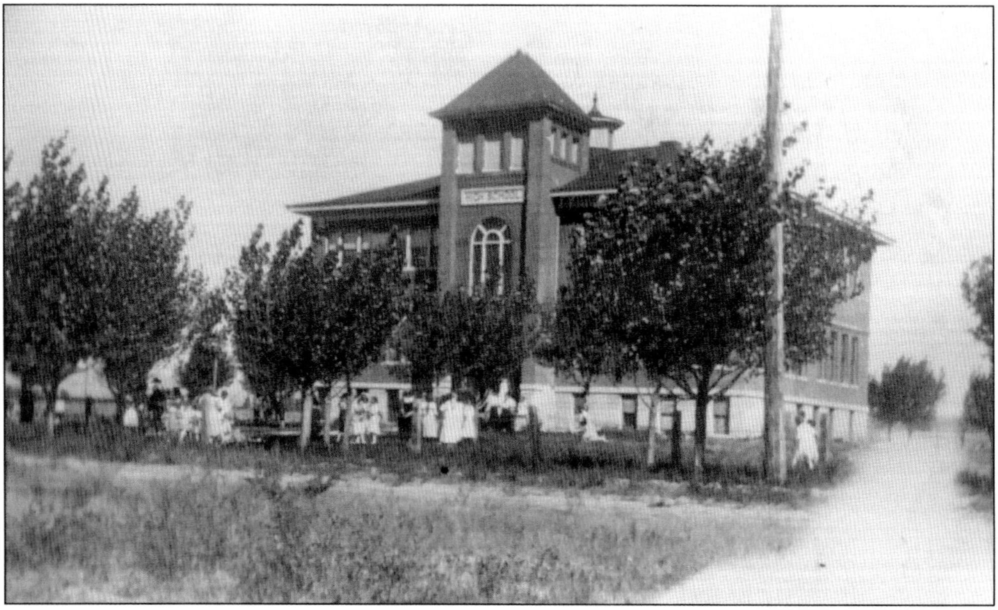

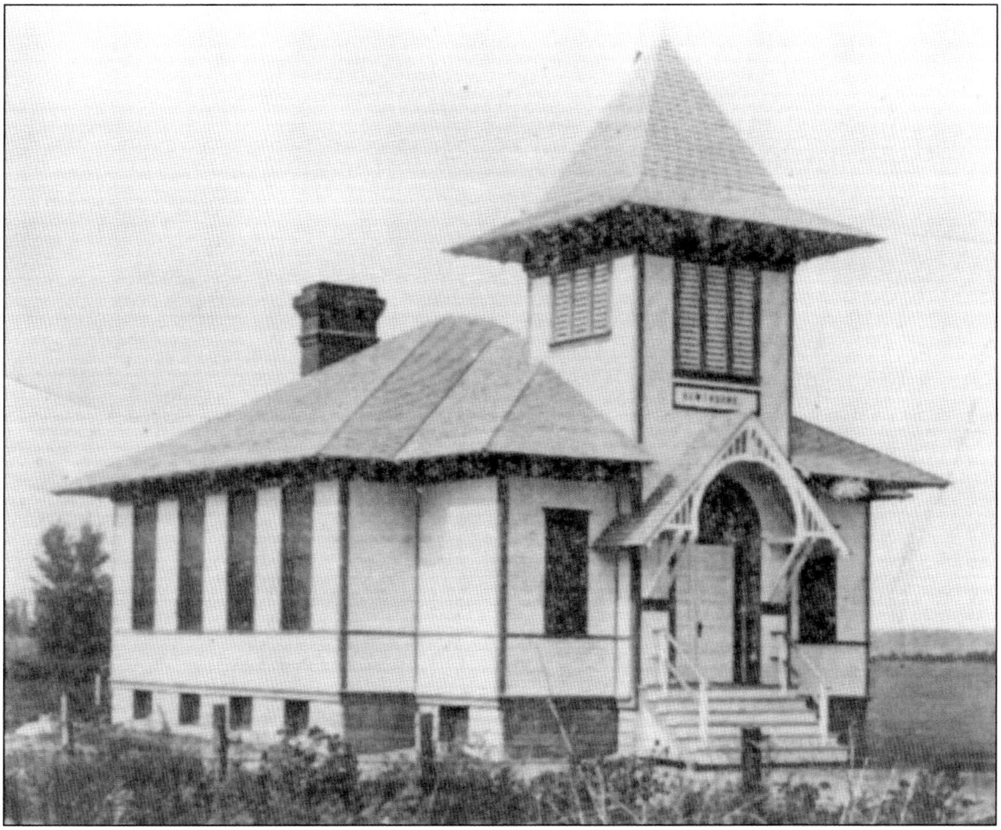

The Hawthorn School was one of eight rural schools that dotted the countryside around Laurel. Not only did country schools provide instruction to children through the eighth grade, they were also the heart of community activities for farming families. (Courtesy of the Laurel Museum.)

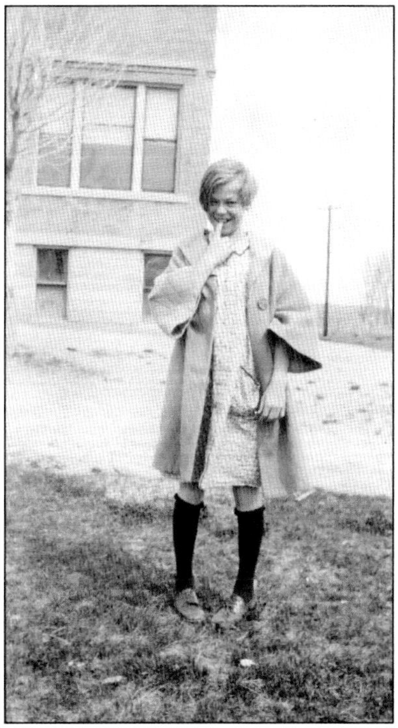

This bashful girl from the White Horse School rode the bus into Laurel to attend high school. (Courtesy of Maxine Allman.)

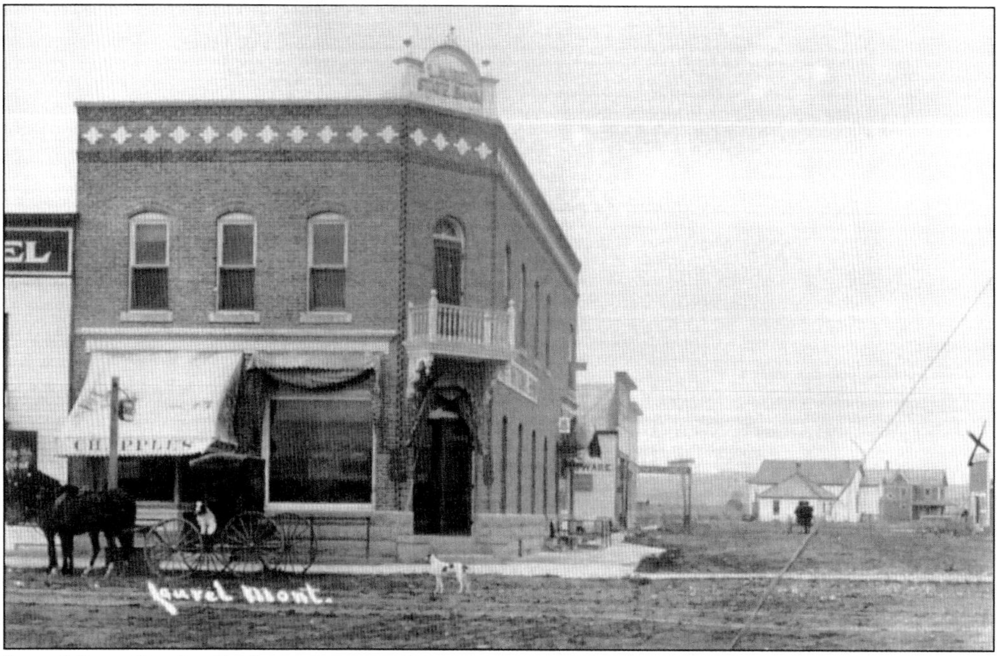

Laurel State Bank, which incorporated in 1906, converted for a short time in 1907 to the First National Bank of Laurel before reverting back to a state bank in 1908 because of lending limitations on real estate. (Courtesy of the Laurel Museum.)

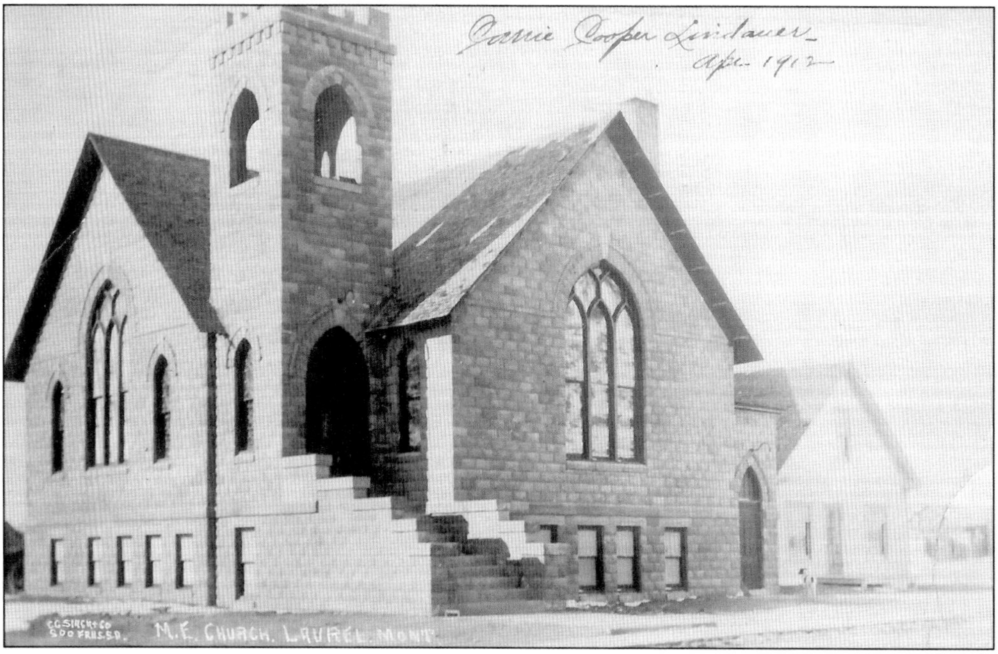

The Laurel Methodist Church offered services from a tent tabernacle in 1908 before a stone church was completed in 1910. This was not the oldest church in Laurel. That honor went to the First Congregational Church, which had been established in Old Laurel in 1891. (Courtesy of the Laurel Museum.)

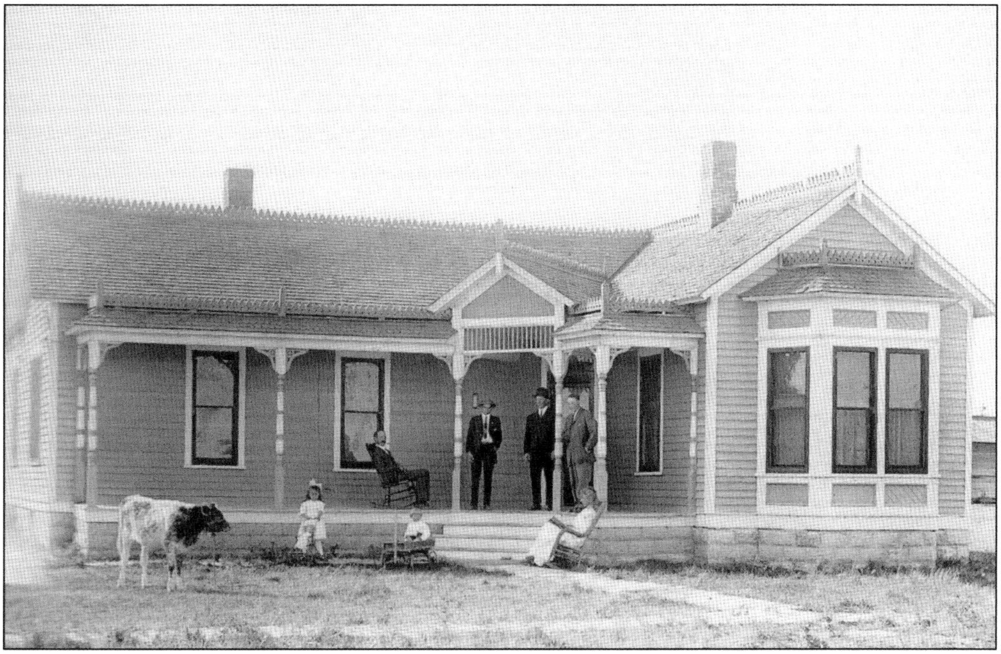

Abraham and Carrie Erb's family poses in front of their home in 1912. By most accounts, this is the oldest house in Laurel, having been built in 1899 by town founders Edgar and Ida Camp. Dr. Martin Young bought the Camp farm in 1907 and moved the house the following year to its current location at 110 Fourth Avenue. He sold the home to his sister Carrie Erb in 1911. (Courtesy of Allison Nys.)

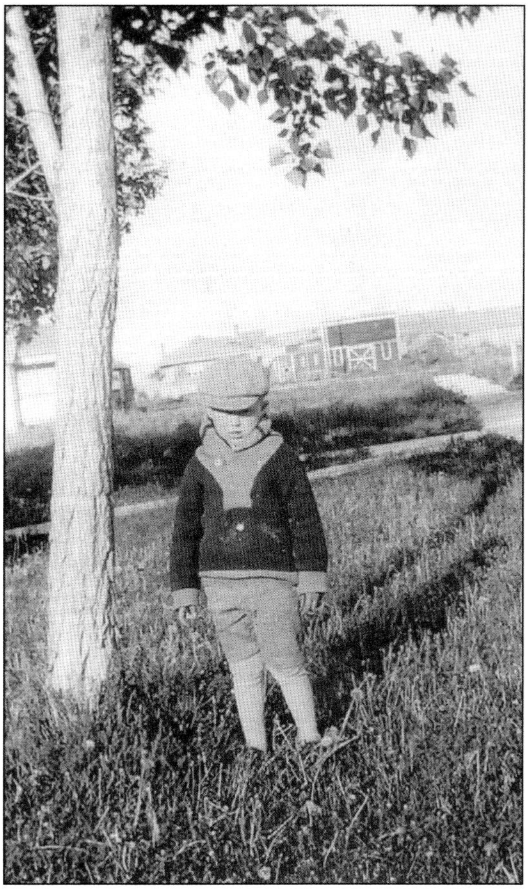

A glimpse of Laurel's growing residential neighborhood, west of downtown in the Young's Subdivision, can be seen behind this glum tyke, identified only as Teddy B. (Courtesy of Allison Nys.)

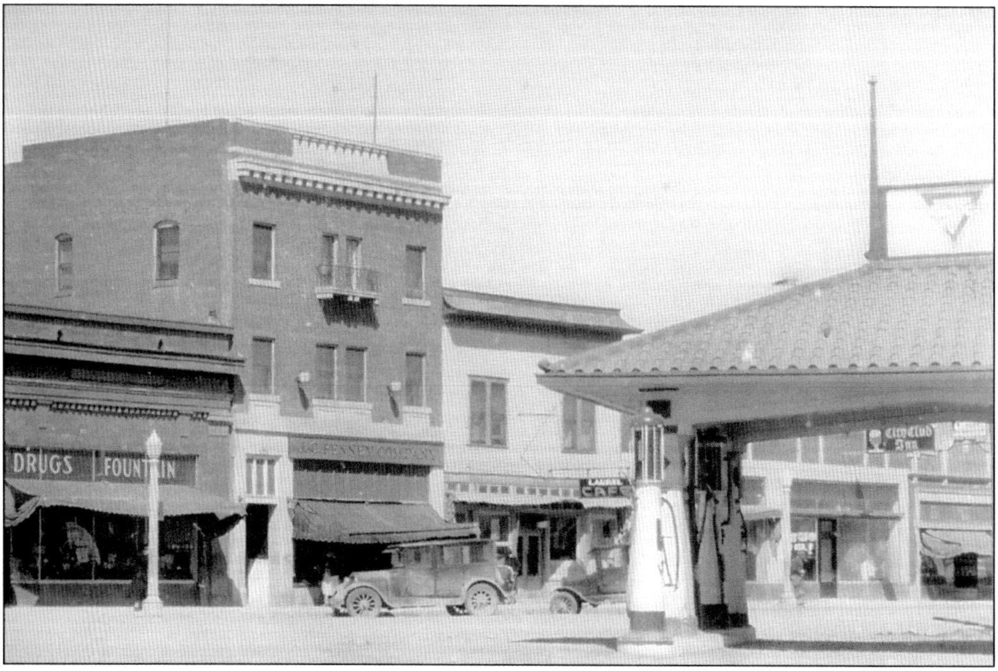

The business district began to expand eastward in 1908, shifting the commercial hub to First Avenue and Main Street. The Laurel Realty Company promoted commercial development along East Main Street, where modern brick commercial blocks accommodated a host of new and established business enterprises. Farther east, toward the new Northern Pacific Railroad facilities, Lucius Nutting developed residential neighborhoods designed for railroad employees. (Both, courtesy of Ryan Mead.)

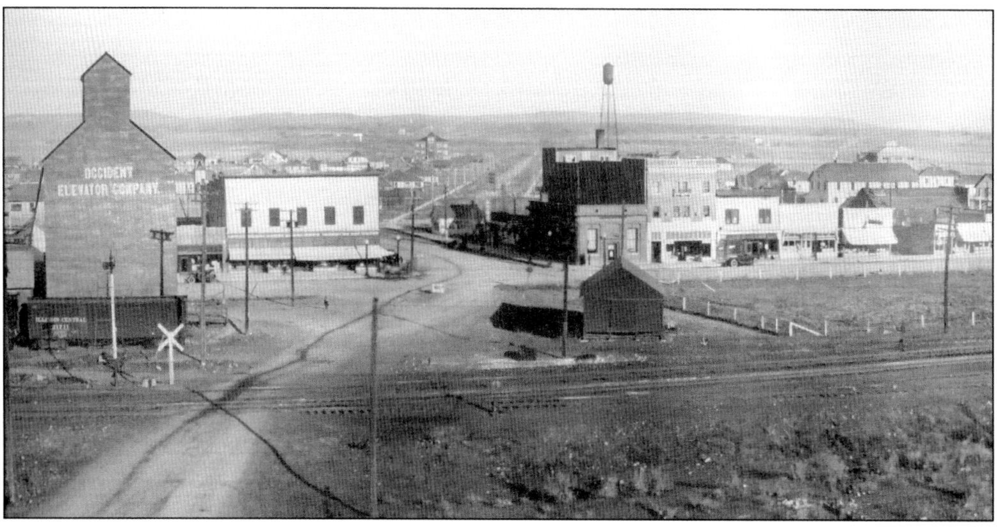

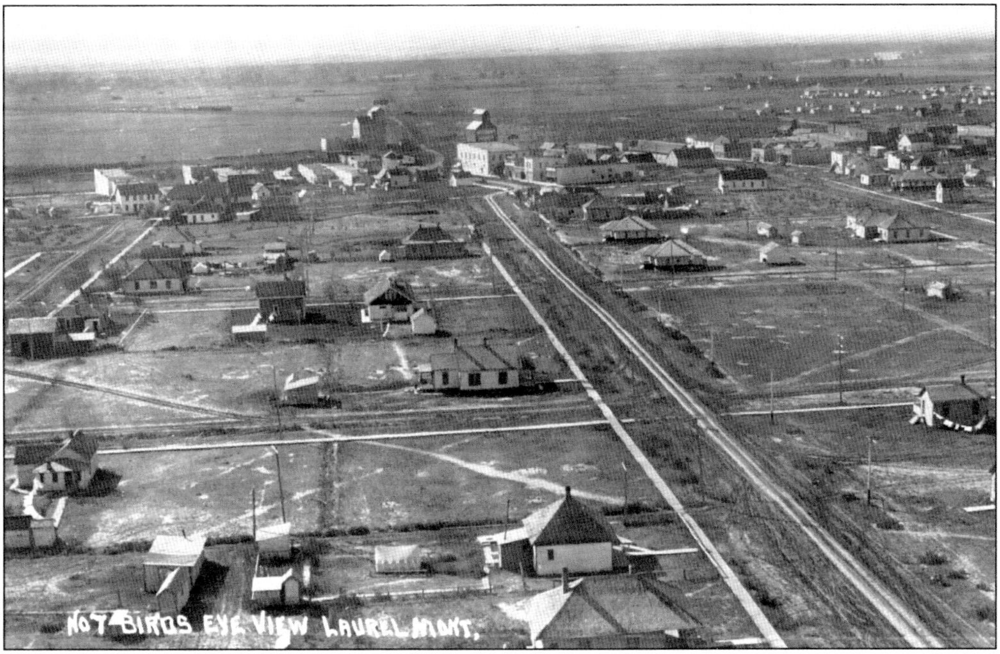

By 1918, the small community of Laurel had grown into a bustling railroad town. This is a view from the water tower to the south toward the Yellowstone River. The neighborhood on the south side of the tracks, known as German Town, can be seen in the distance. (Courtesy of Gerald Shay.)

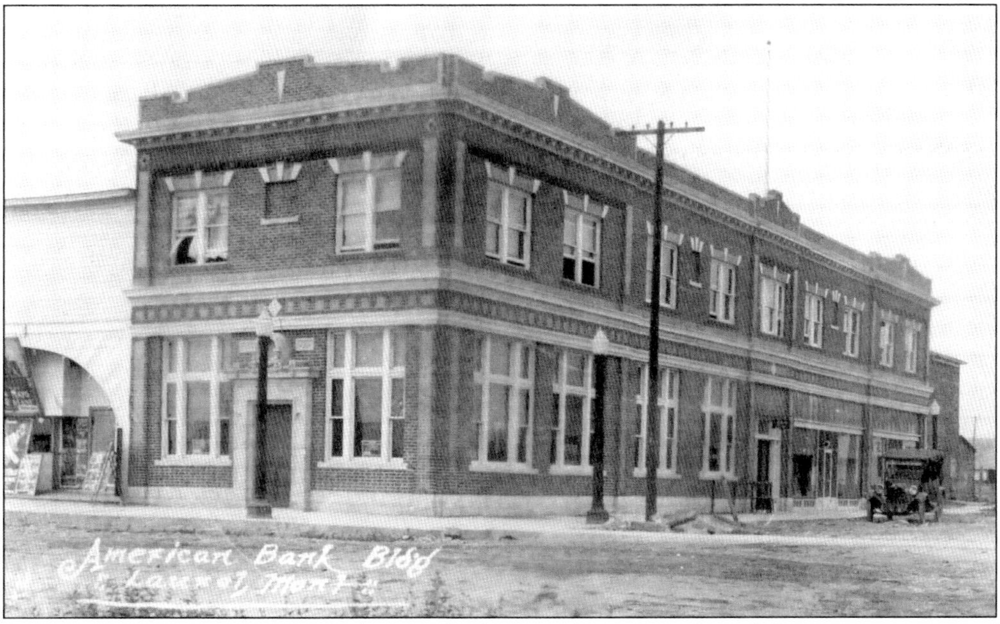

The American Bank of Laurel, along with the Laurel State Bank and the Citizens National Bank, collapsed in the early 1920s when depressed market prices and a long run of droughts caused a rash of farm foreclosures. Laurel was left without a local bank to loan money or cash payroll checks for nearly two years until the Yellowstone Bank opened in 1926. (Courtesy of the Western Heritage Center.)

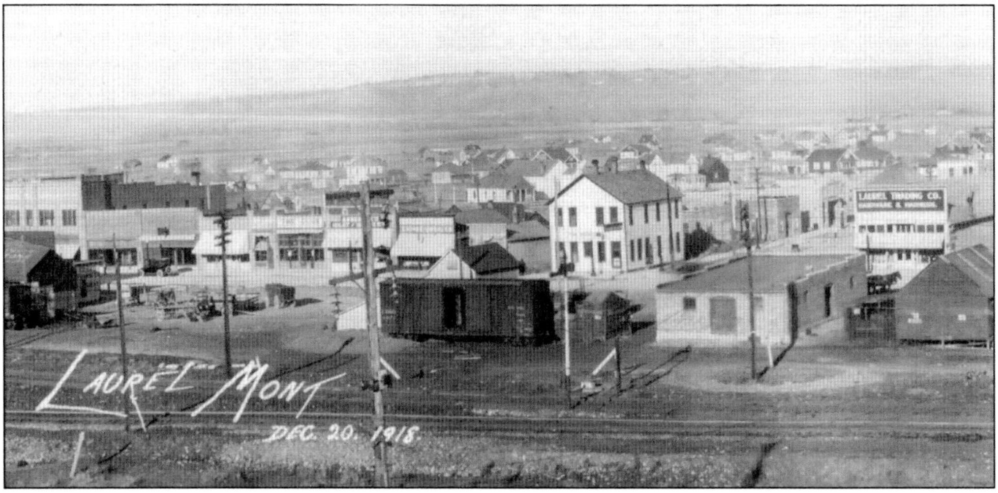

Laurel suffered several devastating fires in the town's early history. The Hotel Malcolm, center, was the lone-surviving building in the 200 block of West Main Street after a 1907 fire tore through the heart of Laurel's commercial district. The hotel and several neighboring buildings fell victim to fire in 1919, the year after this photograph was taken. (Courtesy of Ryan Mead.)

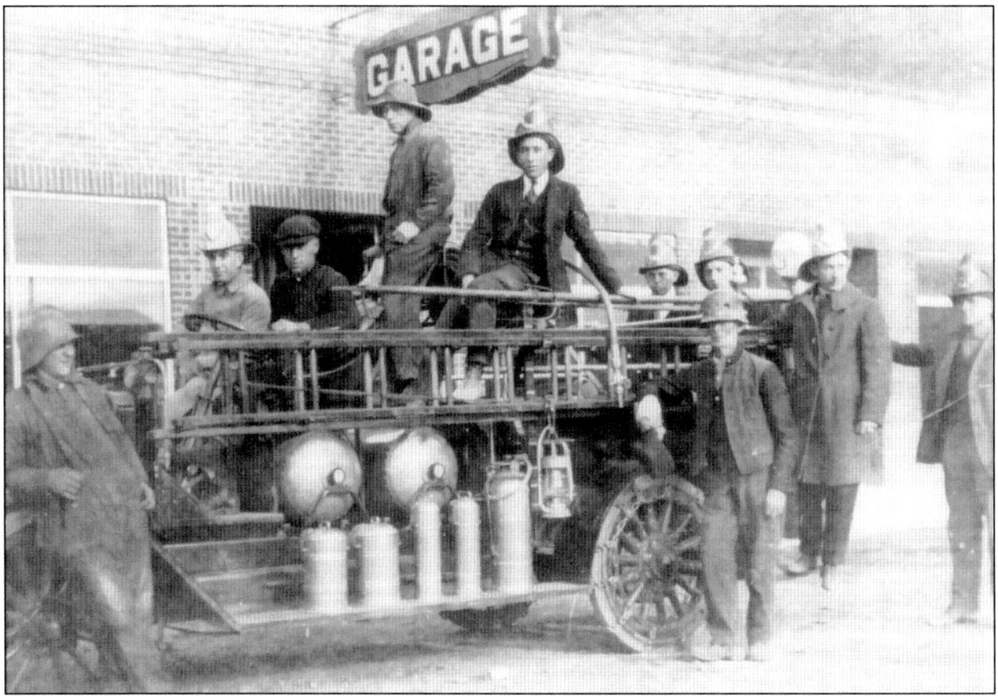

Concerned citizens organized the Laurel Volunteer Fire Department in 1909. Before the fire station installed an alarm system, the Northern Pacific roundhouse aided in fire calls by sounding coded whistles to alert the volunteer firemen of a fire's location. Pictured above is fire chief Reece Price, at the wheel, with his volunteer firefighting crew around 1920. (Courtesy of the Laurel Museum.)

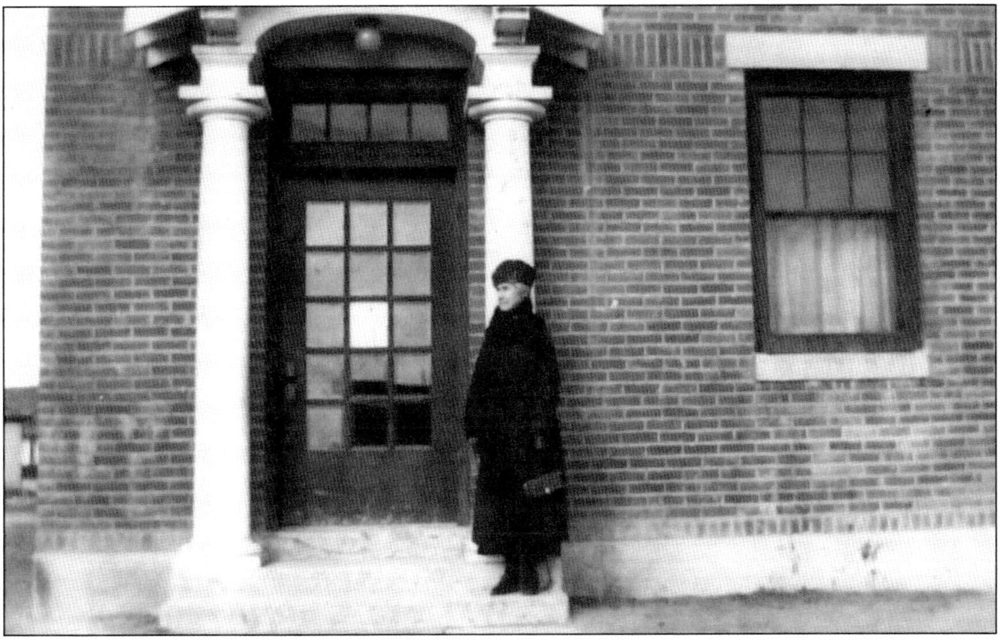

Laurel's first librarian, Carrie Erb, stands on the library steps in 1922. The Laurel Library opened its doors to the public in 1917 in the former dental office of Dr. Marcus and Dr. Chew. (Courtesy of Allison Nys.)

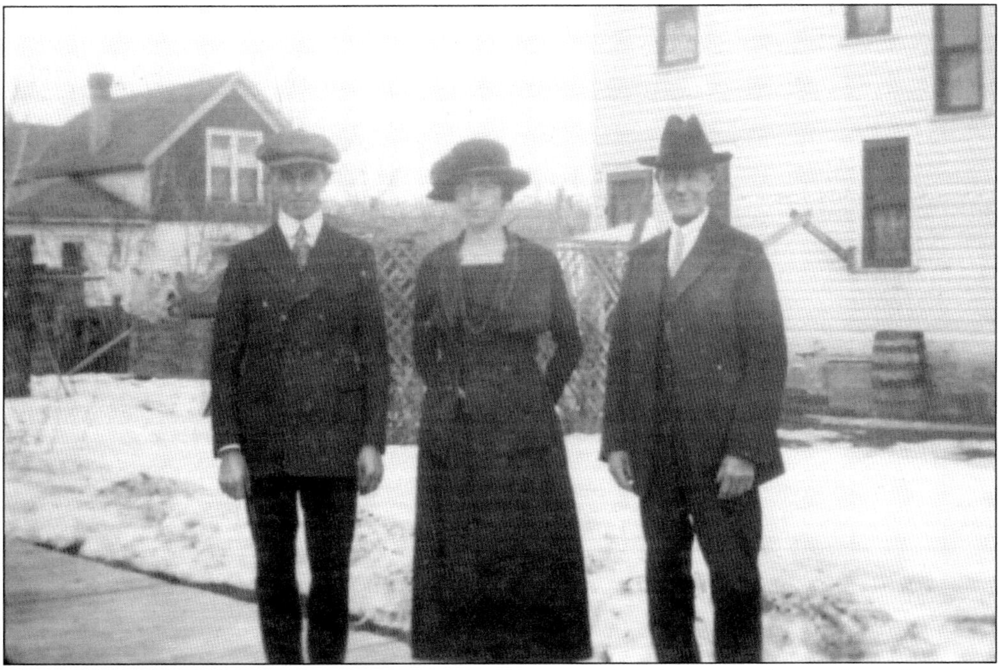

By 1925, many of the dryland farmers from the Wisconsin Settlement had moved into Laurel to live and work, settling into neighborhoods on the east side of town. Pictured here in front of the Jordan home on East Fifth Street is Ruby (Jordan) Winters, flanked by her husband, H. Thomas Winters (left), and her father, James Jordan, who had taken a job with the railroad. (Courtesy of the Laurel Public Library.)

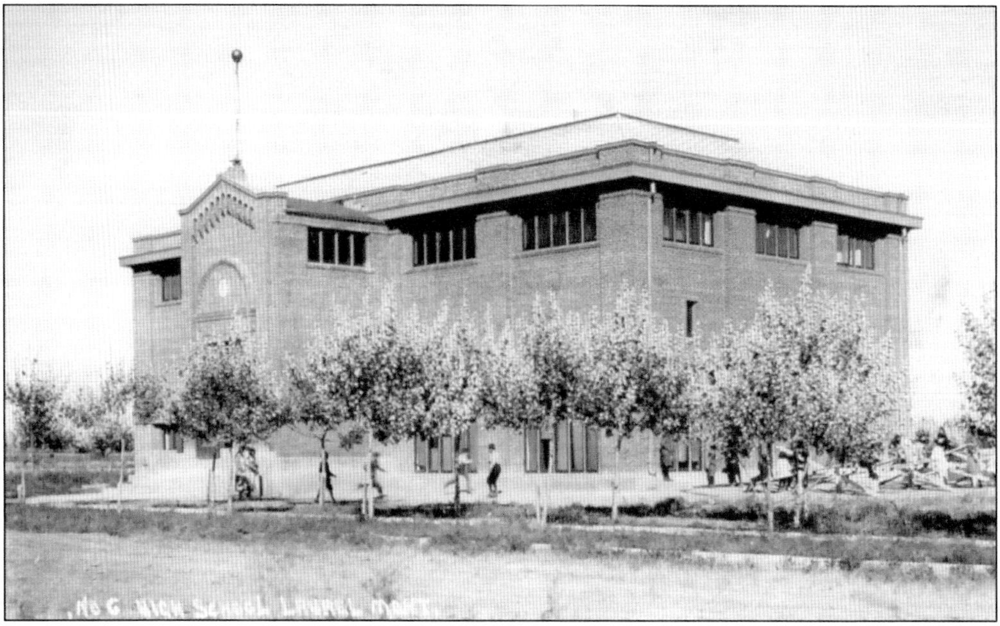

The community welcomed the addition of the school gymnasium in 1914. A blaze left the high school in ruins in January 1916, and classes were held in the lower level of the gymnasium until the high school could be rebuilt. (Courtesy of the Laurel Museum.)

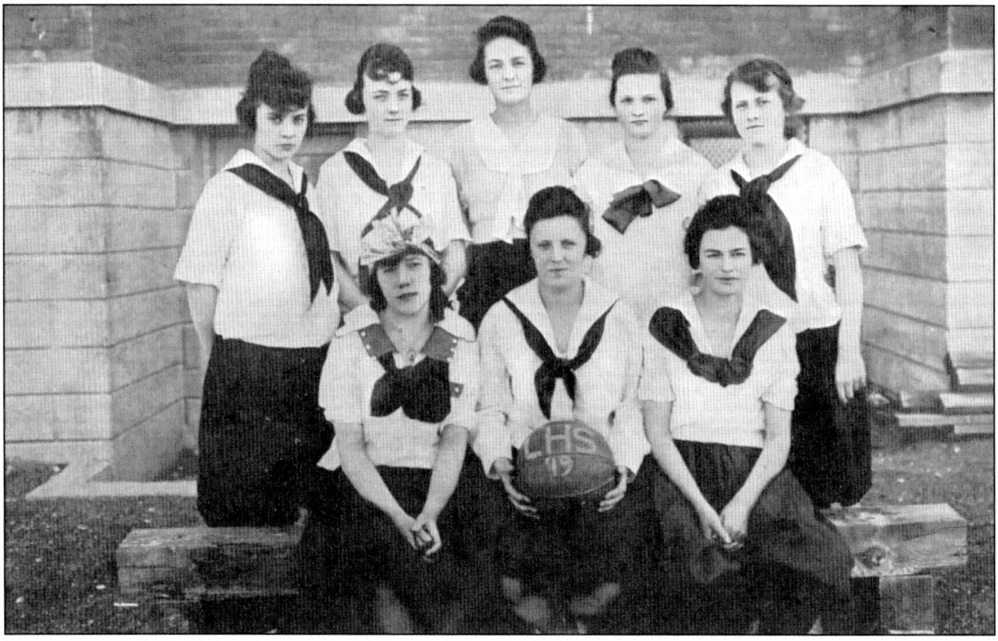

Laurel High School had both a girls' and a boys' basketball team in 1919. (Courtesy of the Laurel Public Library and Laurel High School.)

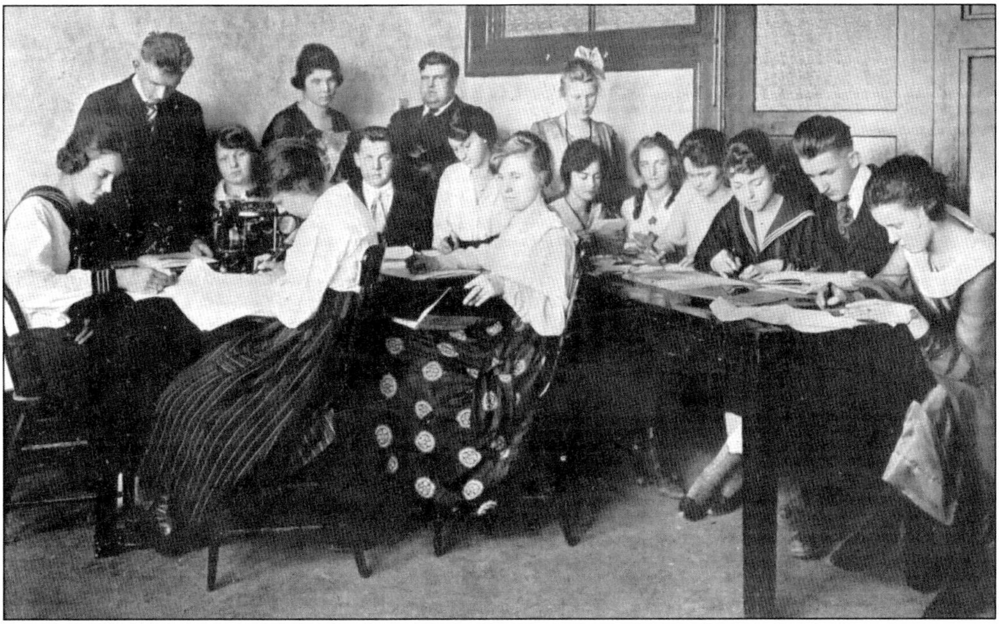

Laurel High School students feign studying for this 1919 yearbook photograph. (Courtesy of the Laurel Public Library and Laurel High School.)

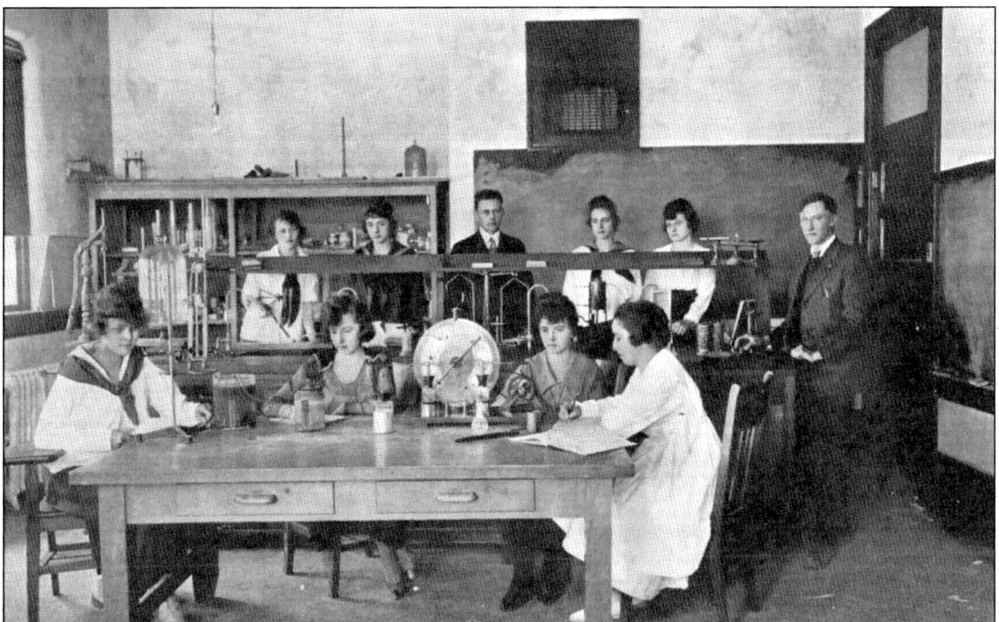

Young women outnumber the lone male student in this 1919 science class at Laurel High School. (Courtesy of the Laurel Public Library and Laurel High School.)

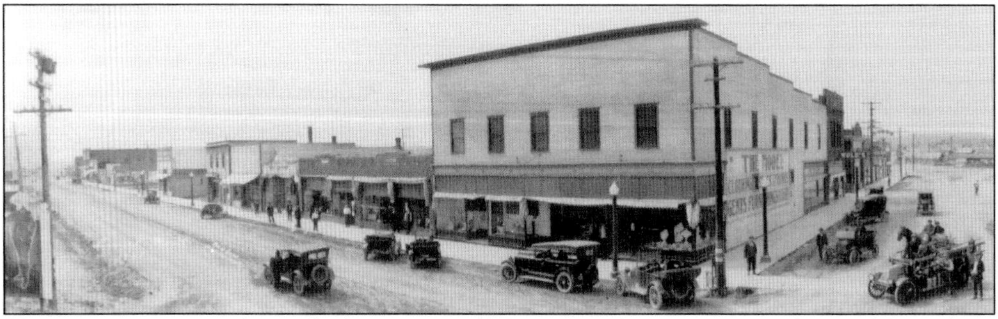

This panoramic view shows the businesses of West Main Street in 1921. The Model, Hjalmar Ahlstrom's clothing store, anchors the corner of the original East Laurel business district. Ole Wold's department store, the new Laurel State Bank building, Sande Drug, and Reese Price's barbershop are to the north on First Avenue. The Strand Theatre is across the street. (Courtesy of Ryan Mead.)

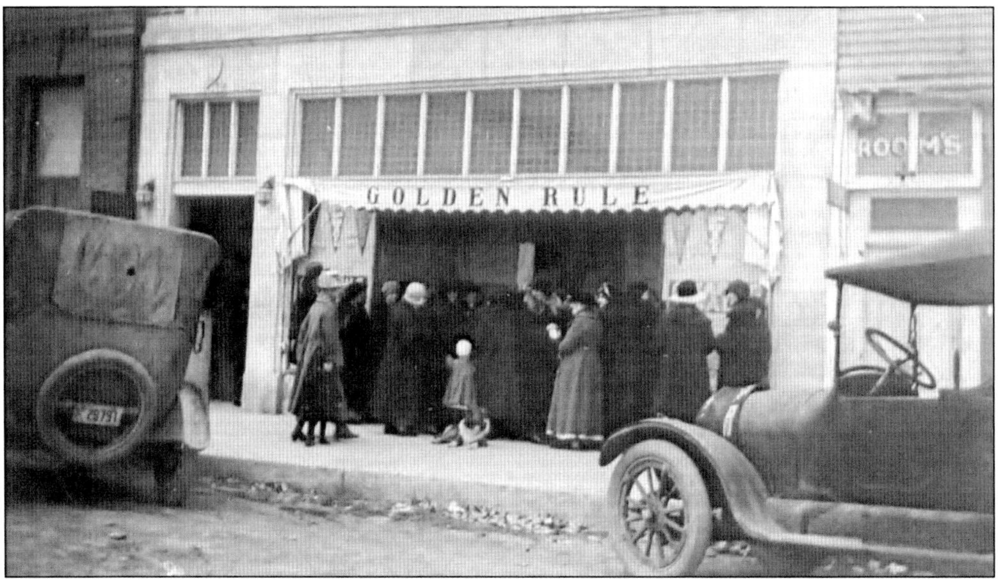

Customers await the grand opening of the Golden Rule at its new location in 1923. The Golden Rule, one of the earliest chain stores to come to Laurel, had moved two doors down from its original location to occupy the lower level of the McCauley-Spencer Building, replacing J.A. Spencer's general store. (Courtesy of Ryan Mead.)

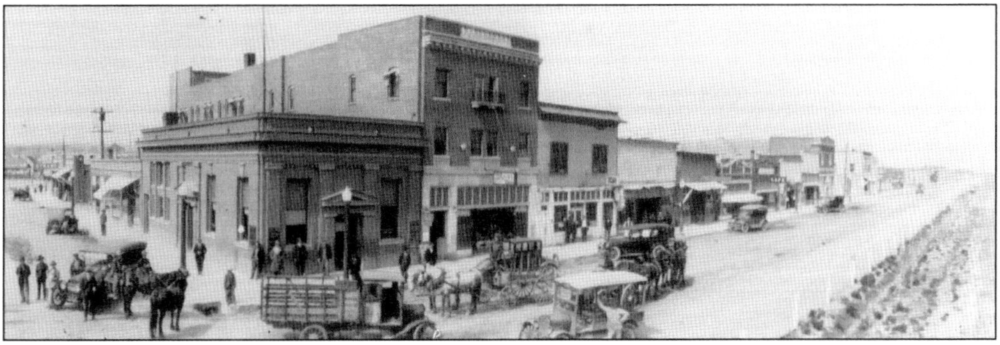

Wagons, trucks, and cars crowd the street along East Main Street in front of the Citizens National Bank and J.A. Spencer's store in 1921. The Davis Transfer Company's truck and the Kasner Hardware Company's delivery truck are parked in the foreground. The American Bank and Frank Valek's general store are visible farther east. (Courtesy of Ryan Mead.)

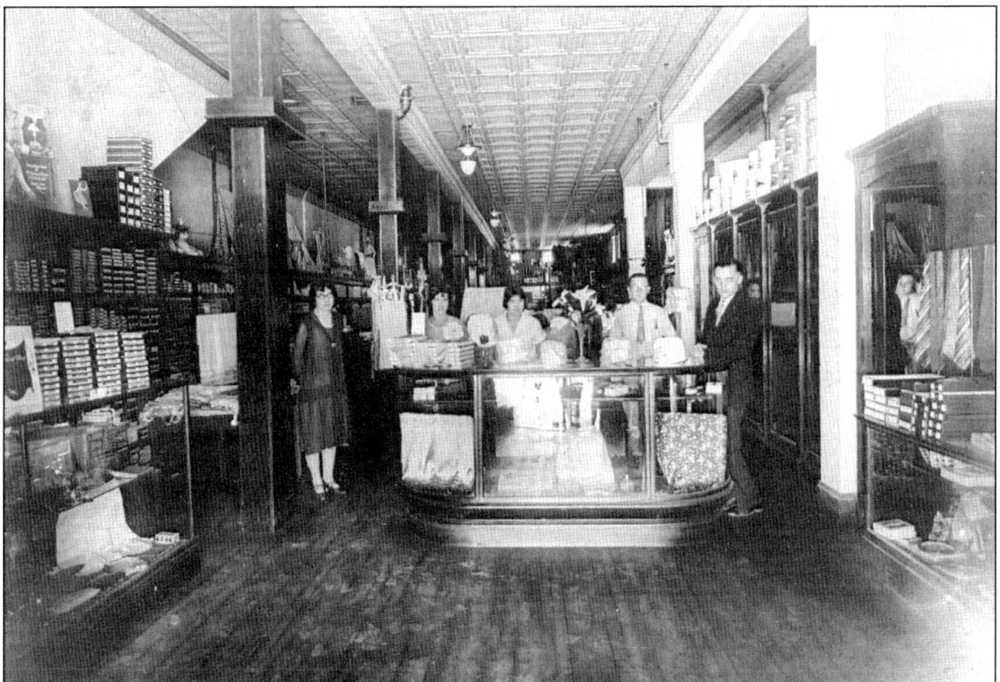

Claude McCracken, far right, operated the Golden Rule dry goods store on East Main Street until it was purchased by J.C. Penney in 1929. The Golden Rule, like other Laurel businesses and stores, stayed open late on Saturday evenings, a day when many farming families came to town to pick up their mail, shop, and socialize. (Courtesy of Ryan Mead.)

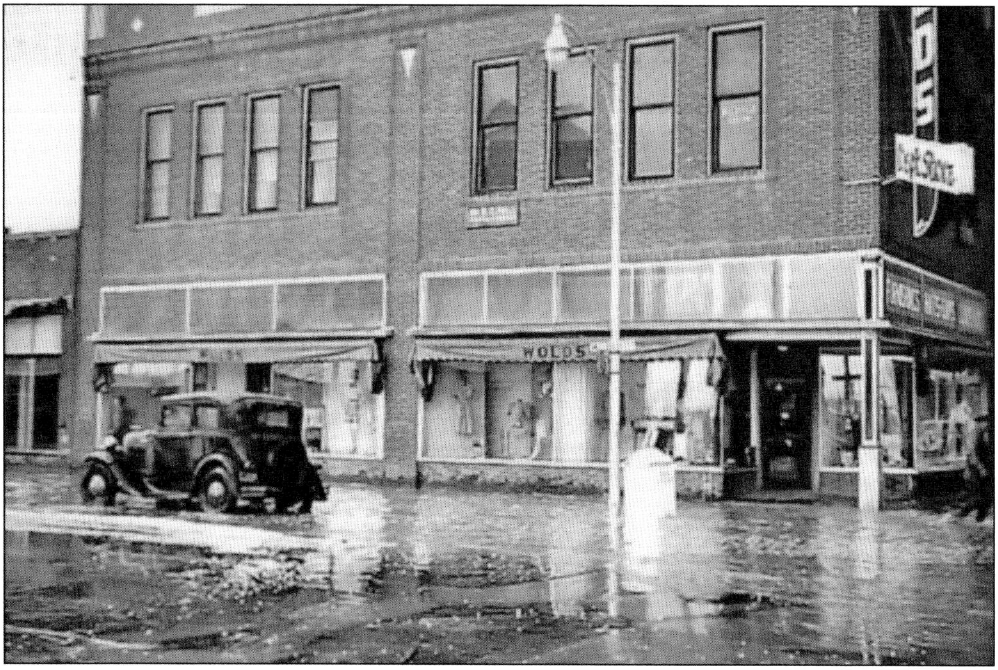

The O.M. Wold Company, advertised as "Laurel's Own Store," was one of the few local department stores to survive the competition from national chain stores, such as J.C. Penney, that started moving into Laurel in the 1920s. The store, first established in the Westbrook-Held Building by Ole M. Wold in 1916, stayed in the family until the Wolds sold it in 1977. (Courtesy of Barbara Nicholas.)

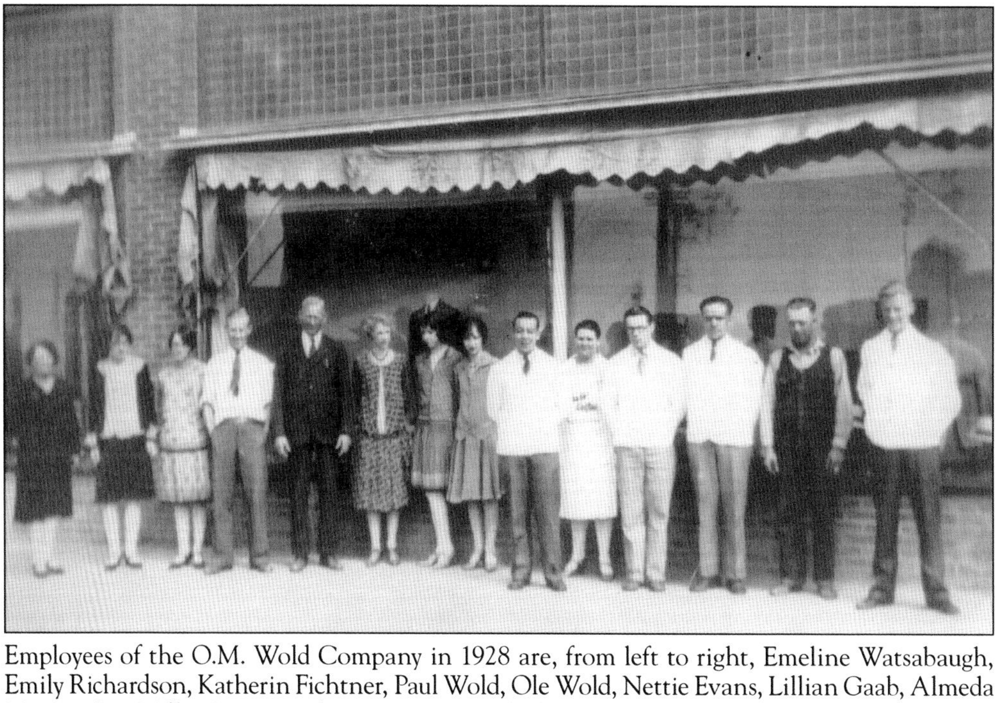

Employees of the O.M. Wold Company in 1928 are, from left to right, Emeline Watsabaugh, Emily Richardson, Katherin Fichtner, Paul Wold, Ole Wold, Nettie Evans, Lillian Gaab, Almeda Marvin, Ray Miller, Jenny Starkey, Vernon Woodard, Bud Kilpatrick, Dale Van Nice, and Oliver Wold. (Courtesy of the Laurel Museum.)

In June 1938, the *Laurel Outlook* reported that torrential rains overflowed ditches and storm sewers, filling the First Avenue underpass and turning east-end neighborhoods into a lake. At the height of the flood, Main Street was under 18 inches of water. Some shopkeepers tried to stave off the floodwaters by sandbagging doorways. Other merchants managed to salvage stock stored in basements, which quickly filled with murky water and mud. The newspaper reported that, although many businesses suffered costly water damage, at least one establishment made the best of the soggy situation. At a restaurant on Main Street, a barefooted waiter with rolled up pants waded through six inches of water to serve hot coffee to patrons at the lunch counter. (Both photographs by Harold Van Nice; courtesy of the Laurel Museum.)

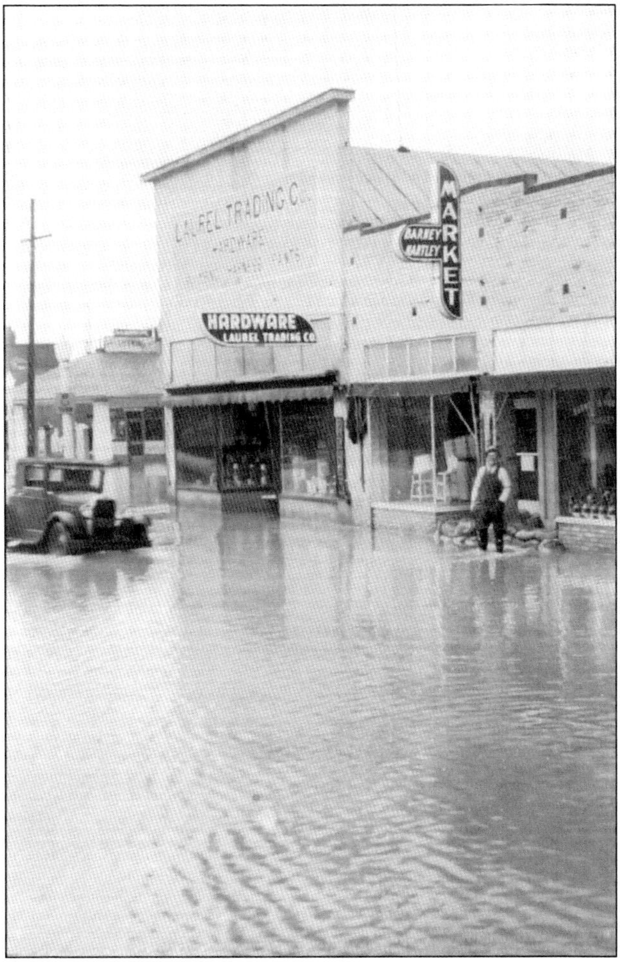

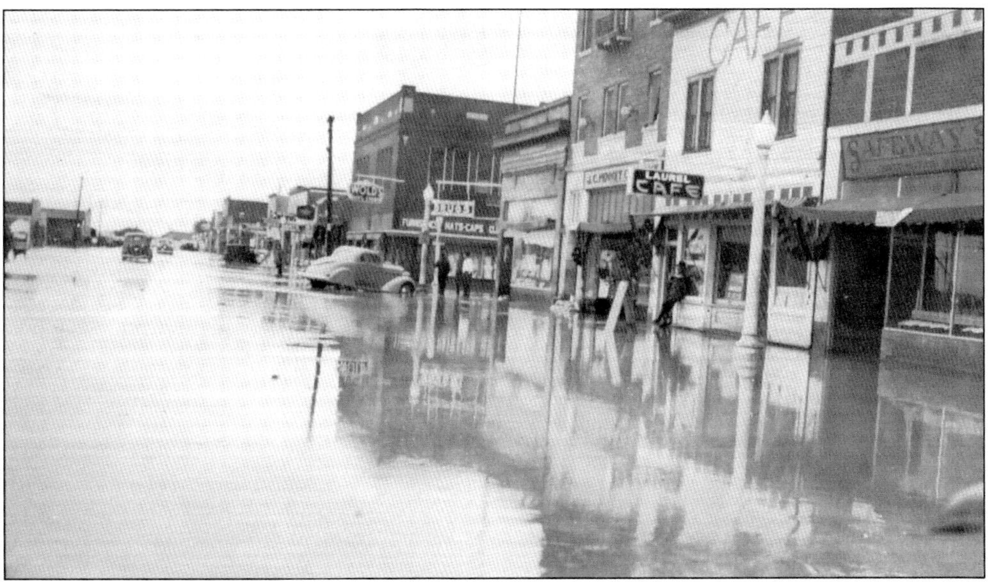

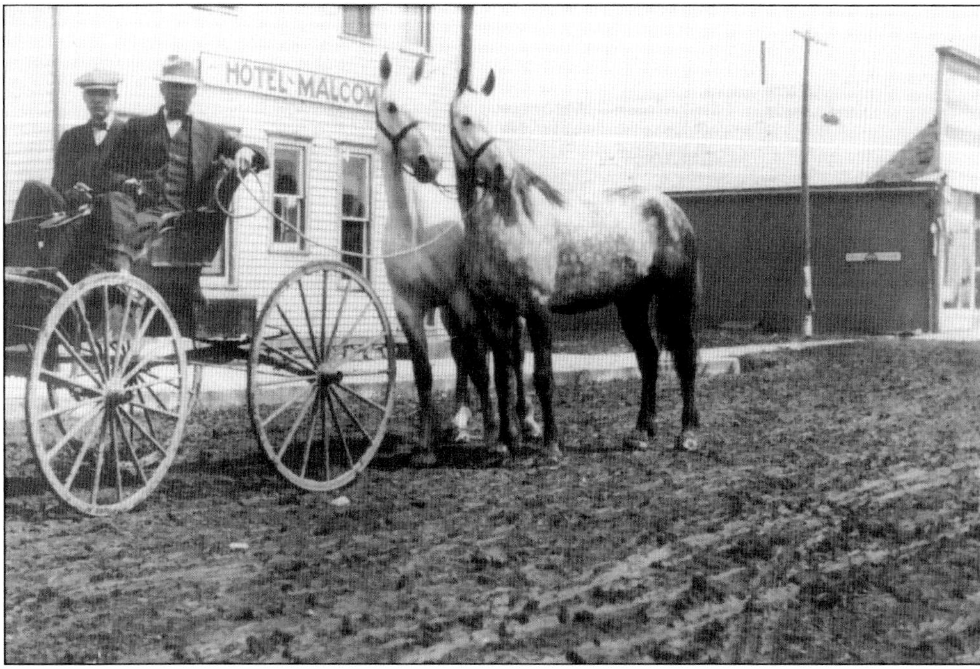

Howard Reeder, left, and Raynus Rutter lead a pair of horses past the Hotel Malcolm on West Main Street in 1911. The men were partners in a wholesale horse trading business, selling horses by the boxcar from stables at a site south of the railroad tracks. (Courtesy of Sedley Barsness.)

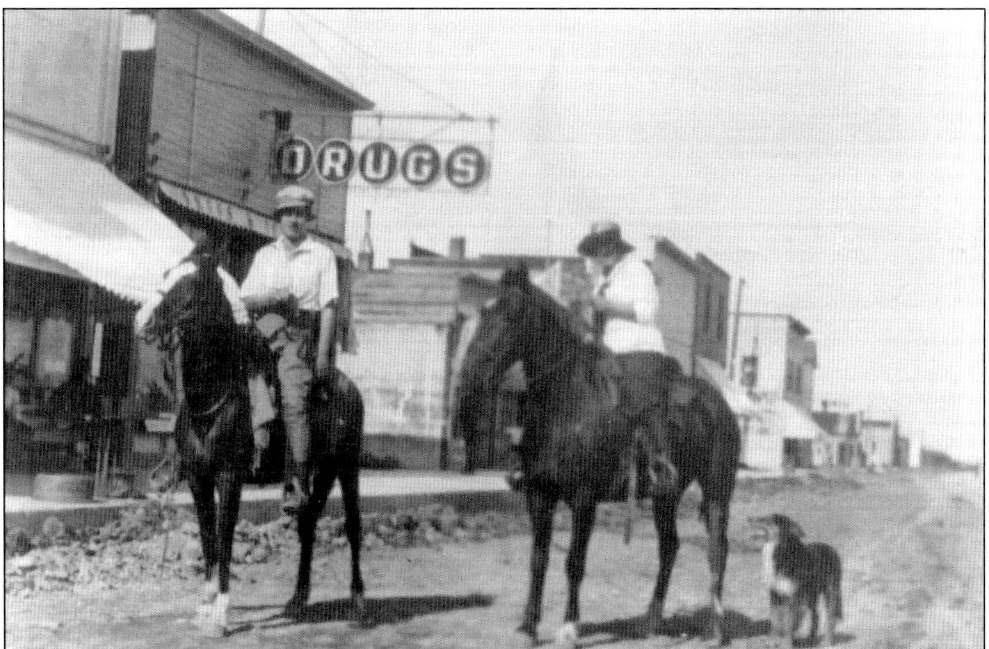

Riders pause in front of Heinz Drug at 111 East Main Street in 1917. Family-run pharmacies, including Gardner Drug and Gene's Pharmacy, have operated from this location for over 100 years. (Courtesy of Sedly Barsness.)

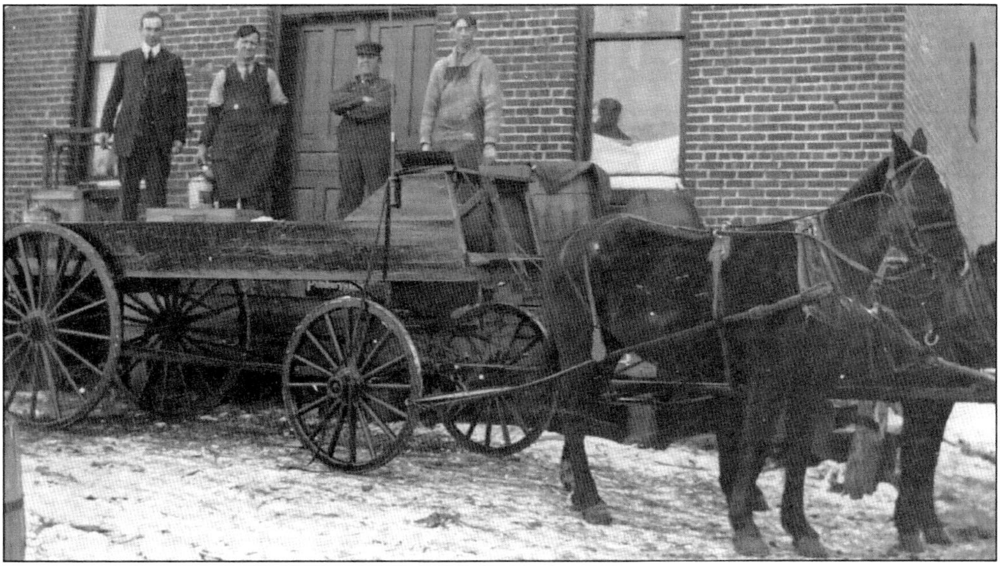

The Laurel Milling Company, founded by Monroe Cramer and Martin Thusen, began producing hard wheat flour in 1914. The mill and grain elevator were built south of the railroad tracks on the former site of the ballpark. In 1921, Stuart Thornton bought a controlling interest in the mill, which reportedly produced over 4,200 pounds of flour daily. (Courtesy of the Laurel Museum.)

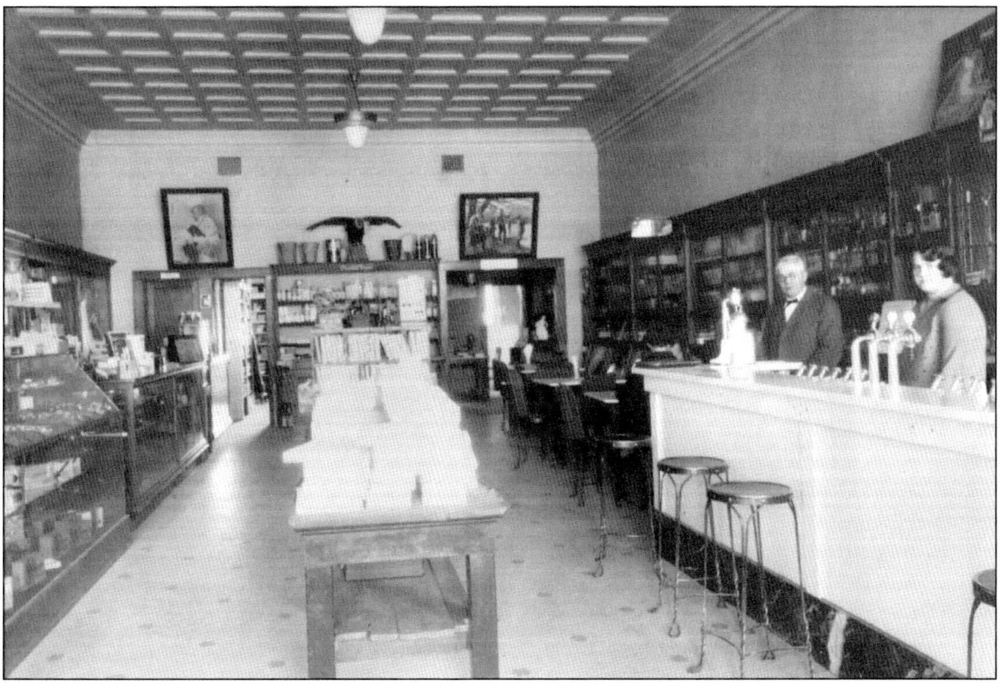

Otis "Chappy" Chapman, proprietor, and a clerk stand behind the counter of the Chapman Pharmacy around 1934. The drugstore was located on the corner of First Avenue and East Main Street in the former Citizens National Bank building. (Courtesy of Sedly Barsness.)

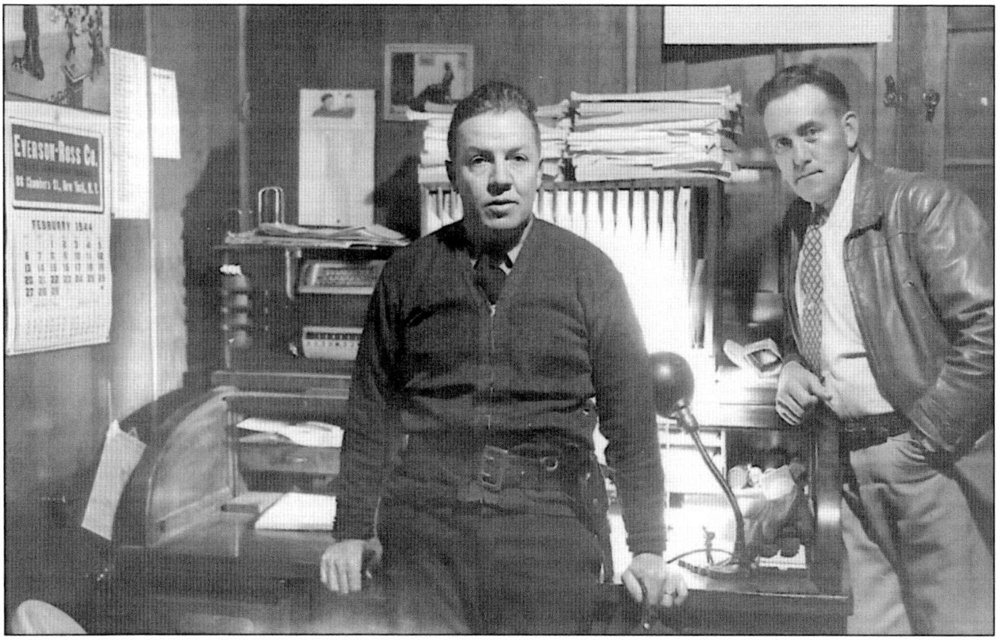

Pictured here are police chief Wayne Willis, left, and deputy sheriff Joe Nicholas in 1944. Law enforcement evolved from a night watchman, who patrolled Laurel's streets on foot, to a mobilized police force in the 1940s. The first police station was housed in the log cabin at Fireman's Park along with the Laurel Commercial Club until 1958. (Courtesy of Barbara Nicholas.)

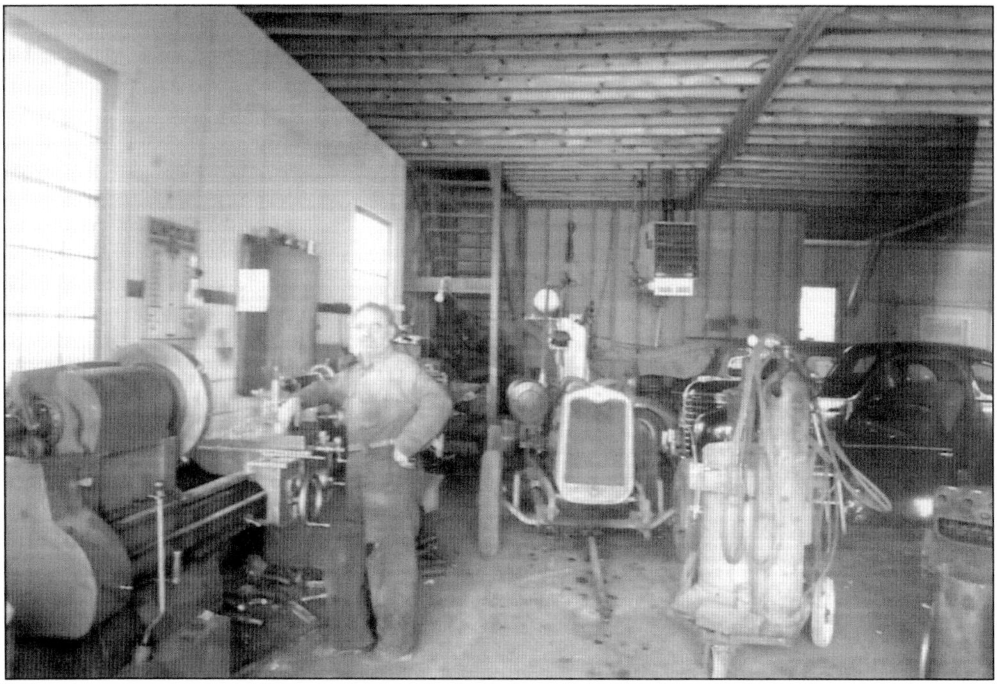

Ben Creasy is at work in the Laurel Machine Shop on East Main Street in the 1940s. (Courtesy of Barbara Nicholas.)

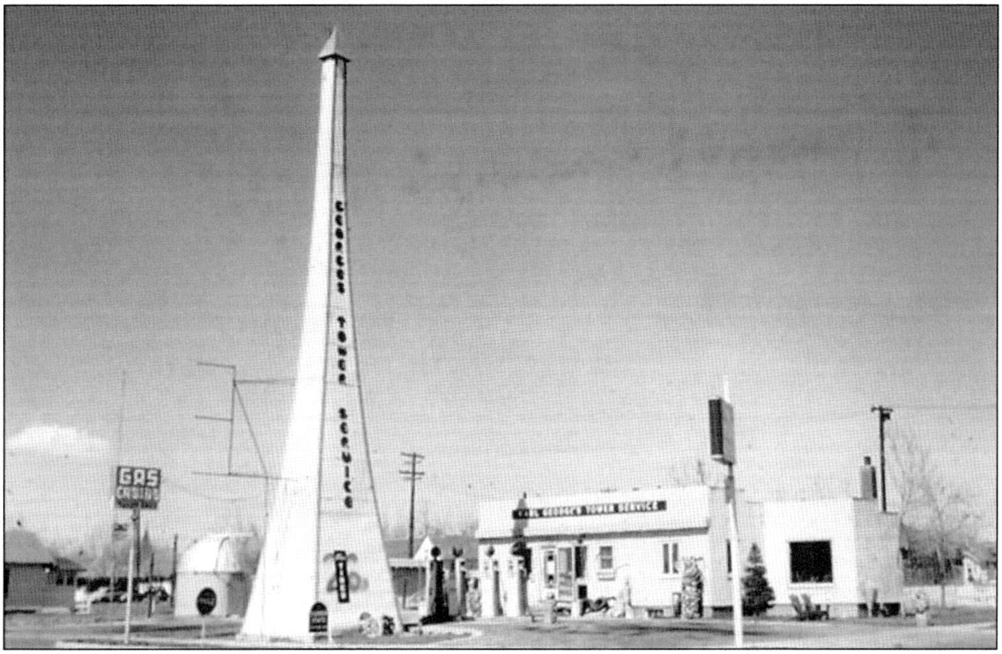

The futuristic tower in front of Karl George's Tower Service Station was an impressive landmark on East Main Street in the 1940s. Karl made a similar mark on the community as a kind-hearted man who helped those in need and, as a thank-you gift, baked an angel food cake for any customer with a bill of $20 or more at his camera and TV repair shop, a later enterprise. (Courtesy of Vance George.)

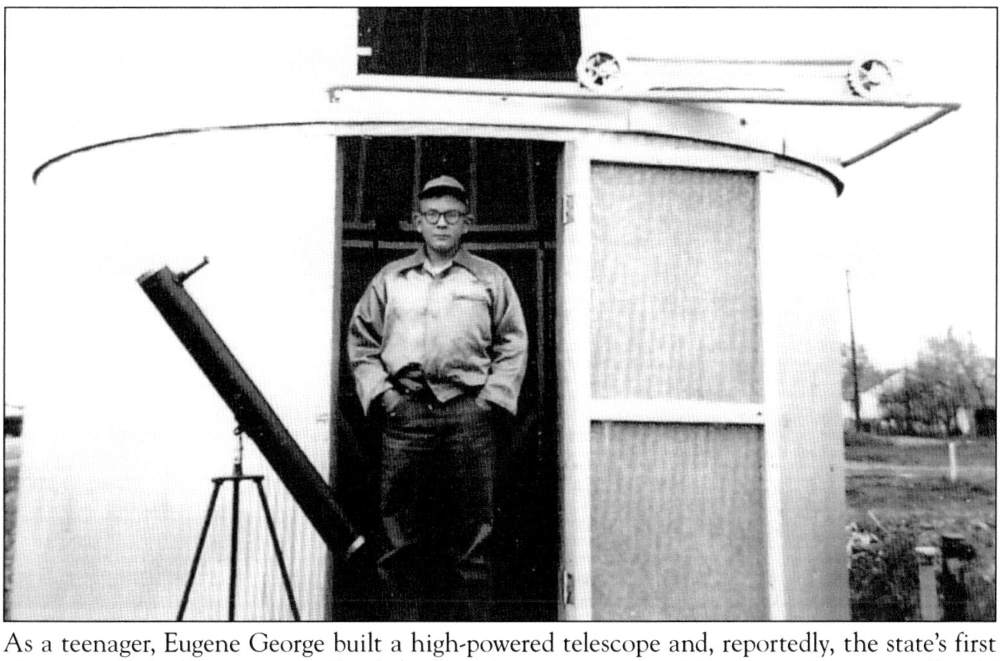

As a teenager, Eugene George built a high-powered telescope and, reportedly, the state's first observatory, which sat in front of his father's service station on East Main Street. He eventually sold the observatory to a farmer who used it as a grain elevator. Eugene went on to pursue a career as an optical physicist for Teledyne Brown Engineering in Alabama. (Courtesy of Janie Duncan.)

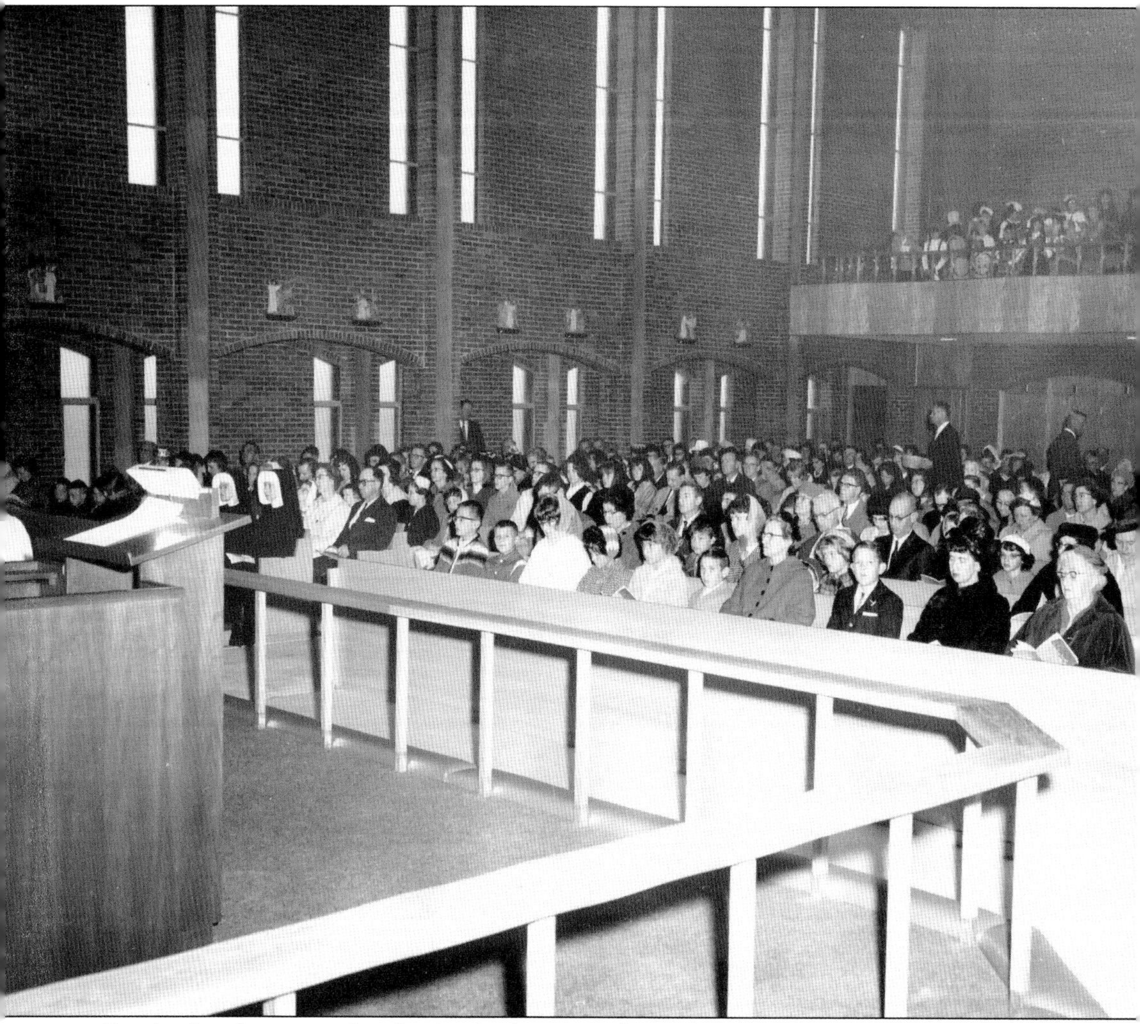

For the first few years after the St. Anthony Parish was founded in 1907, Fr. Charles Treumper held Mass at the homes of Laurel parishioners. The first Catholic church, a modest frame building, was erected in 1910. The parish membership steadily grew as more German families settled in Laurel. In 1927, Fr. Francis Shevlin enlarged the church and added a bell tower. From 1924 to 1931, Father Shevlin also took in and cared for homeless and orphaned boys, providing a home for up to 30 boys at a time in a small house bought by parishioners. The Catholic community of Laurel continued to grow, and a new parish hall was constructed in 1957. Pictured here is the first Mass, celebrated by Fr. John Maher, in the new St. Anthony Catholic Church. (Courtesy of the Western Heritage Center.)

Four

The Laurel Refinery

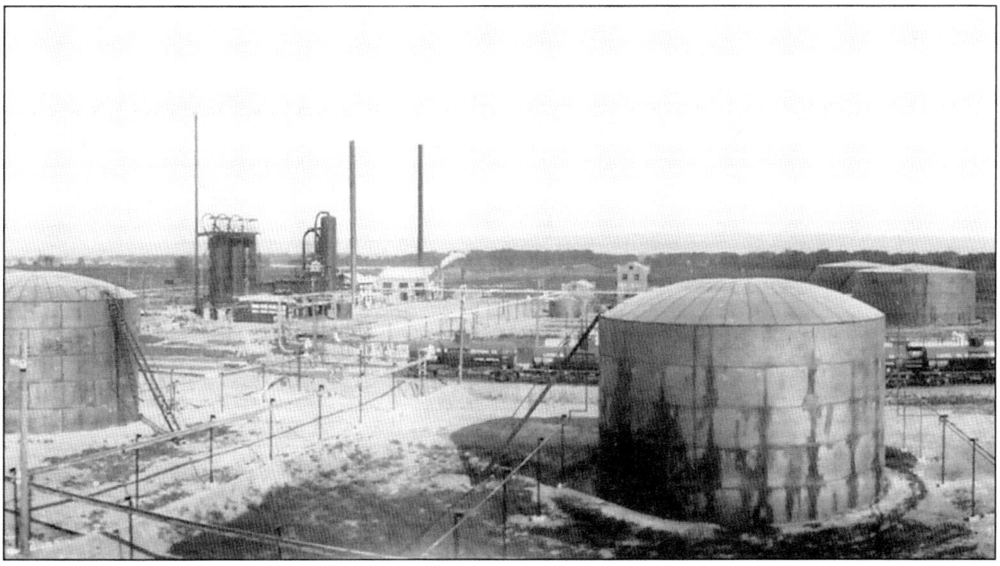

The Laurel Oil and Refining Company organized in 1929 to build a refinery at Laurel. The company selected a site north of the Yellowstone River just outside of town. Investors considered it a prime location that offered a reliable supply of water to refine into gasoline the crude oil shipped from northern Wyoming. The site also had ready access to rail lines to distribute the gasoline throughout the country. (Courtesy of the CHS Refinery.)

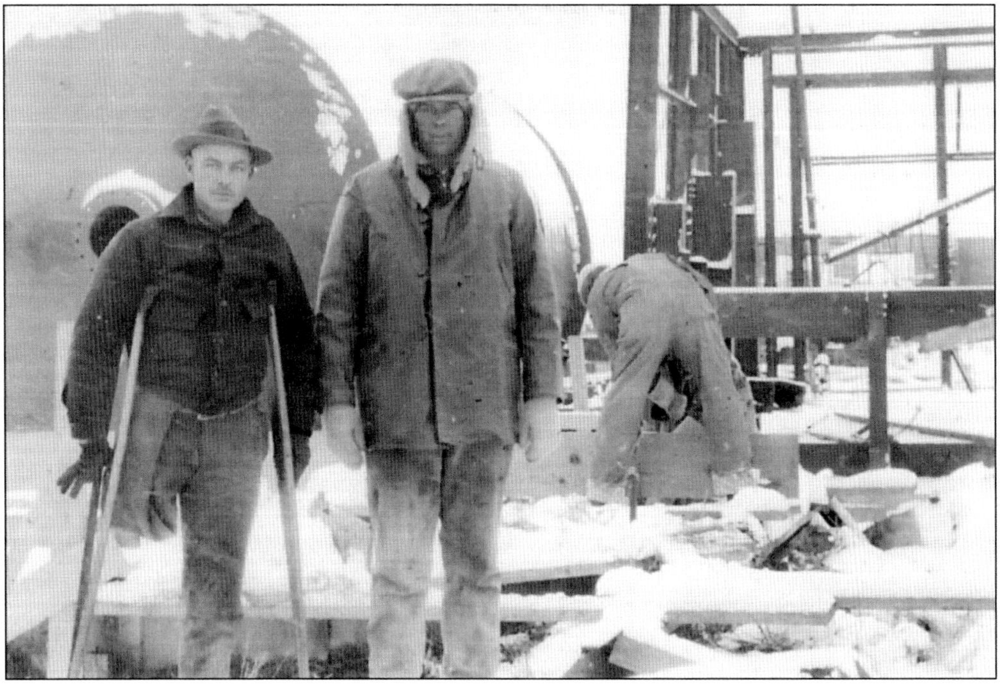

The Smith Engineering Company of Kansas City, Missouri, was contracted to design and build the Laurel refinery for $433,845, with assurances that the facility could refine the sour Oregon Basin crude into auto-grade gasoline. Construction of the refinery began in the fall of 1929, as the rest of the country reeled from the stock market crash. Work continued through the cold winter months into the following spring. (Both, courtesy of the CHS Refinery.)

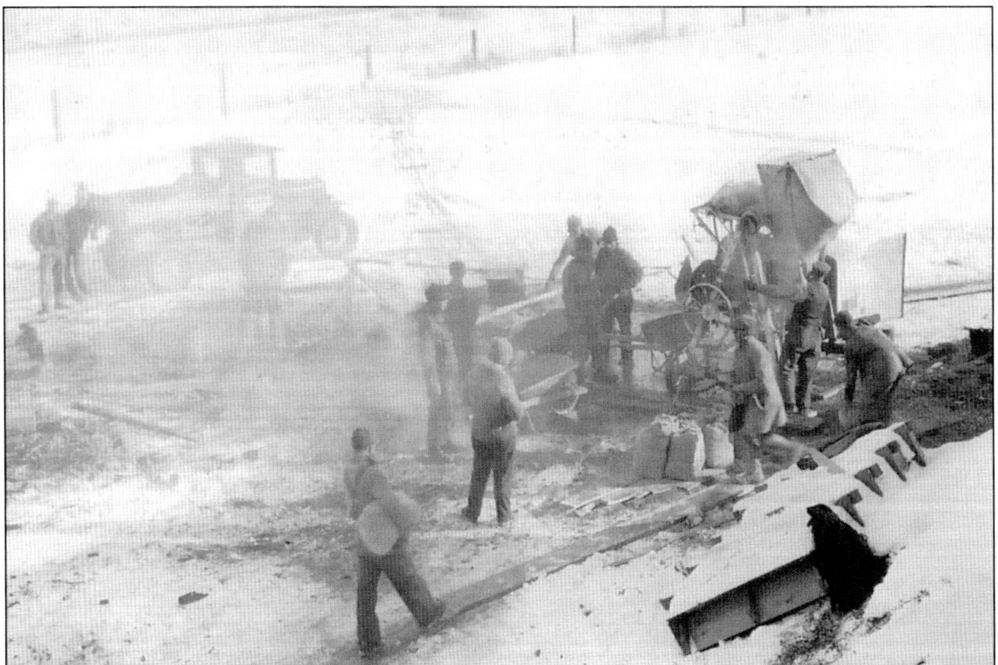

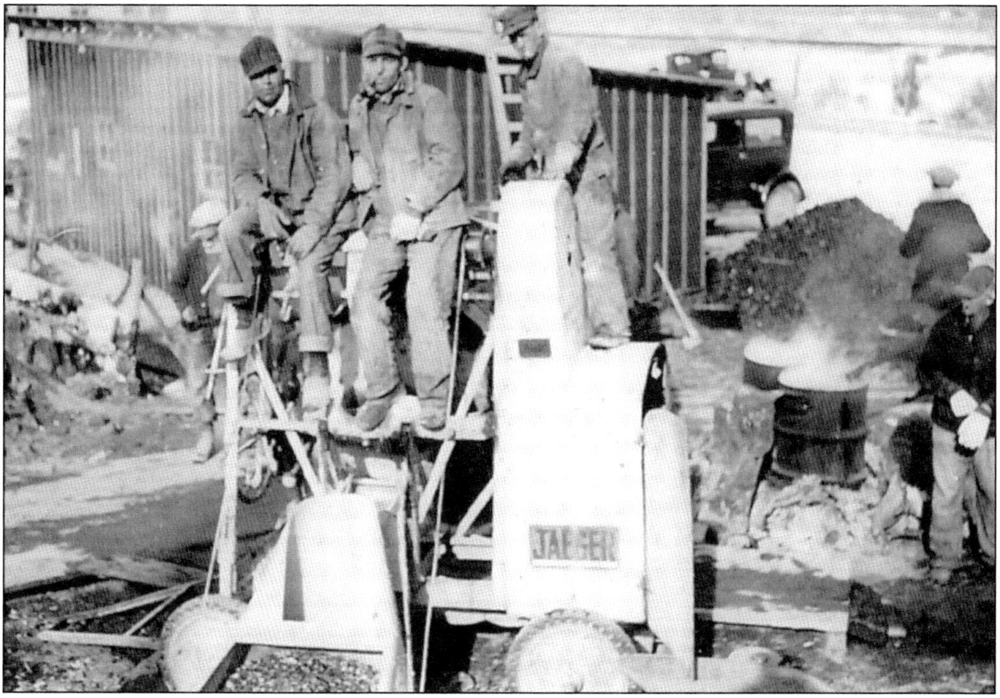

Workmen used shovels to dig foundation trenches and footing holes for the concrete columns of the gasoline treatment plant. Concrete was made one batch at a time in a Jaeger cement mixer and carted up ramps in wheelbarrows to pour into wooden forms. (Both, courtesy of the CHS Refinery.)

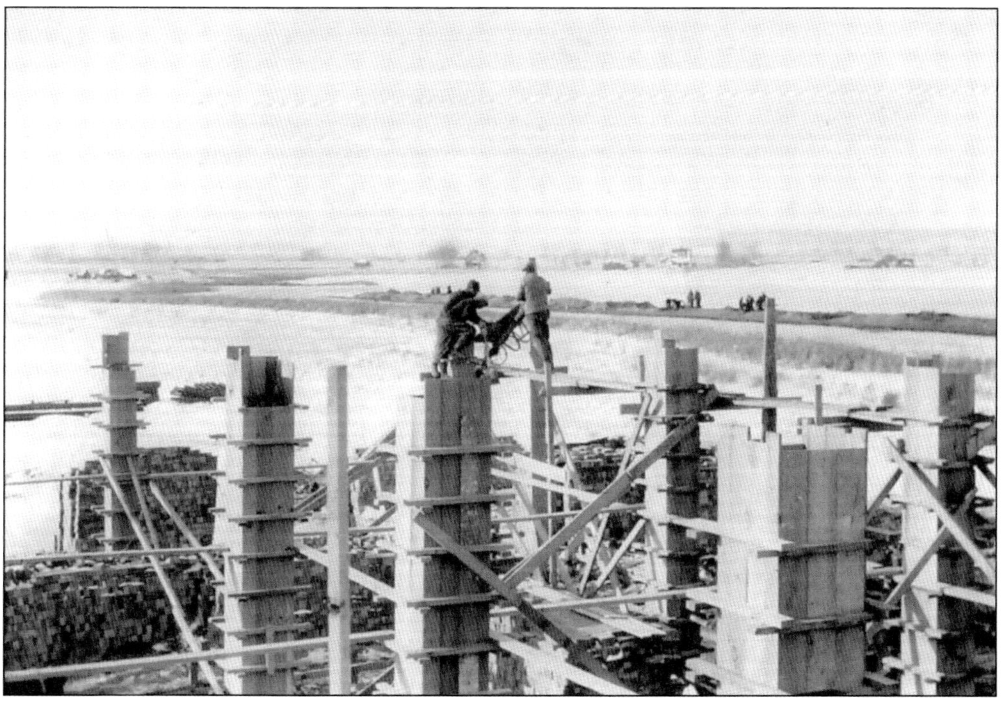

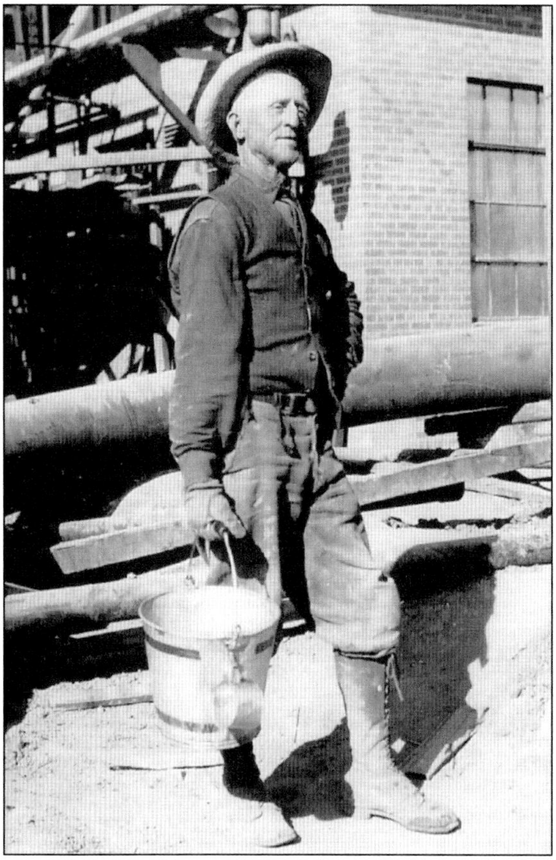

Construction of the refinery was labor intensive. The pace was grueling and the work often dangerous, but local men were grateful to be employed during the economic downturn of the Great Depression. (Both, courtesy of the CHS Refinery.)

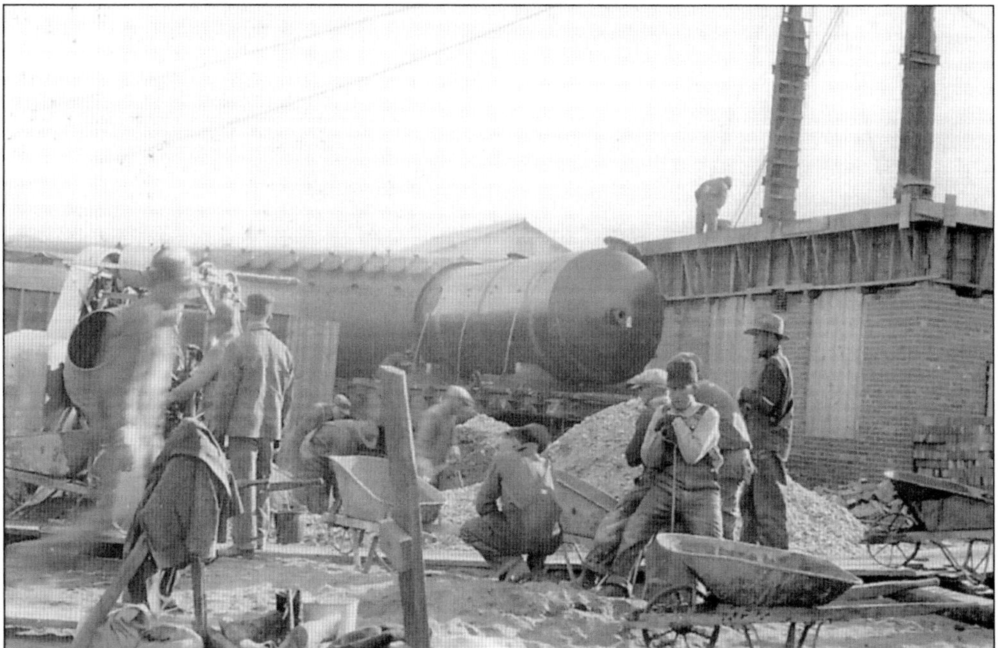

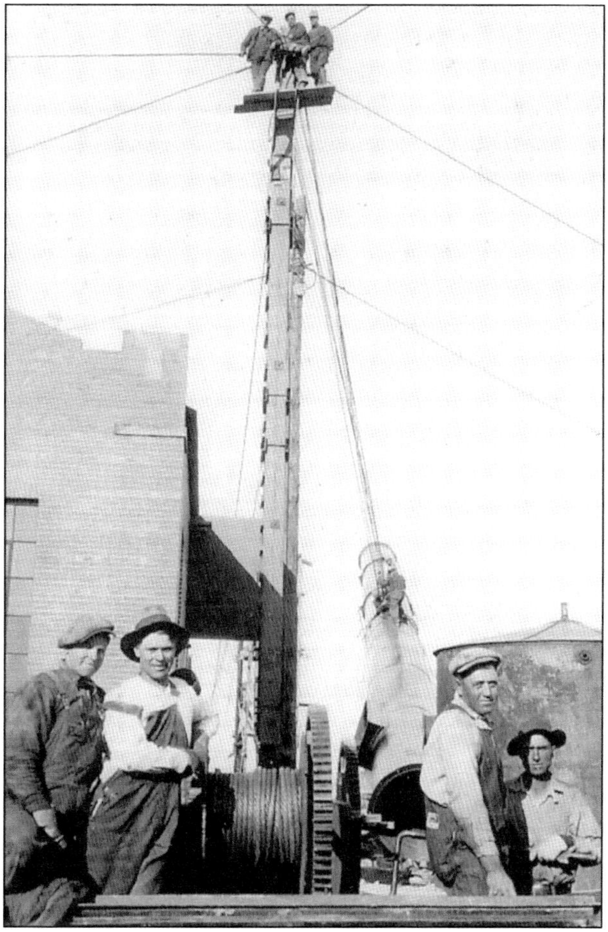

Without a motorized crane, the crew raised and set the 135-foot boiler stack using a block-and-tackle pulley system and guide wires. The men atop the gin pole controlled the trajectory and movement of the stack while the men below used a hand winch to lift it. (Both, courtesy of the CHS Refinery.)

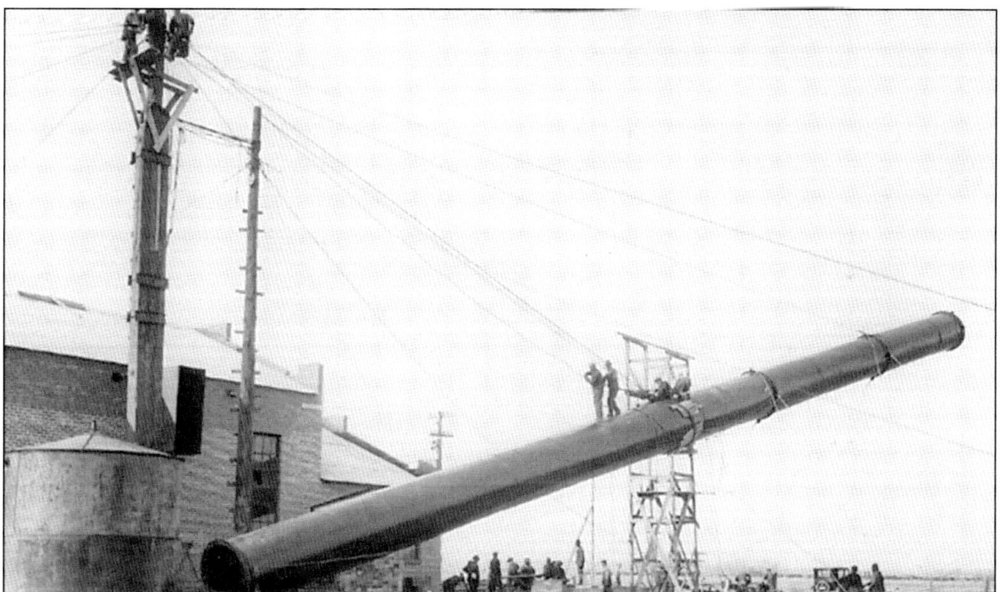

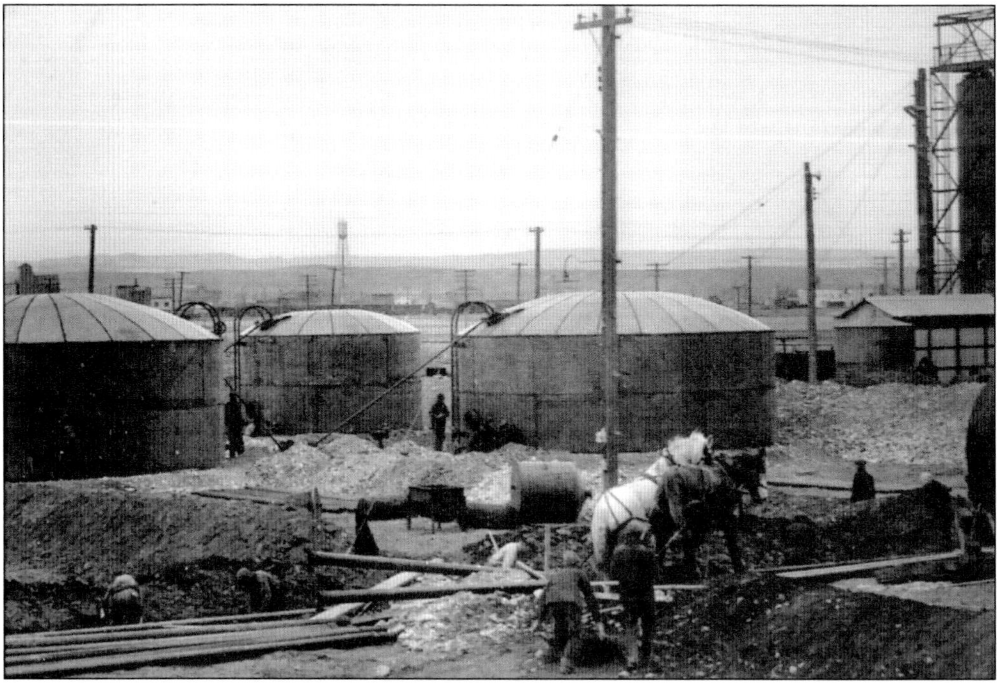

Laborers installed a water pipeline from the pump house at the river to the refinery. They dug the trench for the pipeline with shovels and moved dirt with a horse-drawn skid. (Courtesy of the CHS Refinery.)

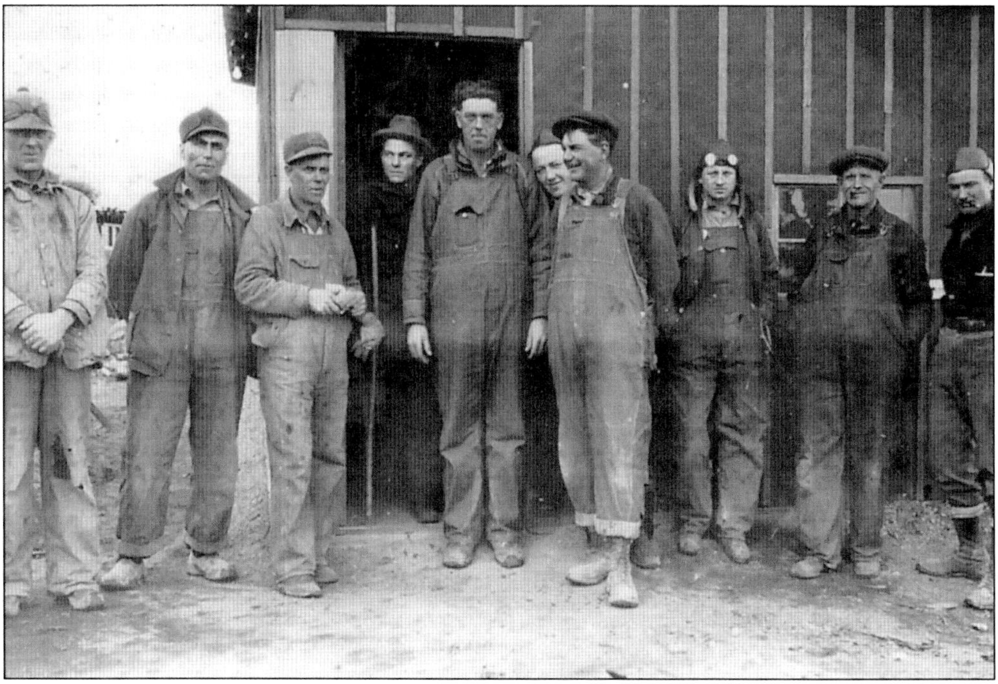

Here, workmen pause for a photograph during construction of the refinery. (Courtesy of the CHS Refinery.)

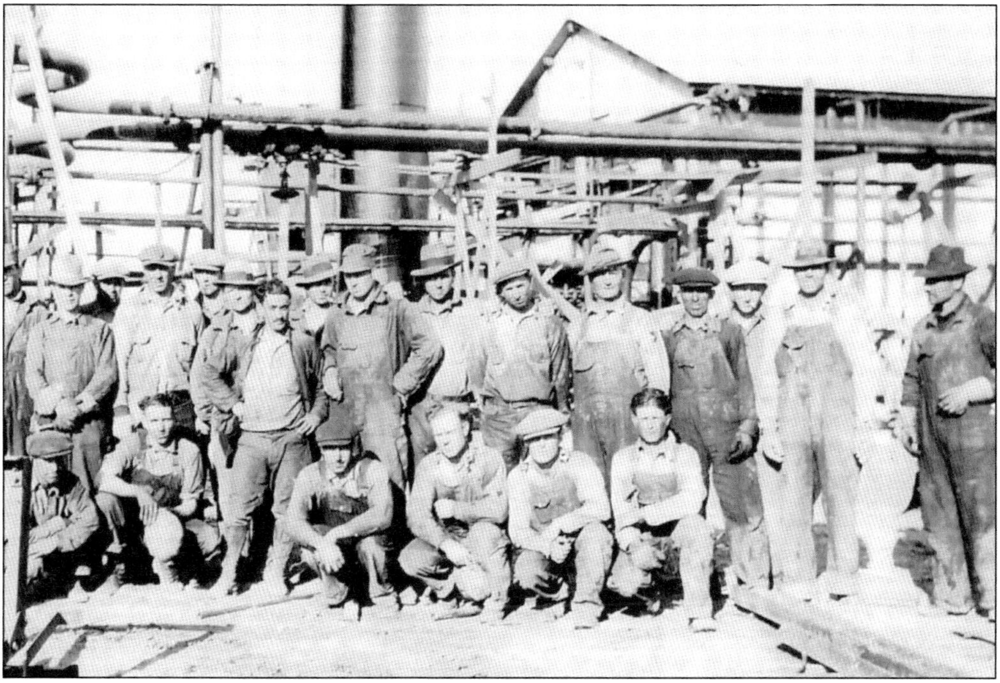

Construction of the refinery was completed in the spring of 1930 at a cost of $535,146. The facility consisted of a thermal cracking unit, a three-drum coking unit, and a gasoline treatment plant as well as storage tanks, a boiler house, a transfer pump house, and an office building. A brick pump house next to the Yellowstone River piped water to the refinery. (Both, courtesy of the CHS Refinery.)

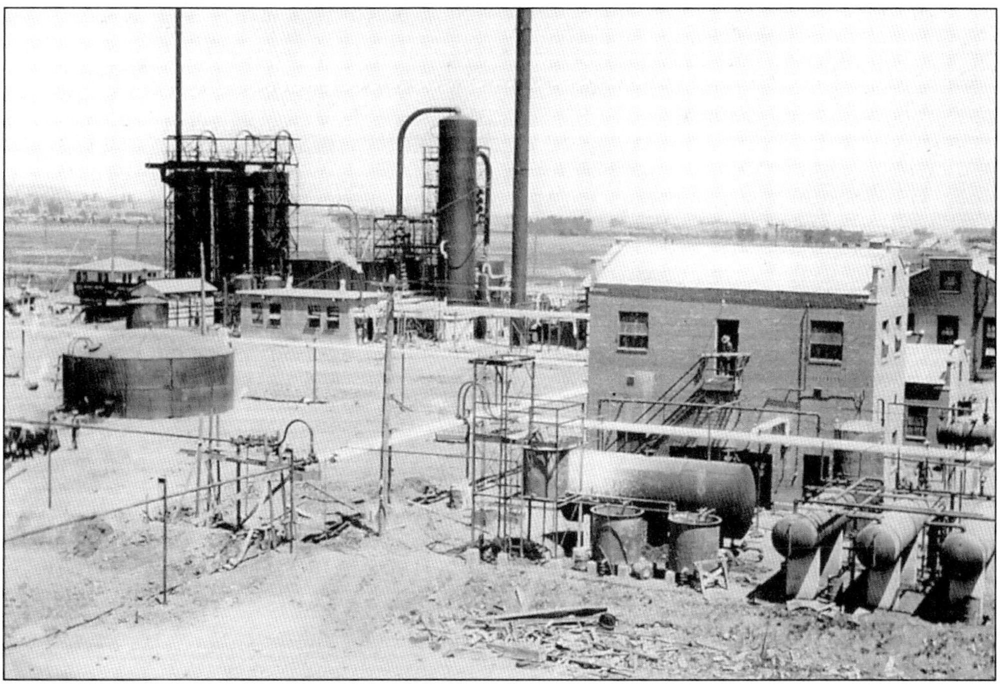

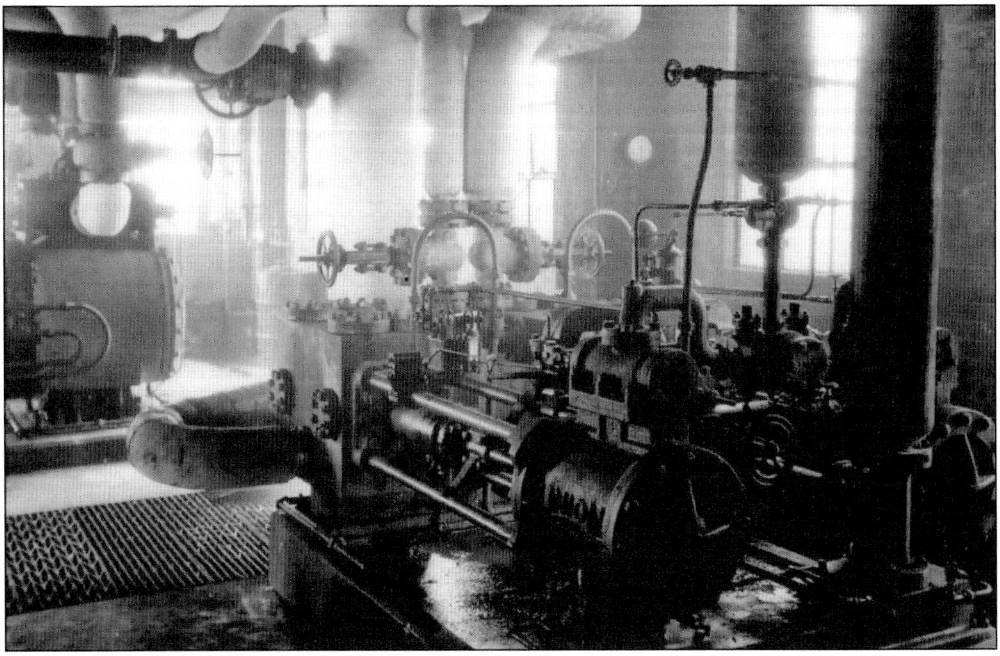

A small crew of workers, under the direction of refinery superintendent Harry Smart and general manager W.A. Manion, began production in May 1930, processing 2,500 barrels of crude oil per day. The refinery immediately encountered setbacks, unable to refine the highly sulfuric crude oil to federal standards for gasoline. The engineering company could not remedy the problem, resulting in years of litigation with the refinery. The refinery overextended its resources rebuilding the gas treatment plant and coking unit, forcing it to shut down operations and declare bankruptcy in 1931. (Both, courtesy of the CHS Refinery.)

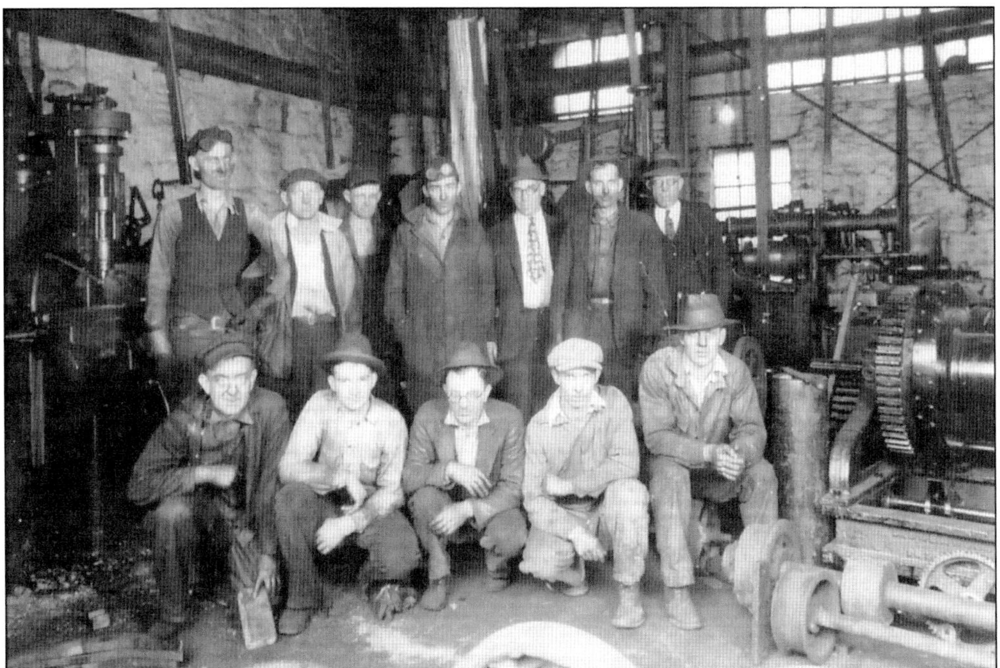

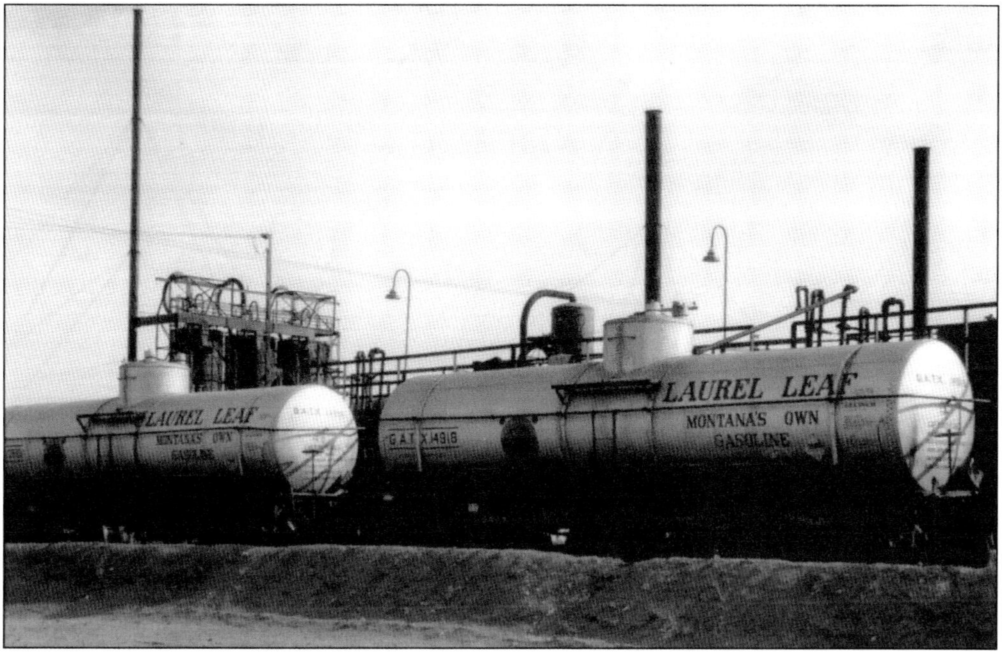

The Independent Refining Company took over the facilities in 1933 and restored operations. With equipment upgrades and a better quality of crude oil, the refinery began producing high-grade gasoline under the Laurel Leaf brand and marketing an expanded product line that included ethyl gasoline, fuel oil, road oil, and asphalt. (Courtesy of the CHS Refinery.)

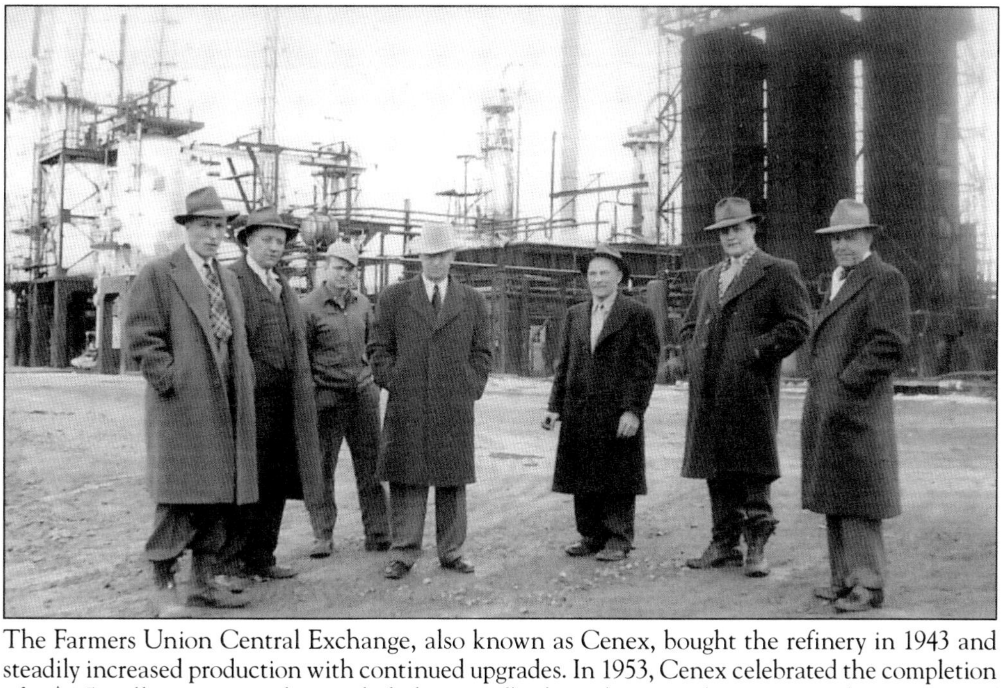

The Farmers Union Central Exchange, also known as Cenex, bought the refinery in 1943 and steadily increased production with continued upgrades. In 1953, Cenex celebrated the completion of a $4.5 million project that included a new fluid catalytic cracking unit and expansion of the refinery's facilities. By 1955, the refinery was processing 15,000 barrels of crude oil per day. (Courtesy of the CHS Refinery.)

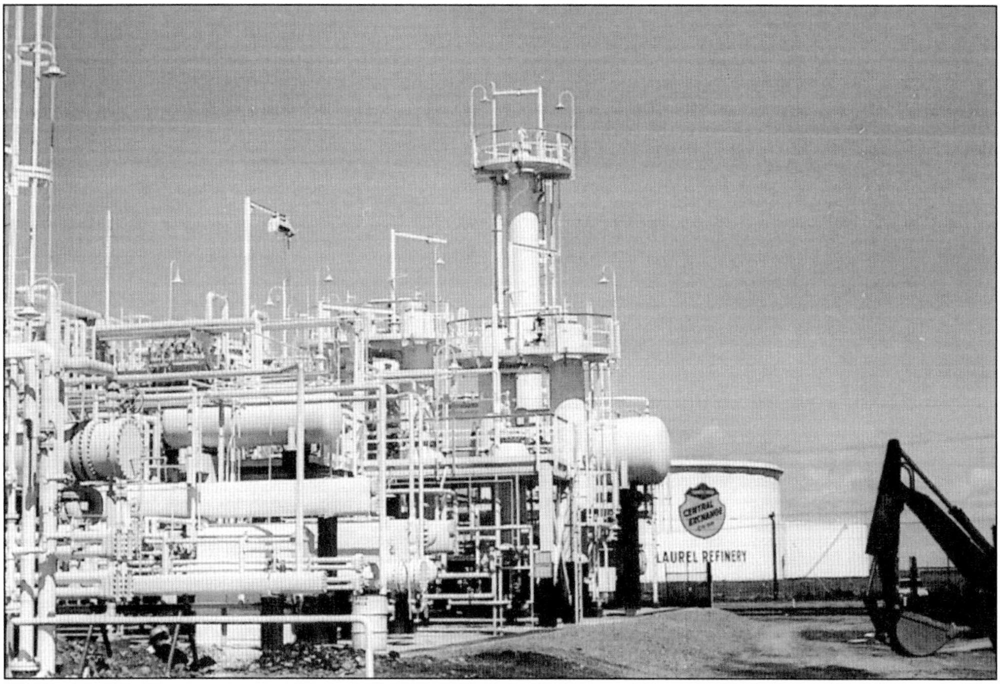

In 1998, Cenex merged with Harvest States Grain. The refinery was renamed the Cenex Harvest States (CHS) Refinery, but it retained the Cenex brand name. (Courtesy of the CHS Refinery.)

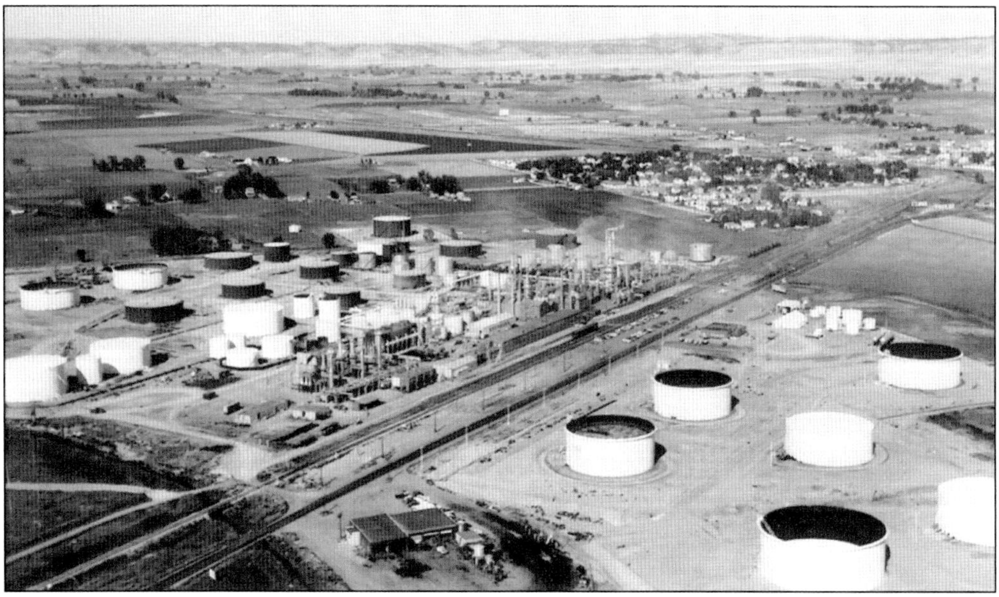

Technological advances and facility improvements have addressed environmental concerns and further increased efficiency and capacity. In 2014, the CHS Refinery reported 300 employees and was operating at a capacity of 60,000 barrels per day. (Courtesy of the CHS Refinery.)

Five

IN GOOD TIMES AND BAD

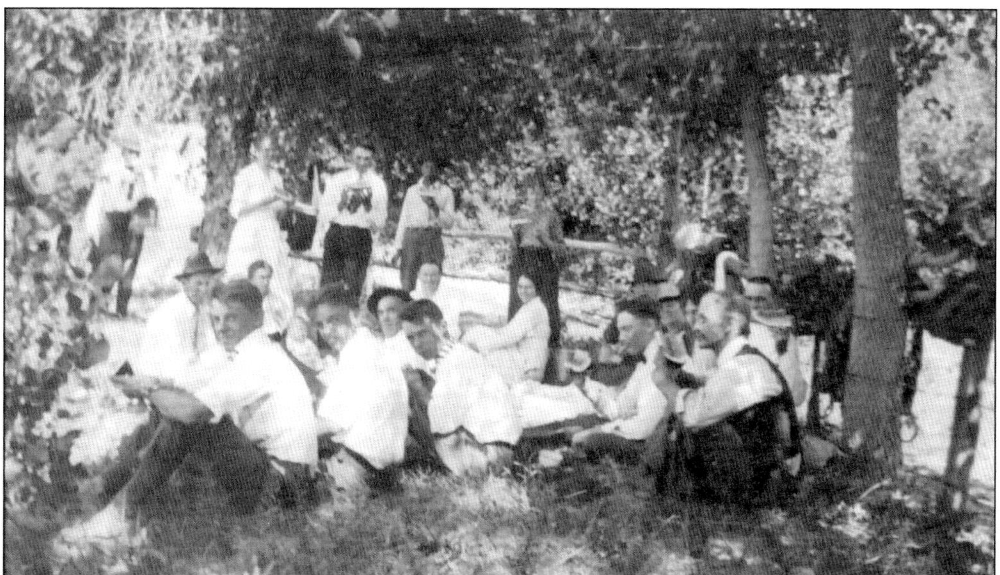

In this photograph, taken around 1921, families from the Wisconsin Settlement savor wedges of watermelon in the shade during an outing to the river. (Courtesy of the Laurel Public Library.)

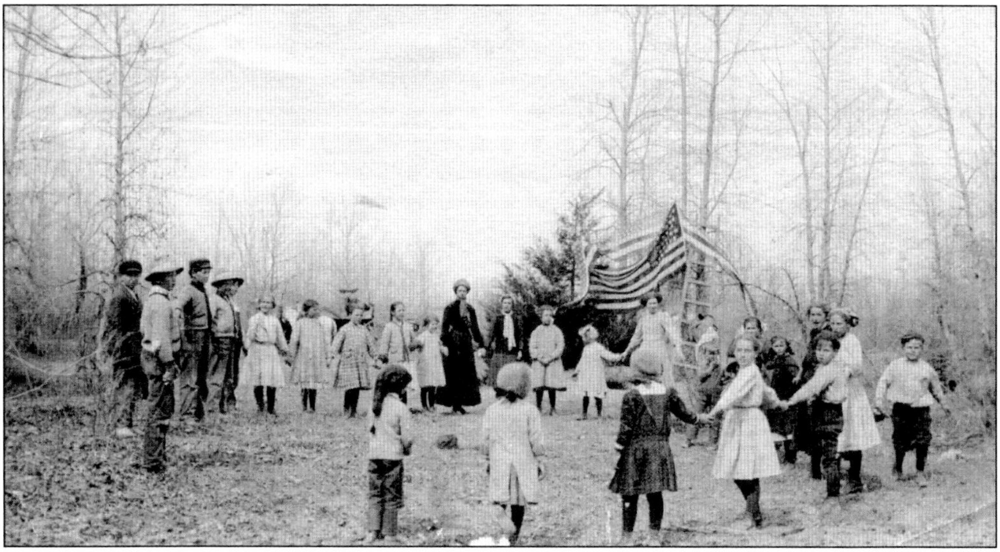

Children from the Allendale School, southeast of Laurel, enjoy an outing to Bode's Grove with their teacher, Aroma Guiler, around 1911. (Courtesy of the Western Heritage Center.)

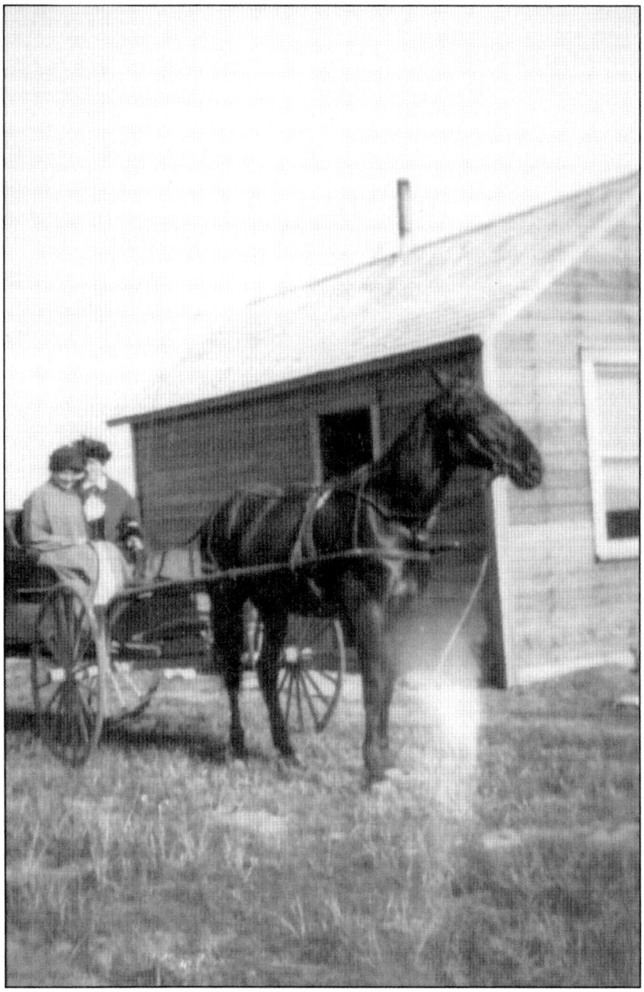

Sisters Anna and Matilda Gilles are pictured in front of Matilda's homestead shack in 1913. Matilda filed a homestead claim southeast of town in 1912 when she came to Laurel as a teacher. Her father, John Gilles, and brothers established farms nearby in 1913 and 1914. Matilda married Ole Brohaugh, a farm implement salesman, in 1919. They had two children, Charles and Ann Brohaugh. (Courtesy of the Laurel Museum.)

This photograph captures the haunting image of a woman gazing at a family portrait while sitting in a sun-kissed field. (Courtesy of the Laurel Public Library.)

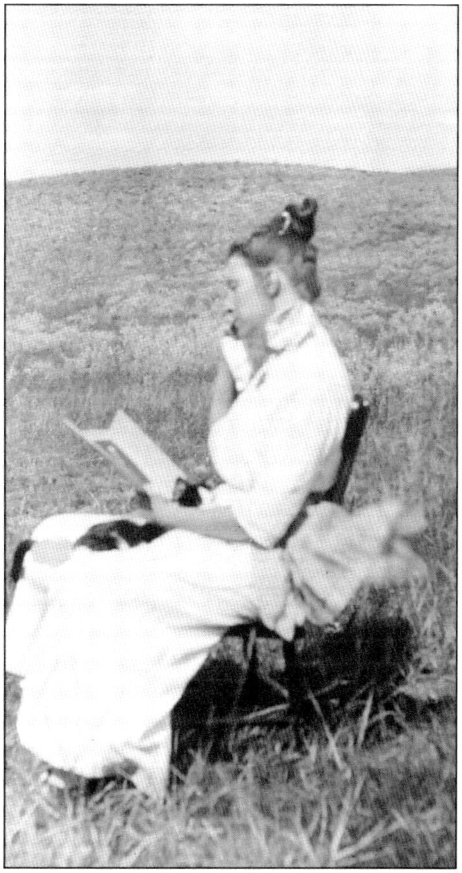

This photograph, labeled only with "sisters," was in a handmade keepsake album belonging to Mary Scammon. Mary grew up as the only child of Sam and Laura Lottie Clare on the Claremont Ranch, south of Laurel along the Clarks Fork River. (Courtesy of Sedly Barsness.)

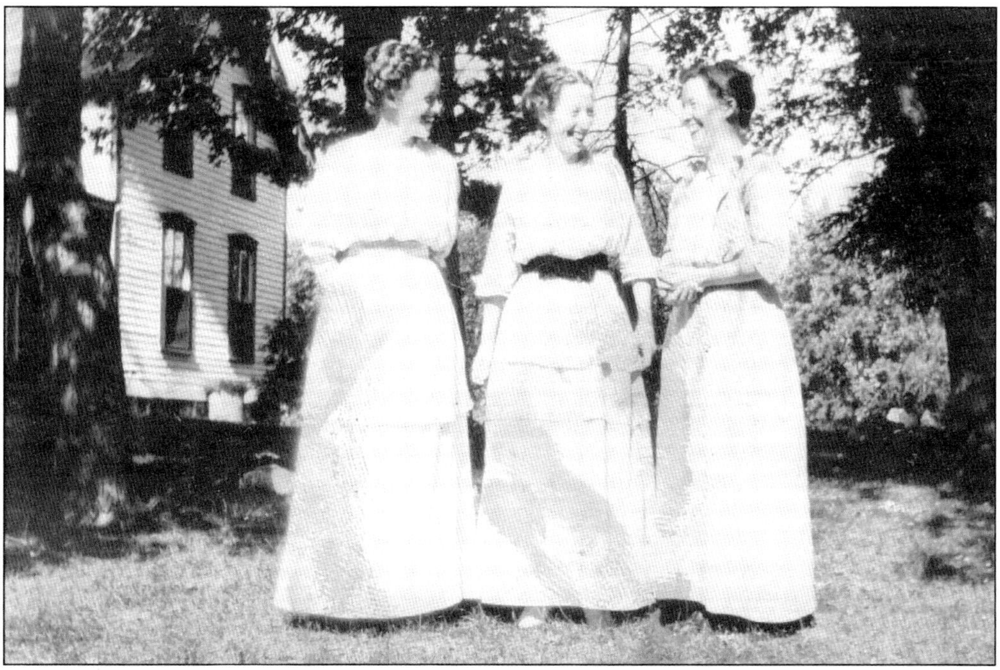

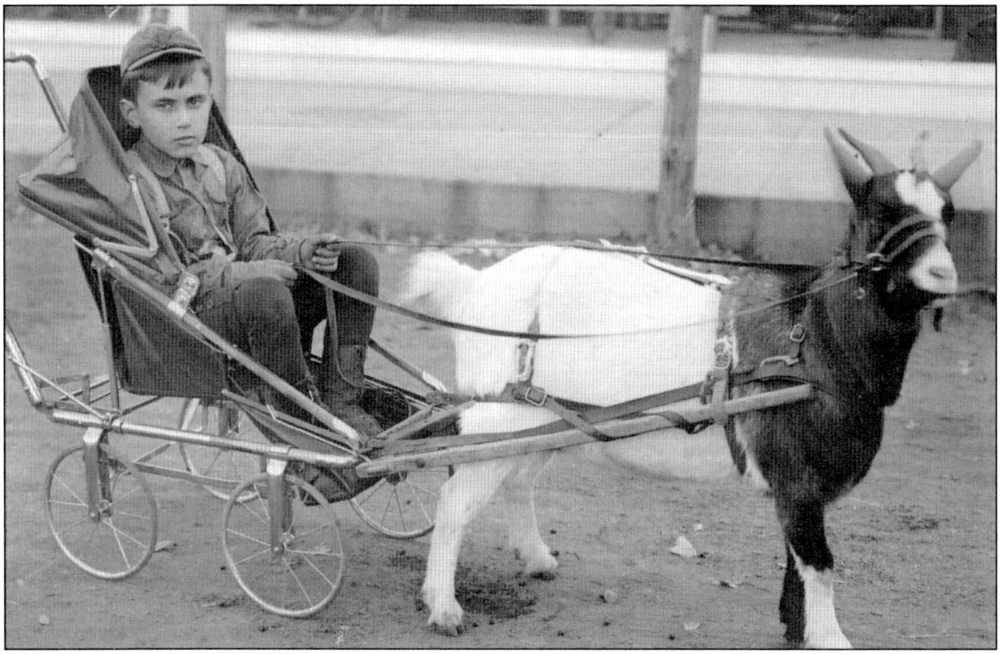

An unidentified youngster poses for a portrait in a goat cart around 1912. The goat cart was a popular prop for traveling photographers at the turn of the 20th century. (Courtesy of the Laurel Public Library.)

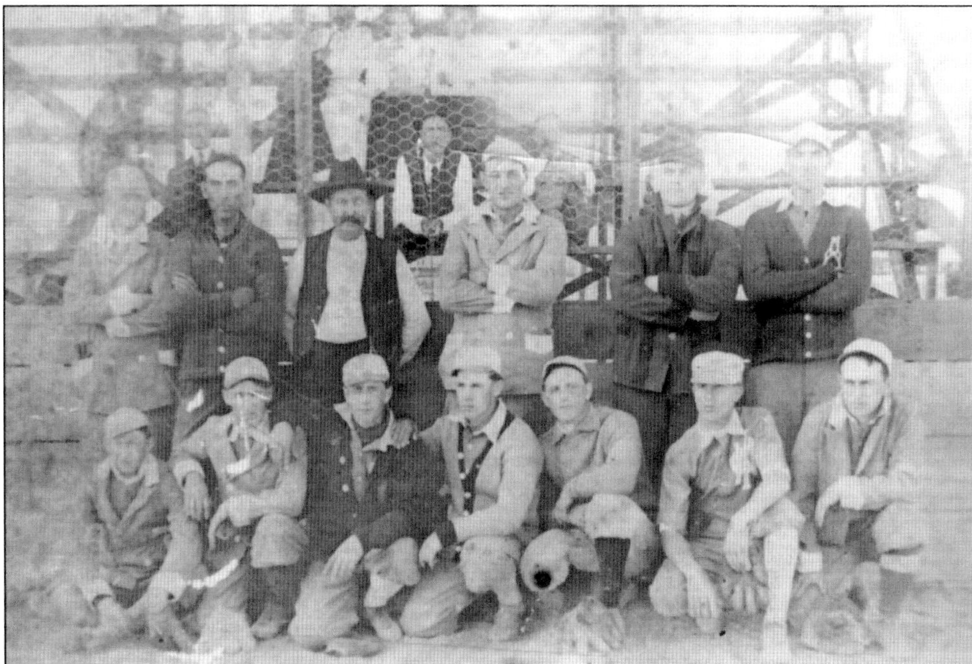

The city had high hopes for another state championship with the 1910 Laurel Boosters baseball team. Local businesses reportedly donated $1,200 in one afternoon to support the baseball club. (Courtesy of the Laurel Museum.)

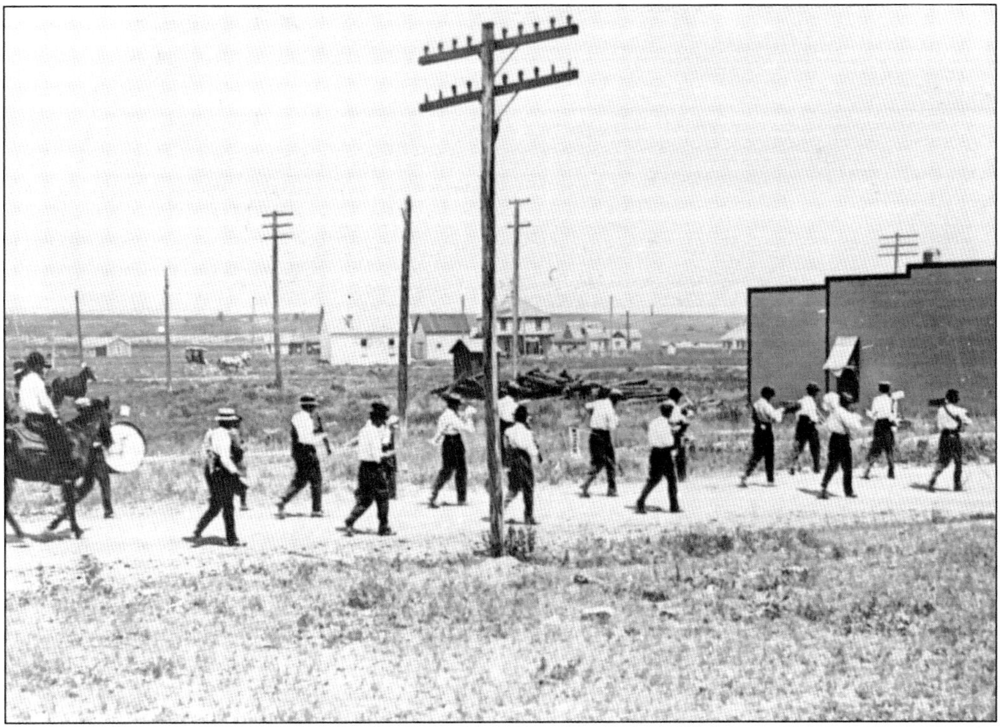

Laurel hosted a Railroad Day spectacular on July 4, 1909, to celebrate the new Northern Pacific terminals. The extravagant affair entertained visitors with a street pageant of elaborately decorated floats and marching bands from Laurel and Billings. Speeches that touted the young city's virtues, and tours of the roundhouse and shops were followed by footraces, steer roping, and a bronc-busting contest. At the ballpark, the Laurel Boosters soundly defeated Red Lodge on the baseball diamond. The celebration continued into the evening with fireworks and a grand ball at the new dance hall. (Above, courtesy of the Laurel Museum; below, courtesy of Janie Duncan.)

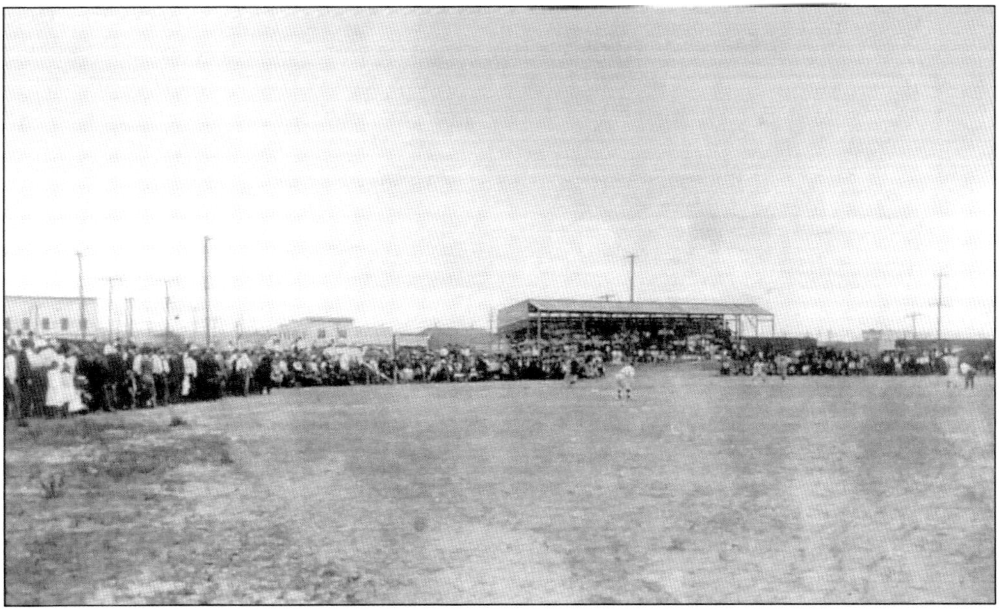

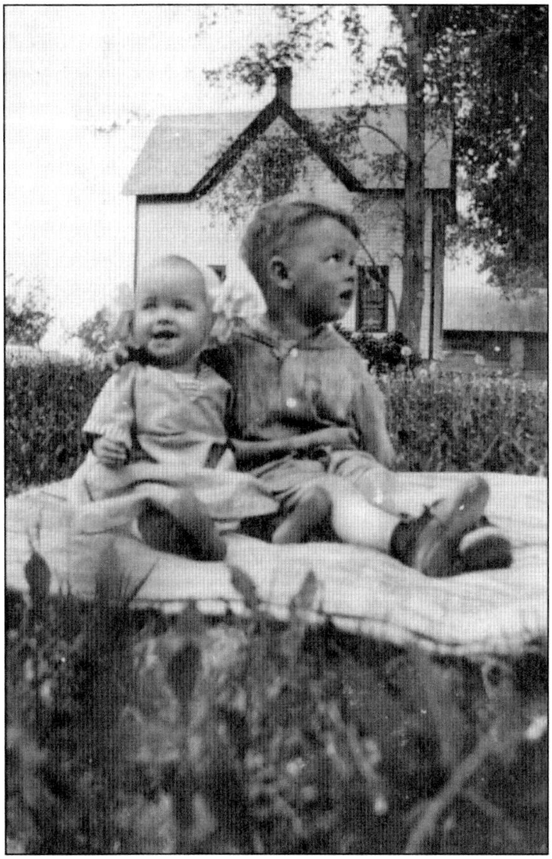

Two young tykes, possibly Virginia and Arnold Neal Shay, the eldest children of Harrison and Ethel Shay, sit for a photograph in front of Melvin and Rachel Shay's farmhouse around 1919. (Courtesy of Gerald Shay.)

The toddler in the wagon was likely Ethel Scammon, Gerald and Mary Scammon's first child, around 1932. Gerald and Mary lived at the Claremont Ranch near her parents, Sam and Laura Lottie Clare. Sam Clare came to Laurel in 1903. He raised sheep and grew wheat on 153 acres along the Clarks Fork River. Sam also sold ponies that he bought on the nearby Crow Indian Reservation. (Courtesy of Sedly Barsness.)

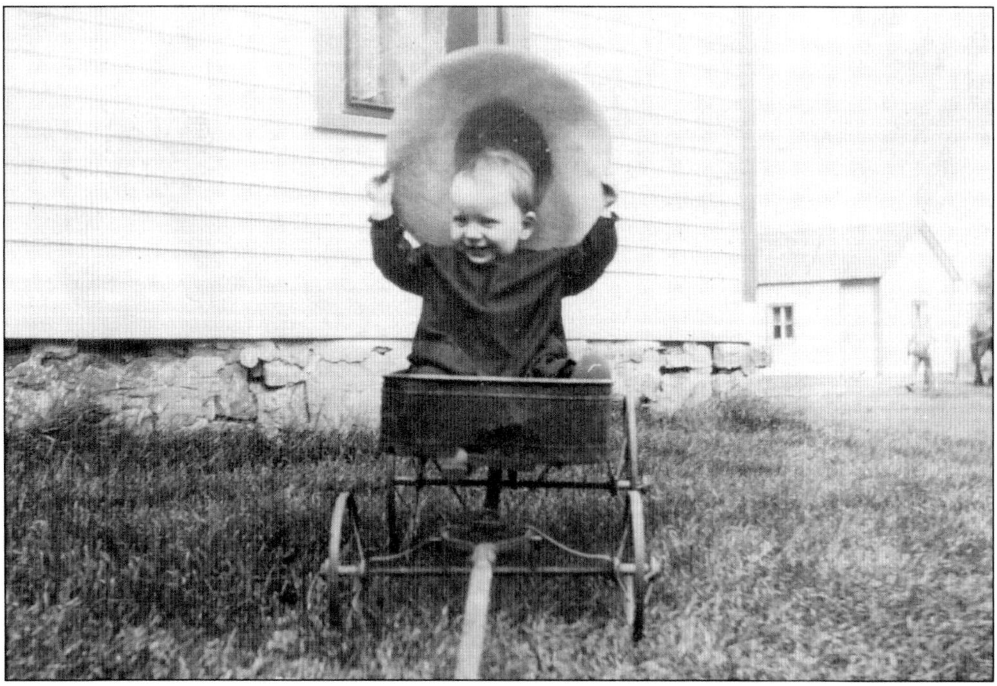

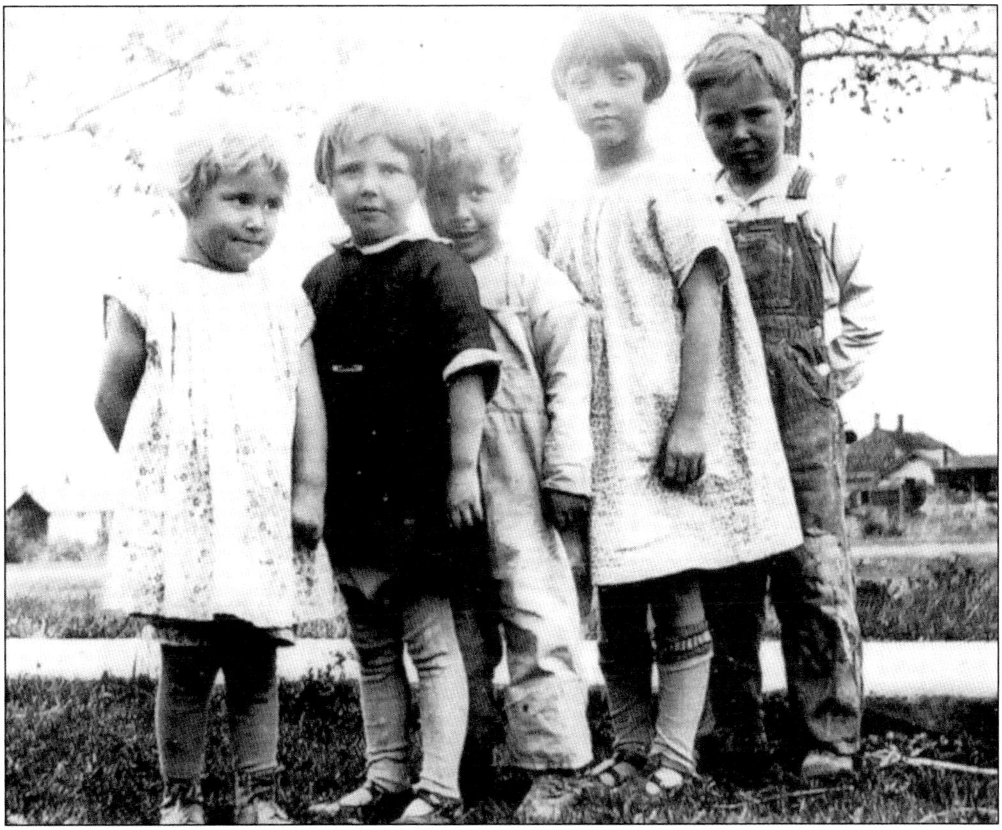

Mildred and Myron Erb, right, take time from playing with three other youngsters to pose for this photograph in front of Carrie Erb's home around 1916. (Courtesy of Allison Nys.)

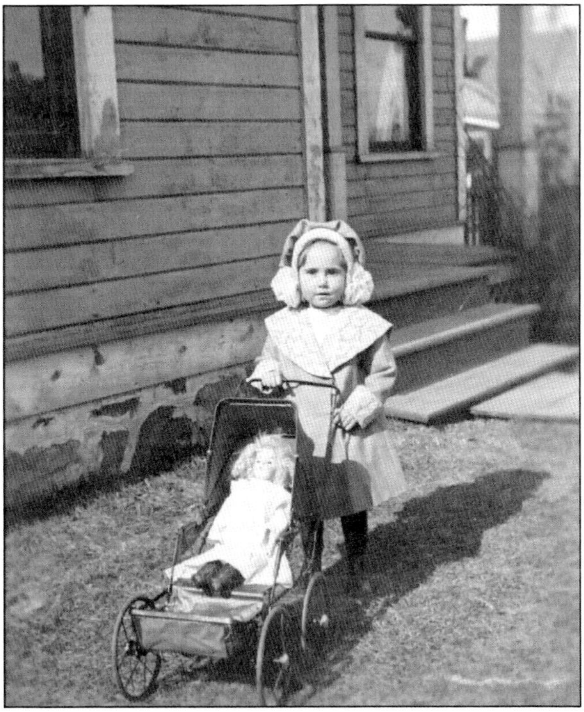

This little girl with her doll in a toy stroller is identified only as Sarah. (Courtesy of the Laurel Public Library.)

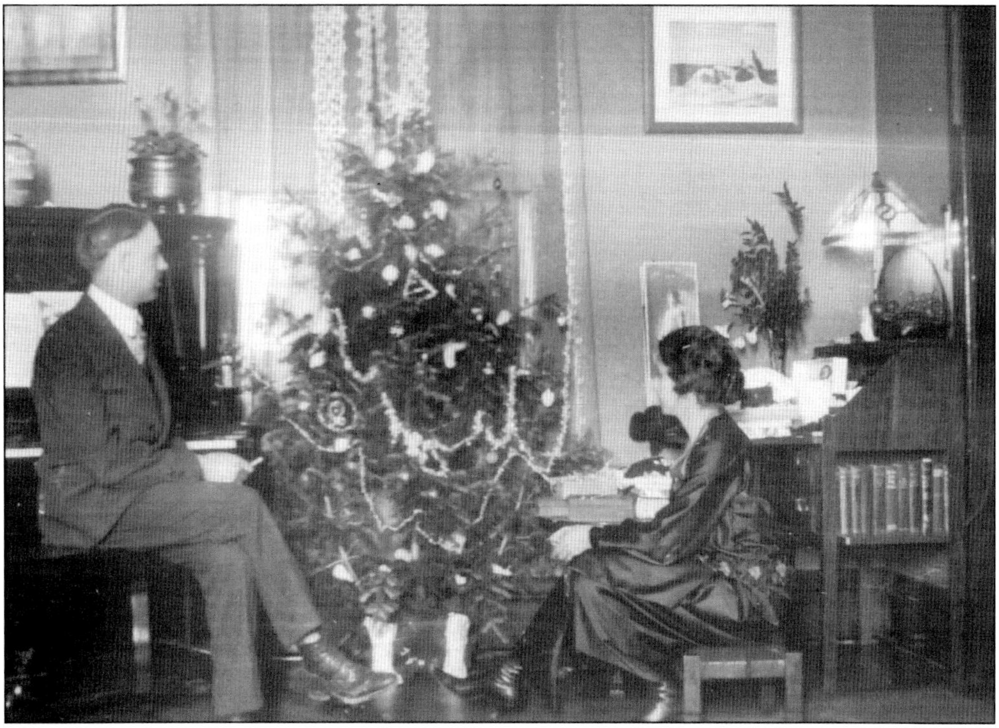

A young couple admires their festively decorated Christmas tree in the 1920s. (Courtesy of the Laurel Public Library.)

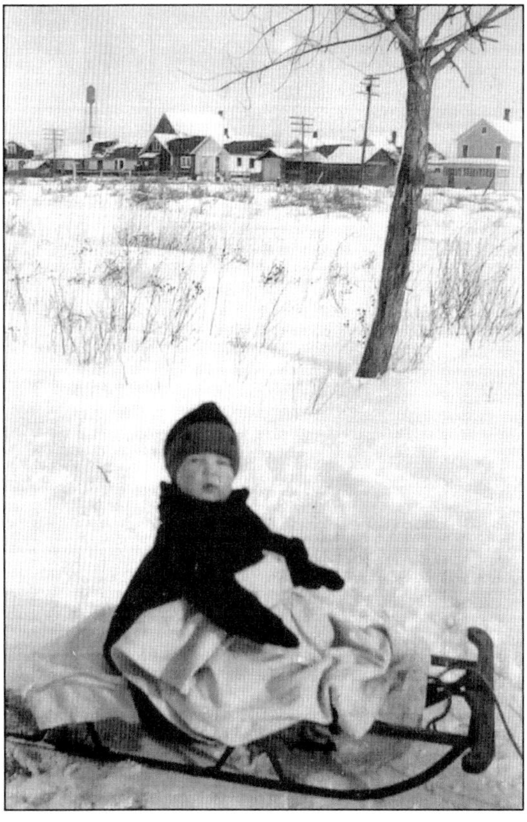

A rosy-cheeked and bundled-up Lilburn Erb goes sledding through the snowy streets of Laurel. Lilburn was the daughter of Roman and Jennie Erb and the granddaughter of Abraham and Carrie Erb. (Courtesy of Allison Nys.)

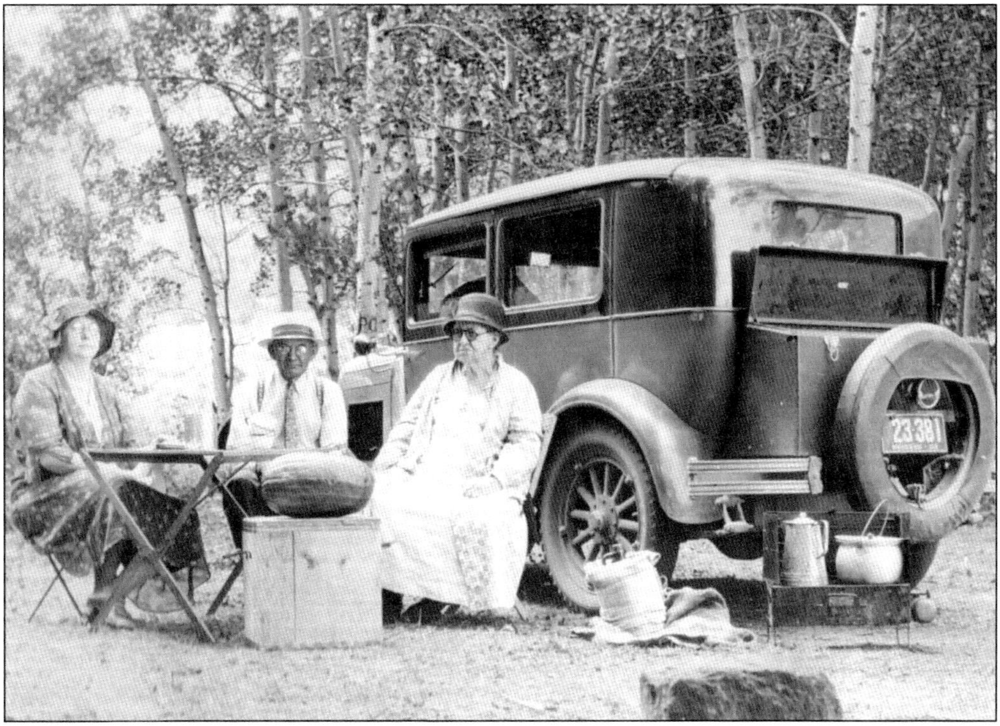

Picnic excursions were a treasured weekend pastime for many Laurelites. Motorcars made it possible for picnickers, like the trio pictured here, to venture farther afield along the river or into the mountains. (Courtesy of the Laurel Museum.)

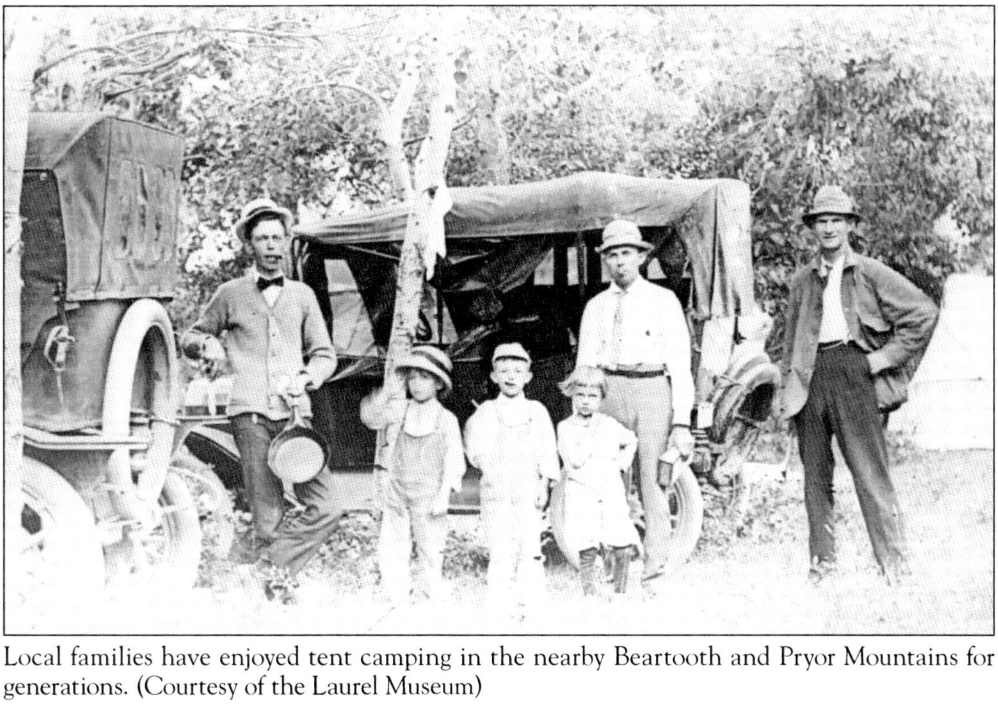

Local families have enjoyed tent camping in the nearby Beartooth and Pryor Mountains for generations. (Courtesy of the Laurel Museum)

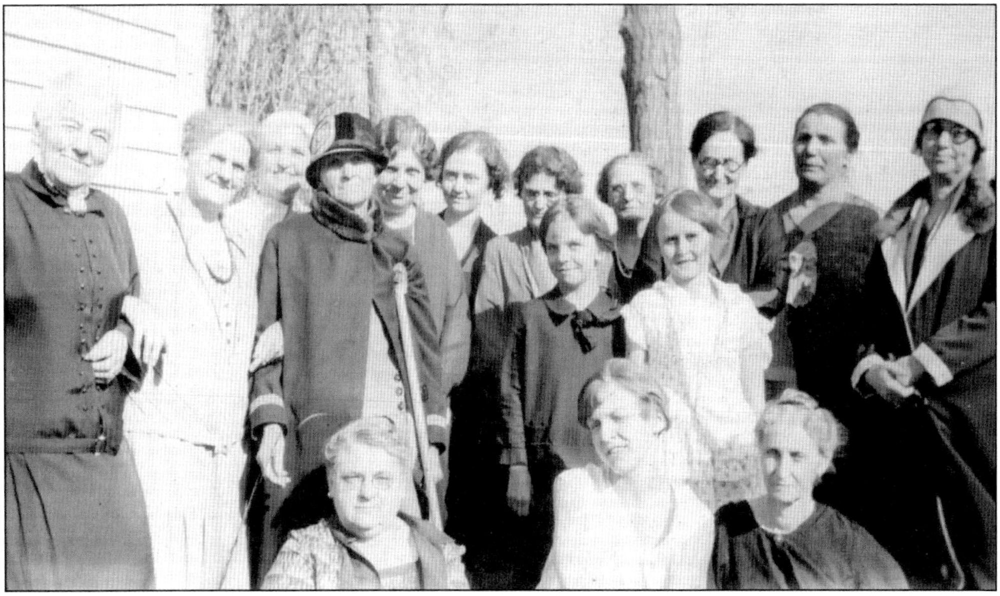

Valma Shay (front center) and her mother, Rachel, entertain guests at their family farm west of Laurel. (Courtesy of Gerald Shay.)

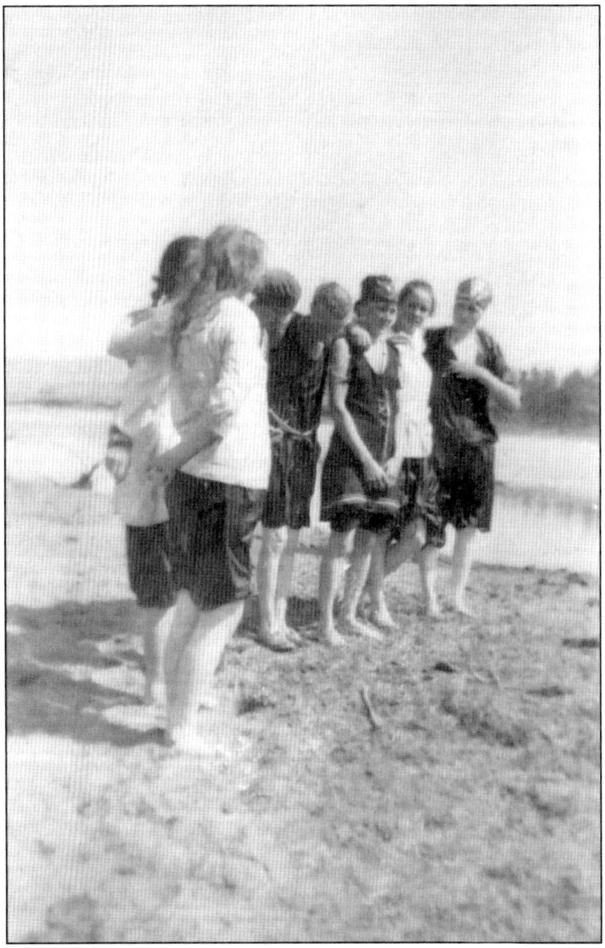

Wet from swimming in the Yellowstone River, these young women pose for a photograph on the sandy beach at the river's edge. (Courtesy of Gerald Shay.)

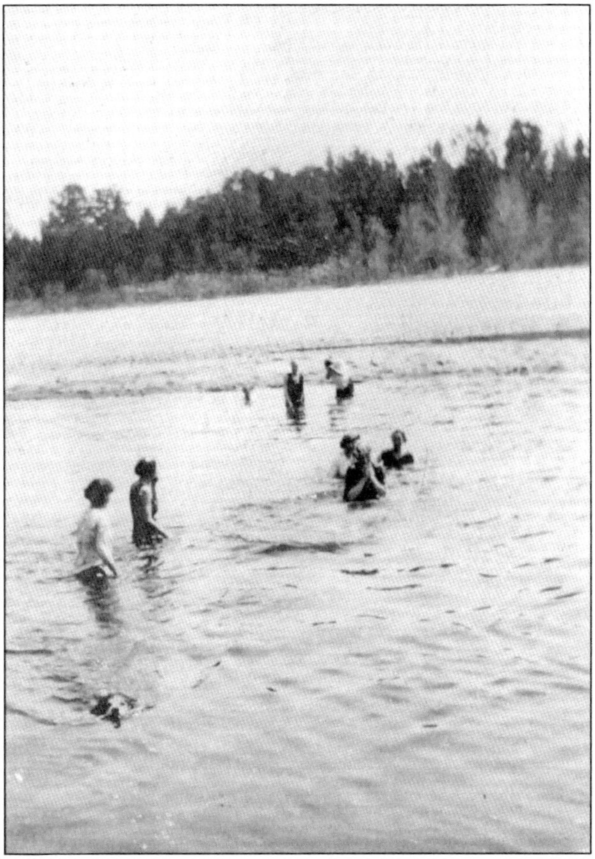

A group of young women swims in the cool currents of the Yellowstone River. The Cove Ditch was another favorite swimming hole before the Laurel pool opened in 1949. (Both, courtesy of Gerald Shay.)

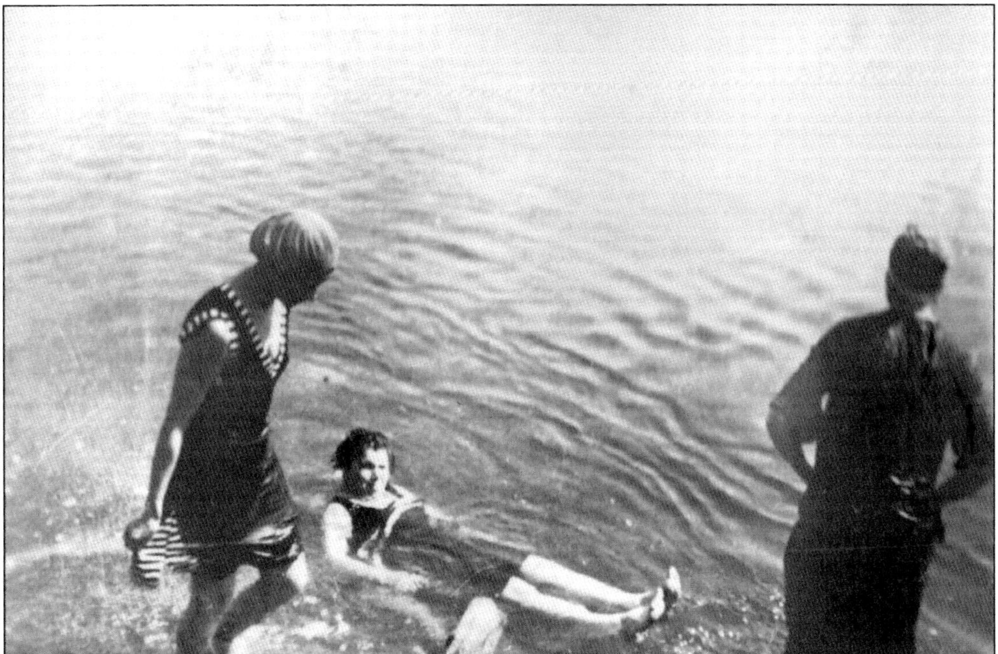

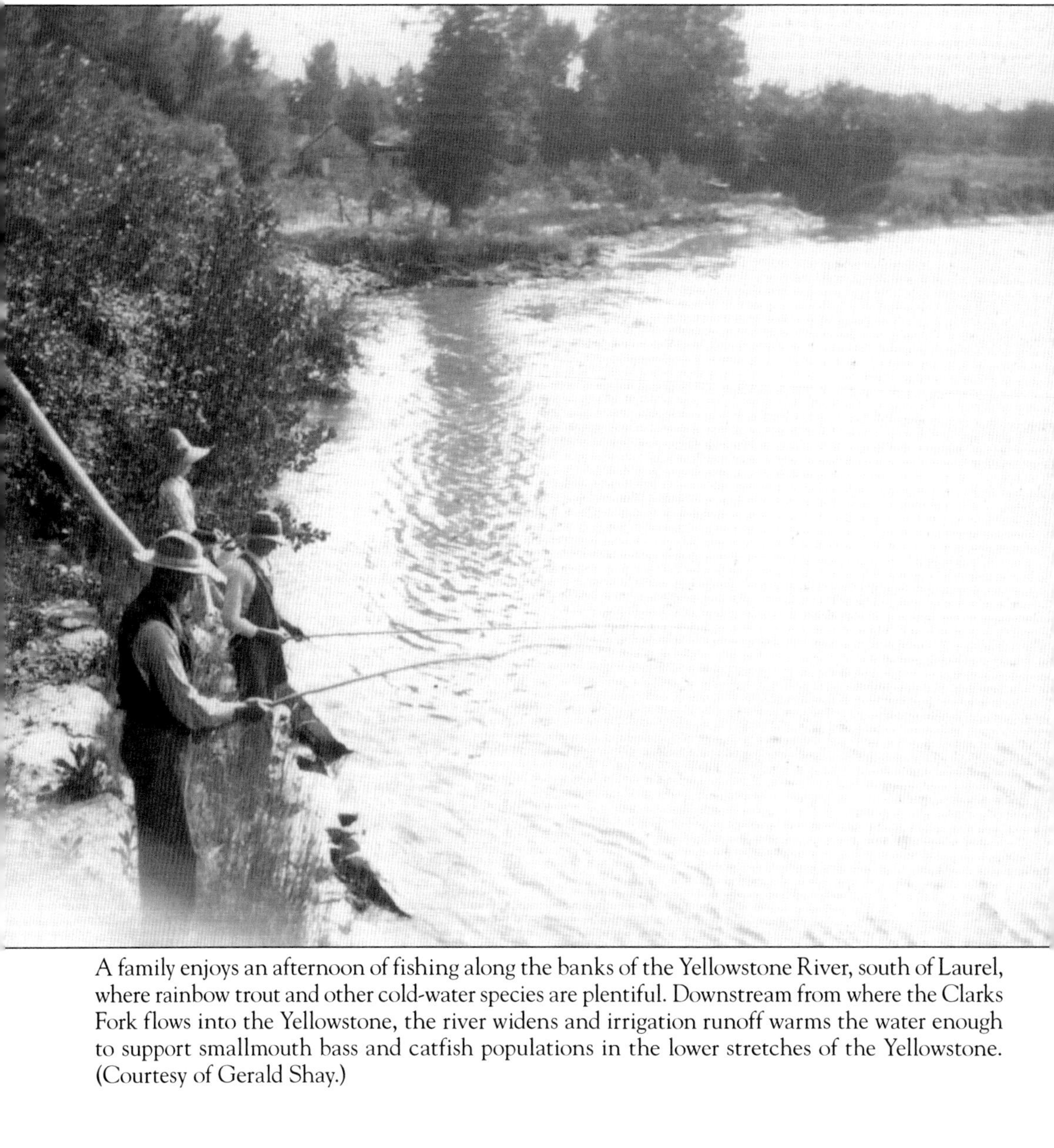

A family enjoys an afternoon of fishing along the banks of the Yellowstone River, south of Laurel, where rainbow trout and other cold-water species are plentiful. Downstream from where the Clarks Fork flows into the Yellowstone, the river widens and irrigation runoff warms the water enough to support smallmouth bass and catfish populations in the lower stretches of the Yellowstone. (Courtesy of Gerald Shay.)

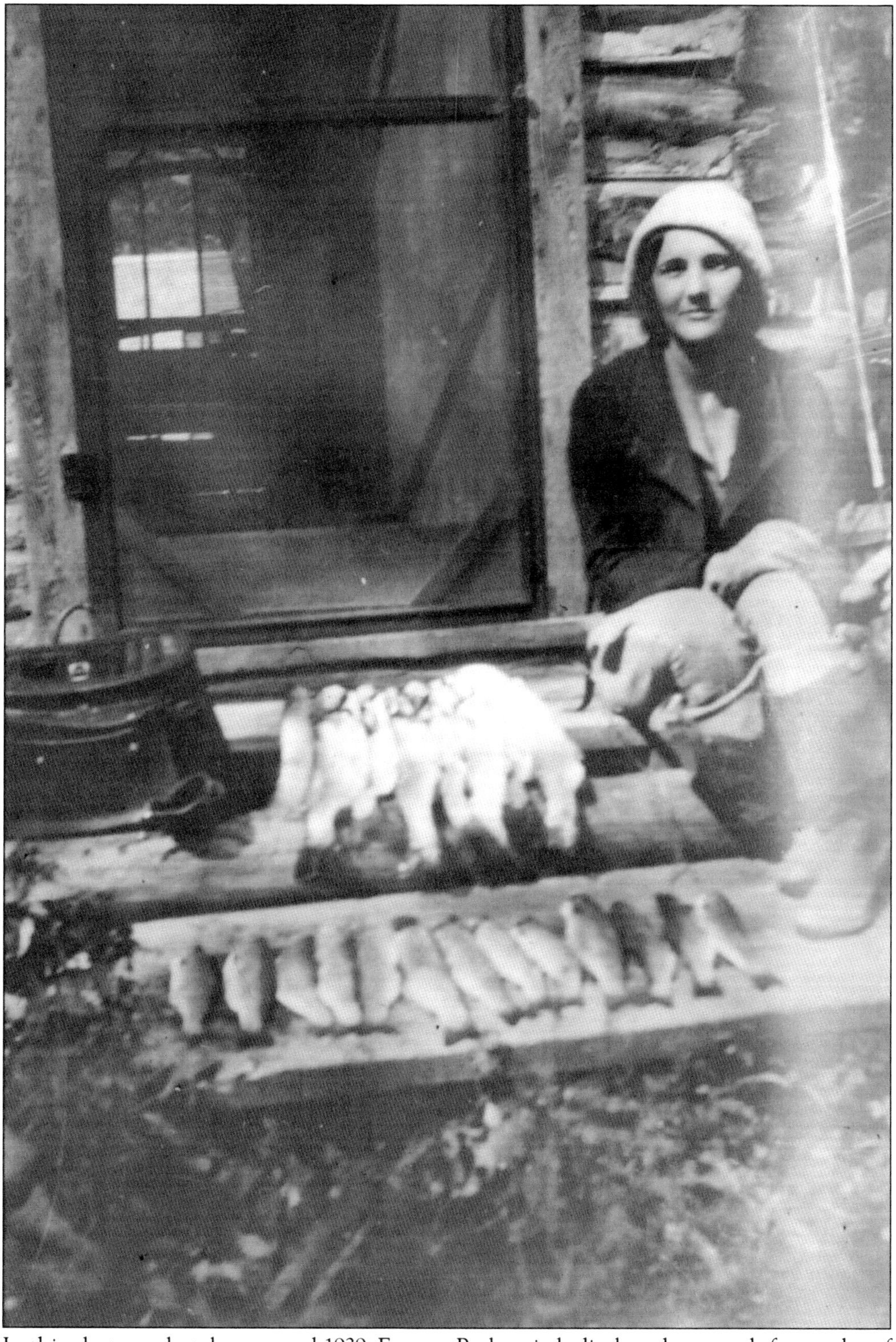

In this photograph, taken around 1939, Frances Beslanwitch displays the rewards from a day of fishing. (Courtesy of the Laurel Public Library.)

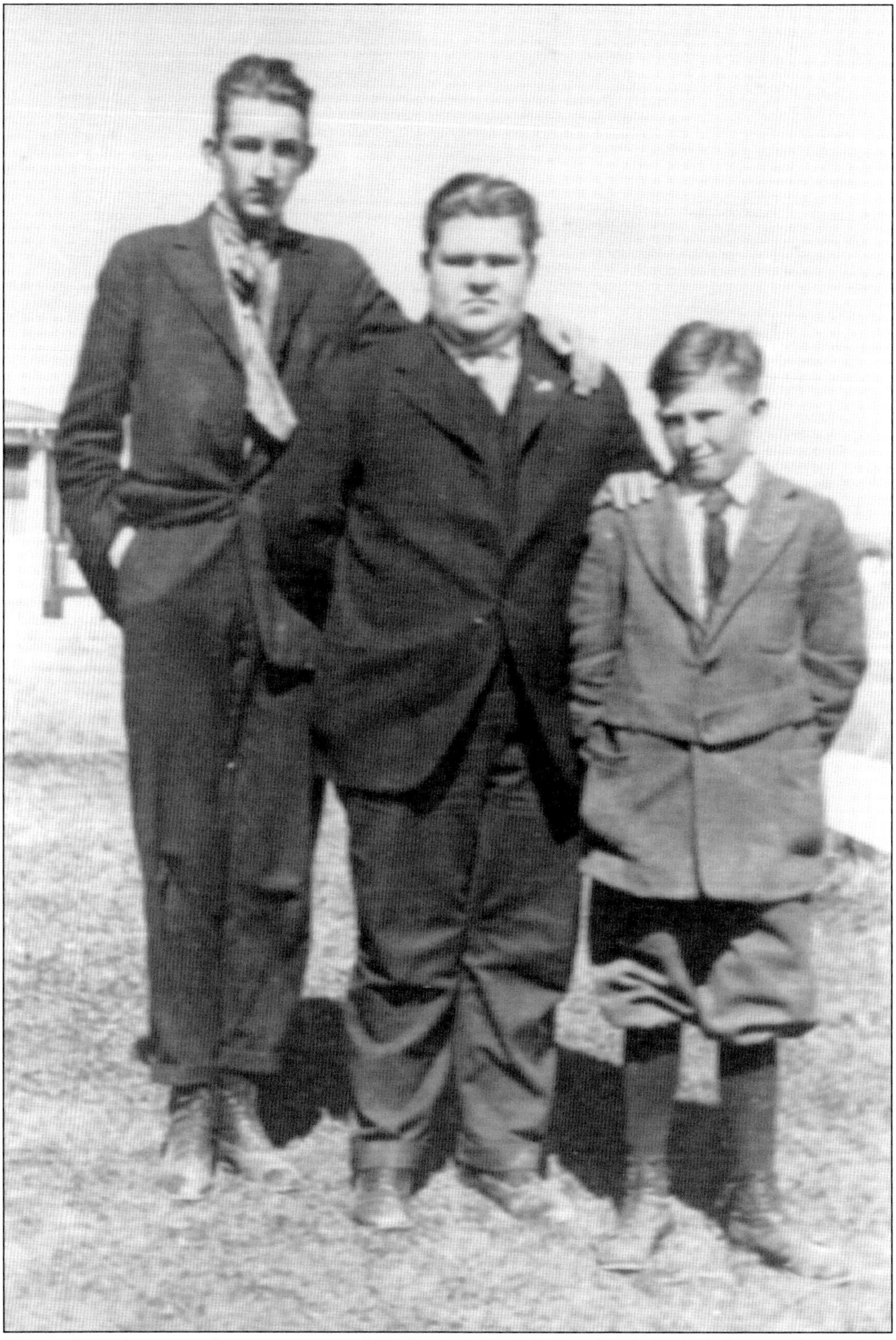

These three boys are the same age and in the same grade at school. From left to right are Bill Burla, Franklin Parker, and Jack Leigh. (Courtesy of the Laurel Museum.)

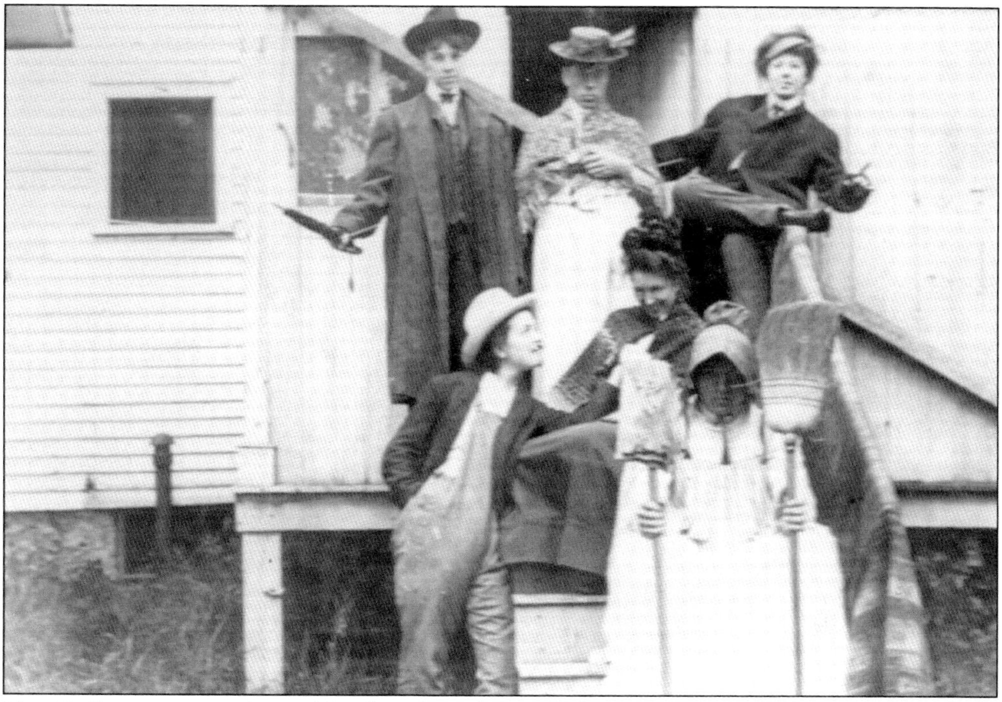

Matilda Stevens, top right, and her friends strike a pose during a costume party in Laurel. Matilda was a trained nurse who was married to Dr. Lawrence Stevens, the Northern Pacific Railroad's local physician. (Courtesy of the Laurel Museum.)

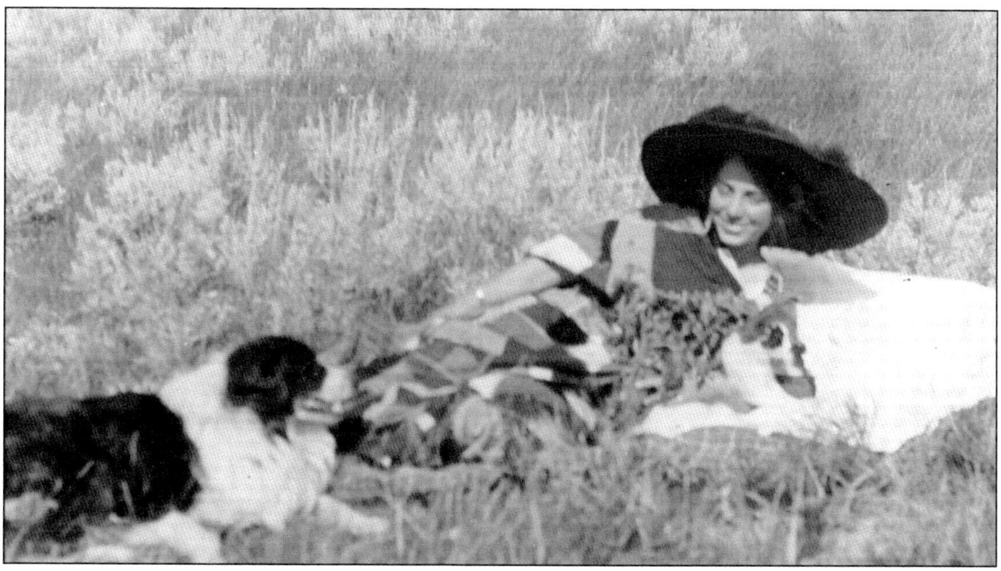

A young woman, possibly Emma Brickman, lounges in the sun next to her dog. (Courtesy of the Laurel Public Library.)

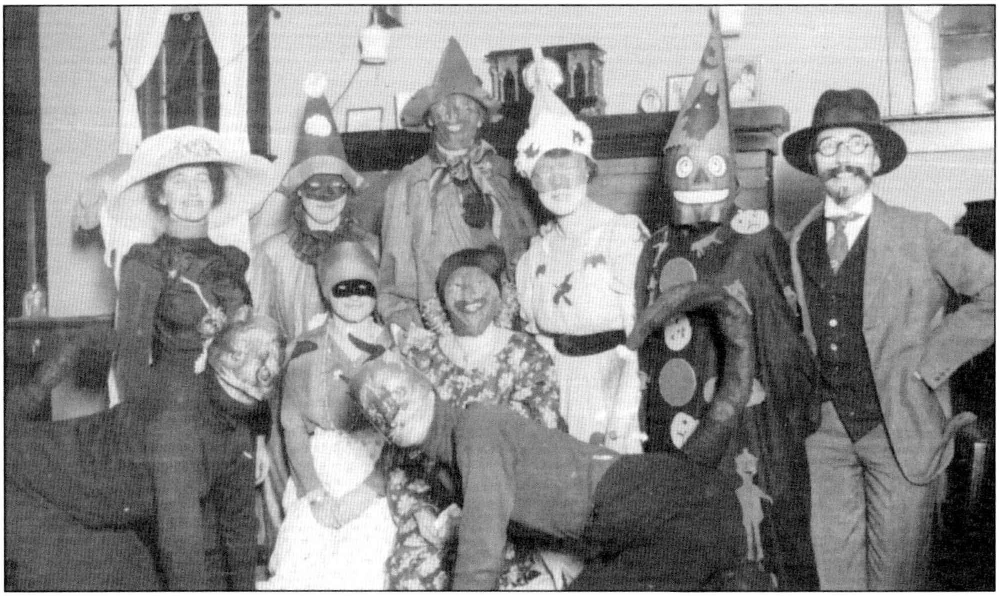

Costume parties and skits were popular entertainment at holiday gatherings. Above, friends of Thomas and Ruby (Jordan) Winters donned handmade masks and costumes for a Halloween dinner party in the 1920s. Below, young women act out a skit about true love's triumph during a Christmas get-together. (Both, courtesy of the Laurel Public Library.)

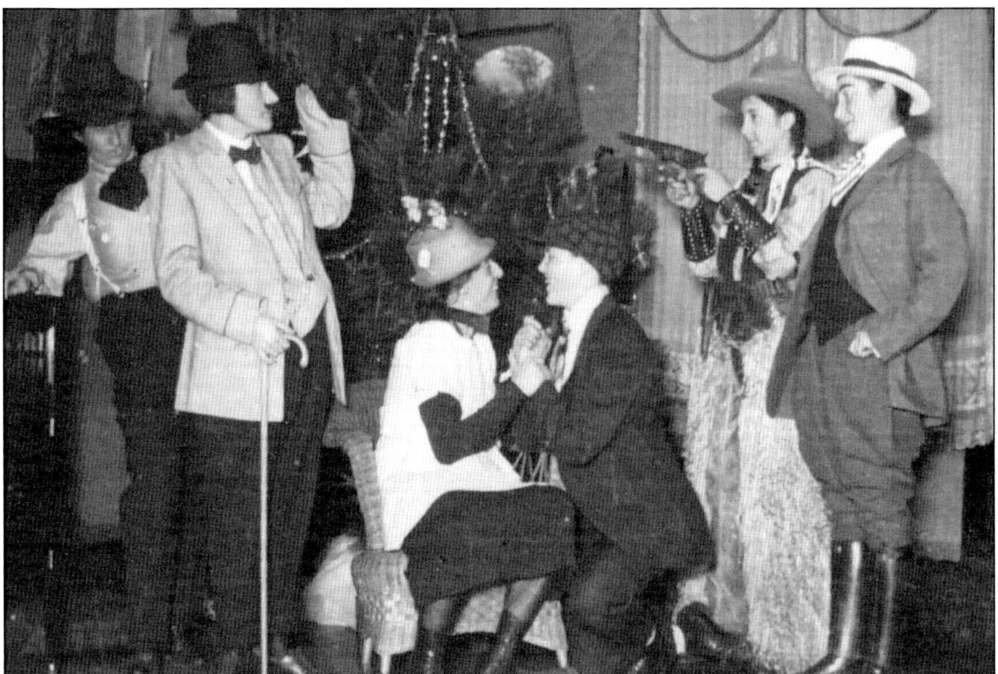

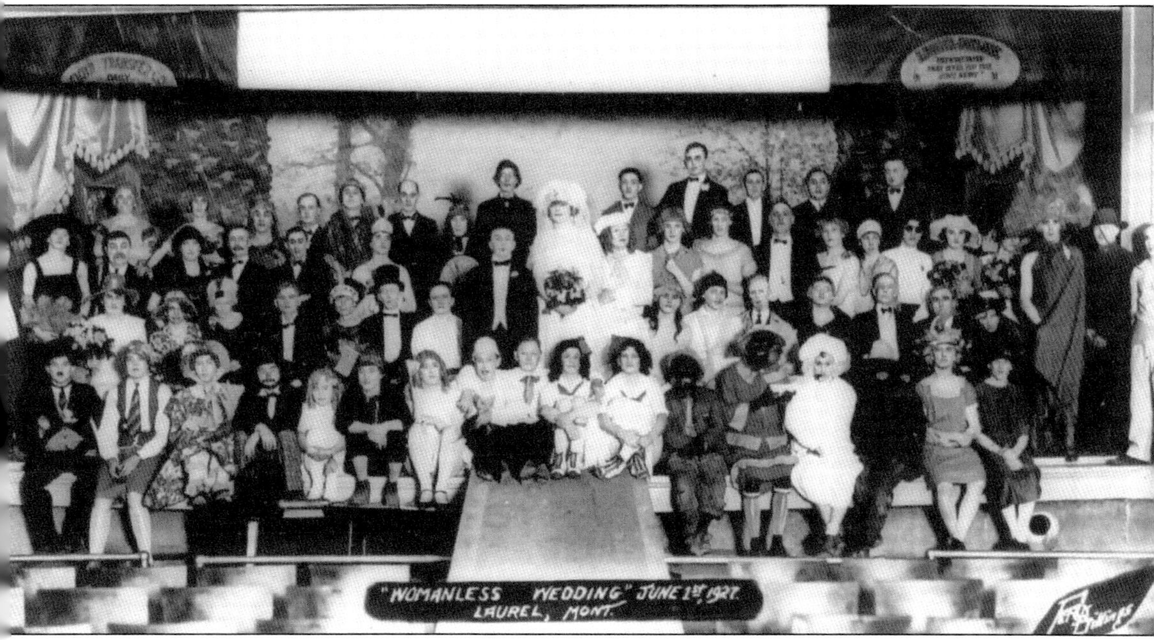

The Congregational Ladies' Circle sponsored a Womanless Wedding production at the Strand Theatre in 1927. The farcical wedding sold over a thousand 50¢ tickets, drawing spectators from far and wide for the two-night show. Banker Bert Harris and barber Reese Price starred as the bride and groom in the all-male cast of 60. Other notable community figures in the play were physician Dr. Warren Tupper, dentist Dr. Daniel McCauley, school superintendent Fred Graff, magistrate Frederick Scheidecker, city engineer Thomas Rigney, and Northern Pacific roadmaster Nels Vordahl. The cast also included merchants Charles Morris and Ole Wold, hotel manager Bernard Berger, and pharmacist Charles Sande, along with three former mayors: insurance agent Edwin Fenton, contractor Clarence Laird, and attorney Benjamin Price. (Photograph by John Petek; courtesy of Allison Nys.)

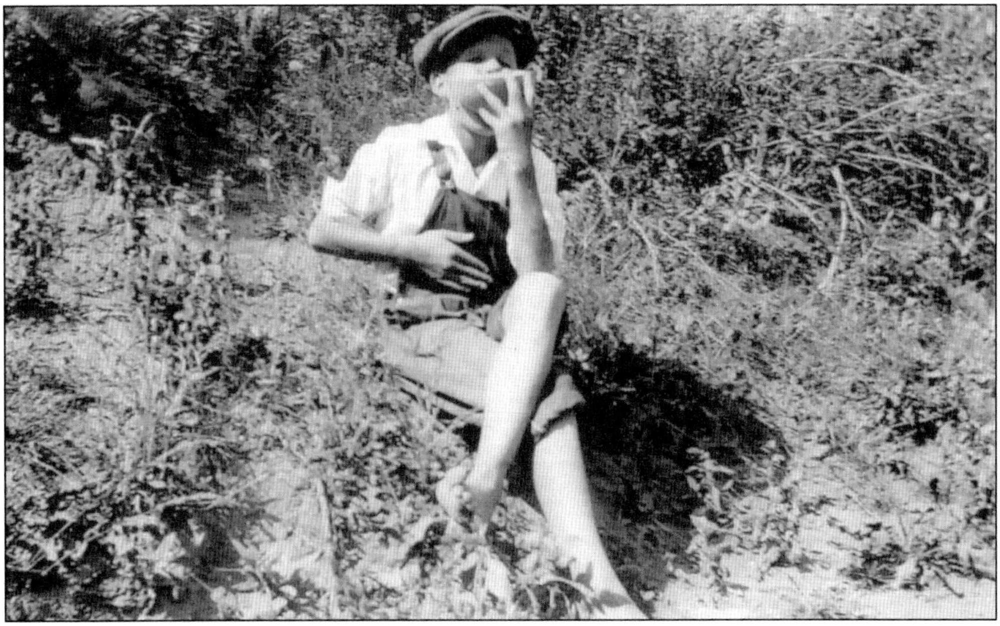

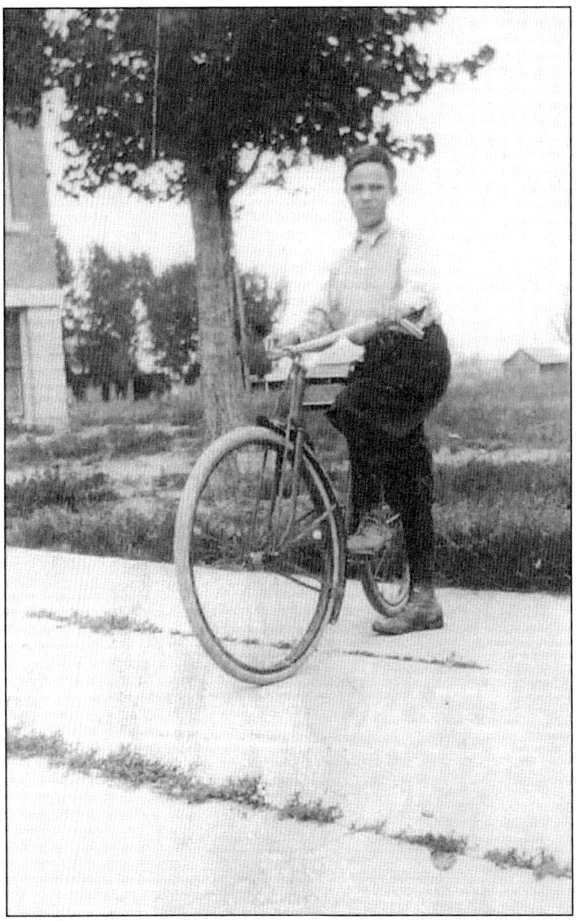

Myron Erb enjoys a slice of watermelon on a hot summer day. (Courtesy of Allison Nys.)

Earl Arnold readies to ride his bicycle after school. Earl was the son of Martisha and William Arnold, who owned Laurel's first flower shop. (Courtesy of Allison Nys.)

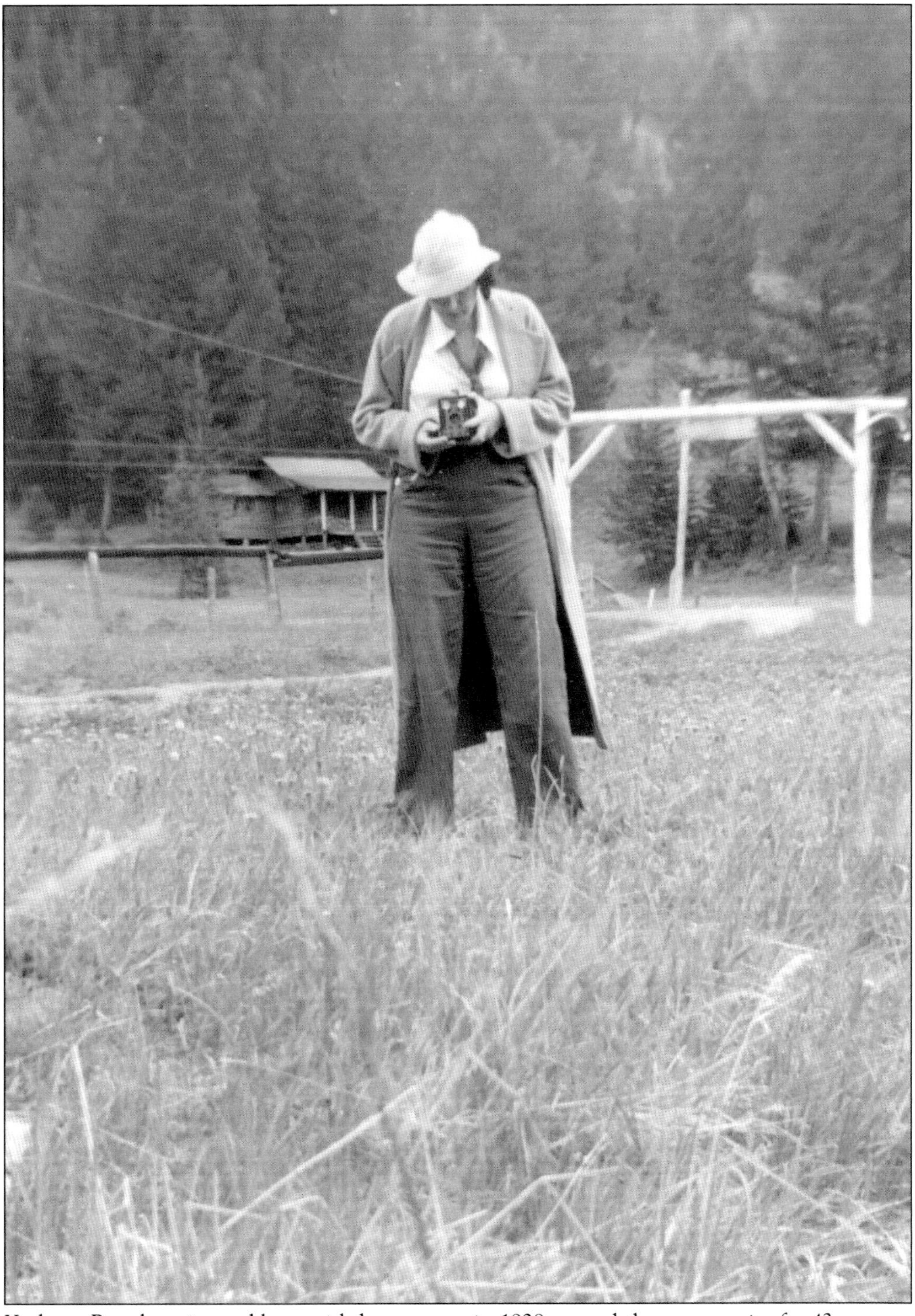

Kathryn Royalty, pictured here with her camera in 1938, served the community for 43 years as the Mountain States Telephone Company's chief operator. Kathryn was the daughter of Lucinda and Charles Rugg, an English immigrant who was among the first to settle in the Yellowstone Valley in the late 1870s. (Courtesy of the Laurel Public Library.)

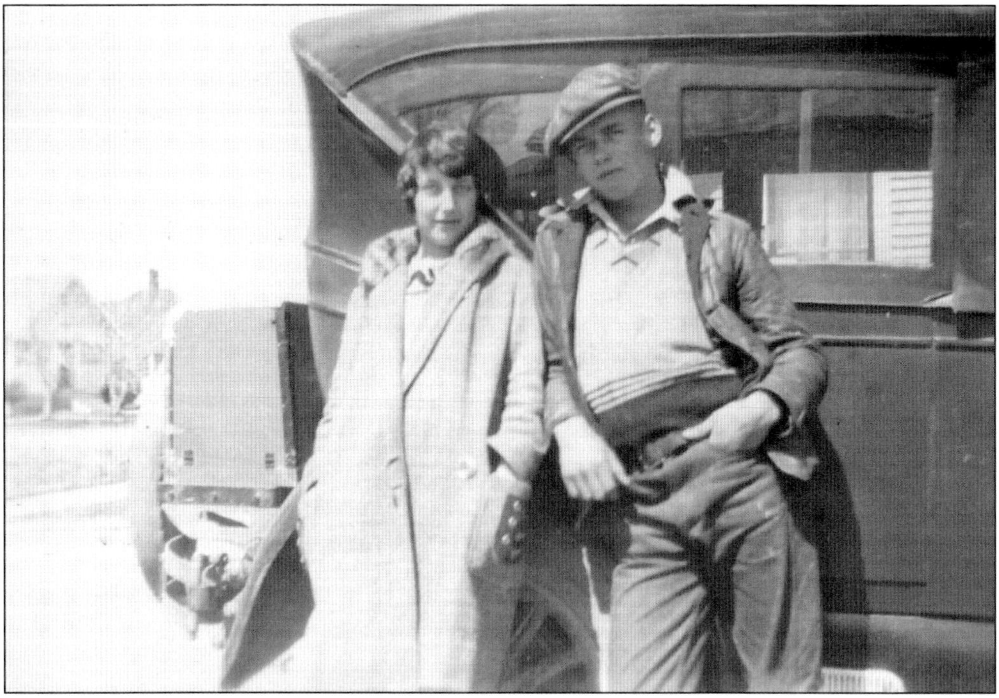

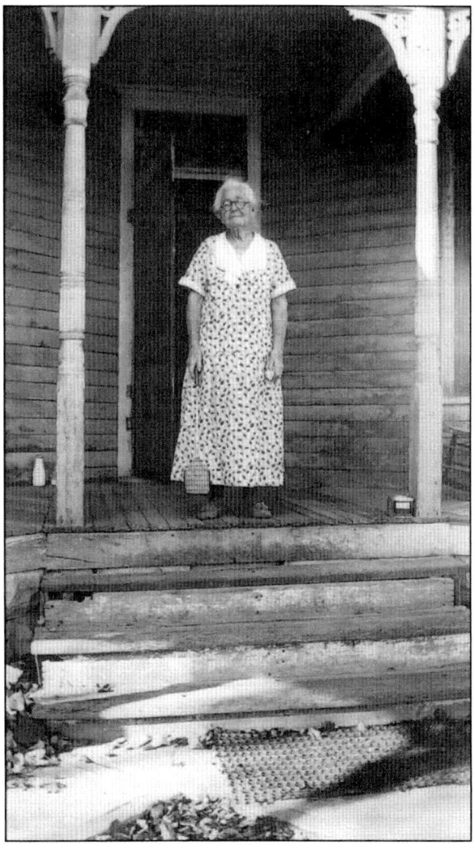

Pictured are Marion Jackson and a friend from high school. Marion, the daughter of Charles and Ada Jackson, grew up on a farm south of Laurel and rode the bus into town to attend high school. (Courtesy of Maxine Allman.)

Mary Jackson stands on the porch of the Erb house in 1936. Mary and Frank Jackson were among the earliest homesteaders in the area, joining the Ripon Colony near Park City in 1882. The Jacksons bought land west of Laurel in 1887 and farmed it for over 25 years before moving to Washington. Mary moved back to Laurel after Frank's death, boarding at the Erb apartments. (Courtesy of Allison Nys.)

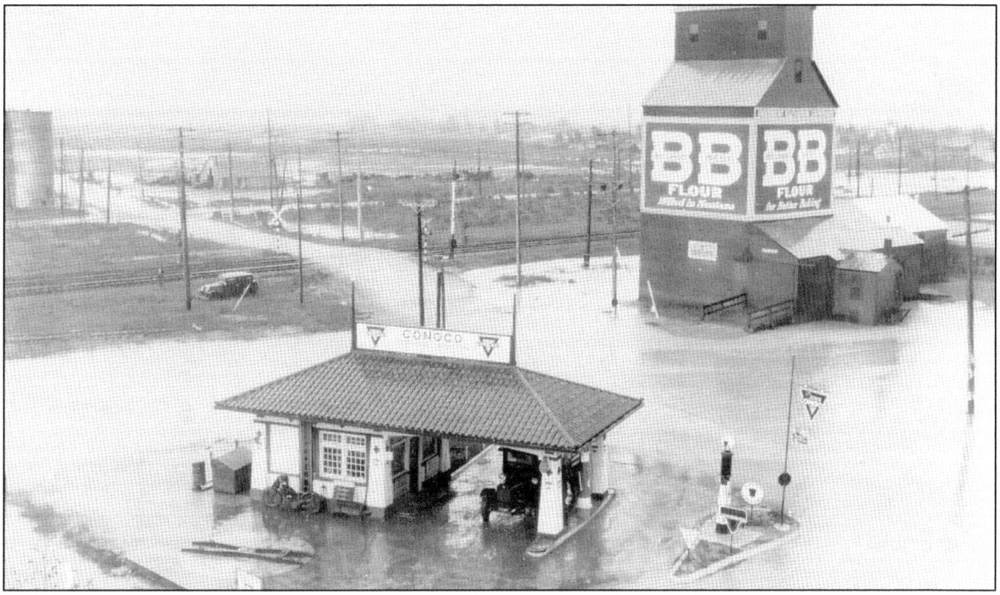

Laurel has suffered several severe floods over the years. In 1924, a sudden storm caused the Cove and Big Ditches to break. The highway and railroad tracks east of town were submerged under nearly three feet of water, weakening the railroad bed enough that some of the tracks collapsed. In June 1937, a hailstorm followed by heavy rain breached the Cove, High, and Big Ditches, drowning livestock and crippling irrigation for weeks. In the photograph above, a storm floods the streets of Laurel before the underpass was built between the Occident grain elevator and the Conoco service station, then owned by Bert Sherrow. Below, Otis "Chappy" Chapman, center right, stands in galoshes outside his drugstore as floodwaters recede in 1937 or 1938. (Above, courtesy of the Laurel Museum; below, courtesy of Barbara Nicholas.)

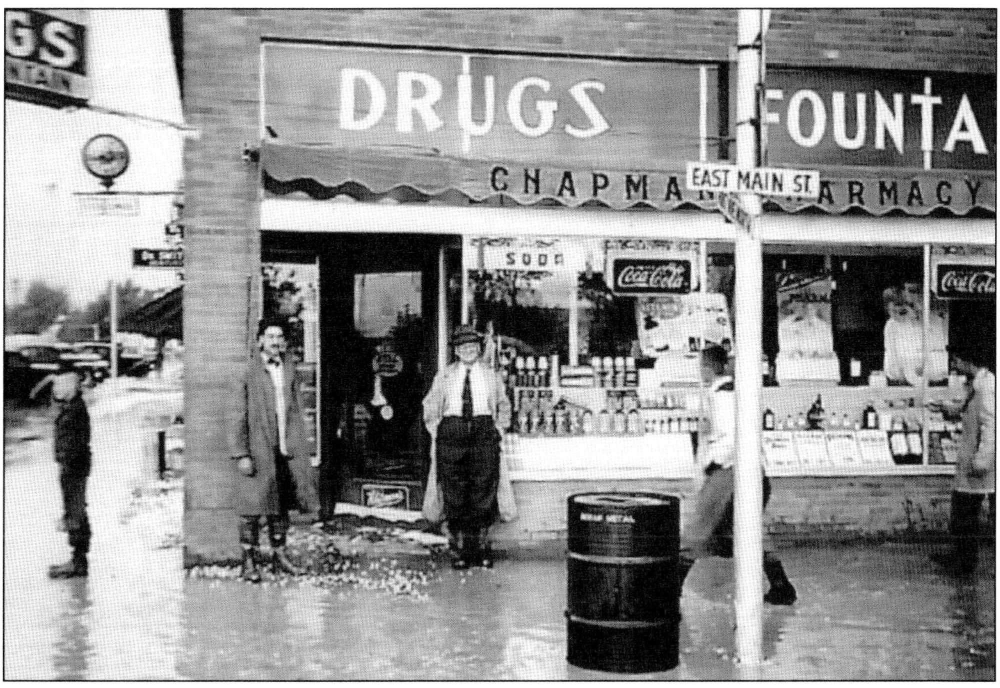

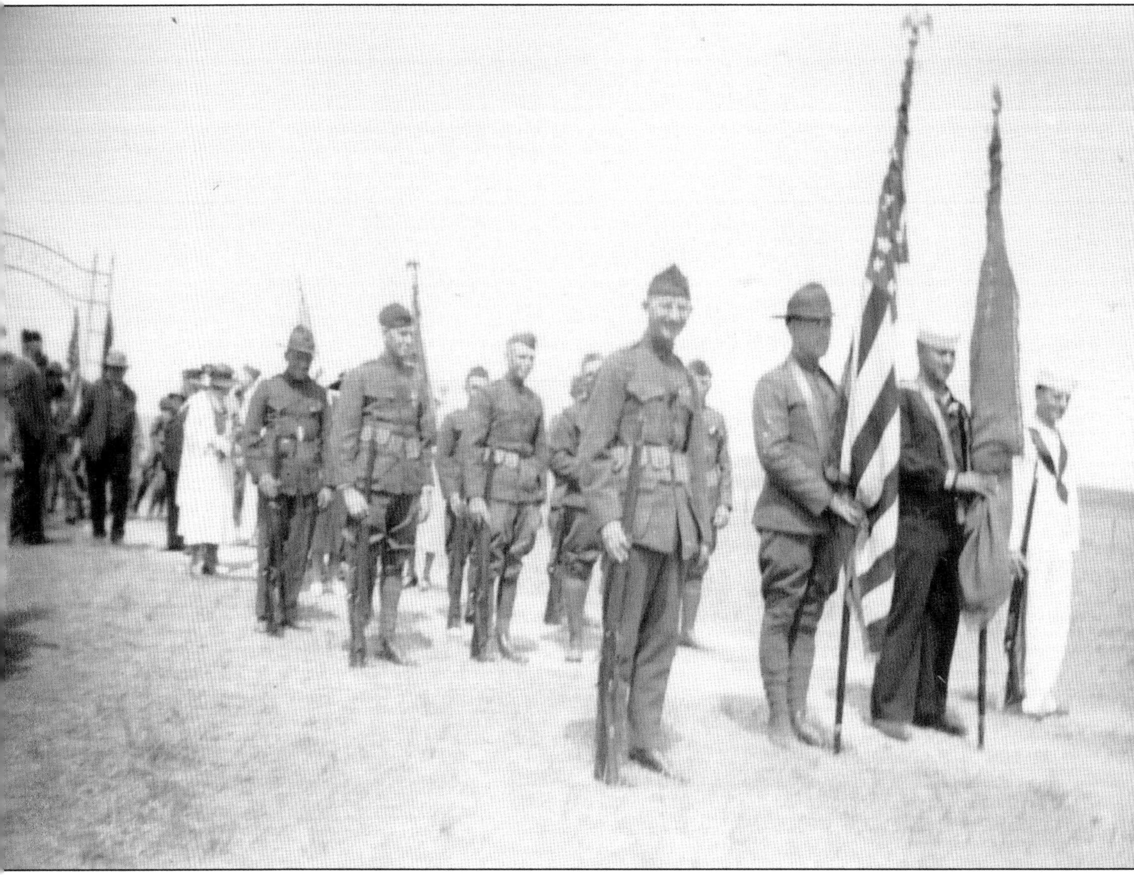

Bill Fenton carries the US flag in the 1934 Memorial Day procession at the Laurel Cemetery. Members of the American Legion Auxiliary placed wreaths on servicemen's graves, and the Legionnaires fired a 21-gun salute to honor the men and women who had served their country in the armed forces. (Courtesy of the Laurel Public Library.)

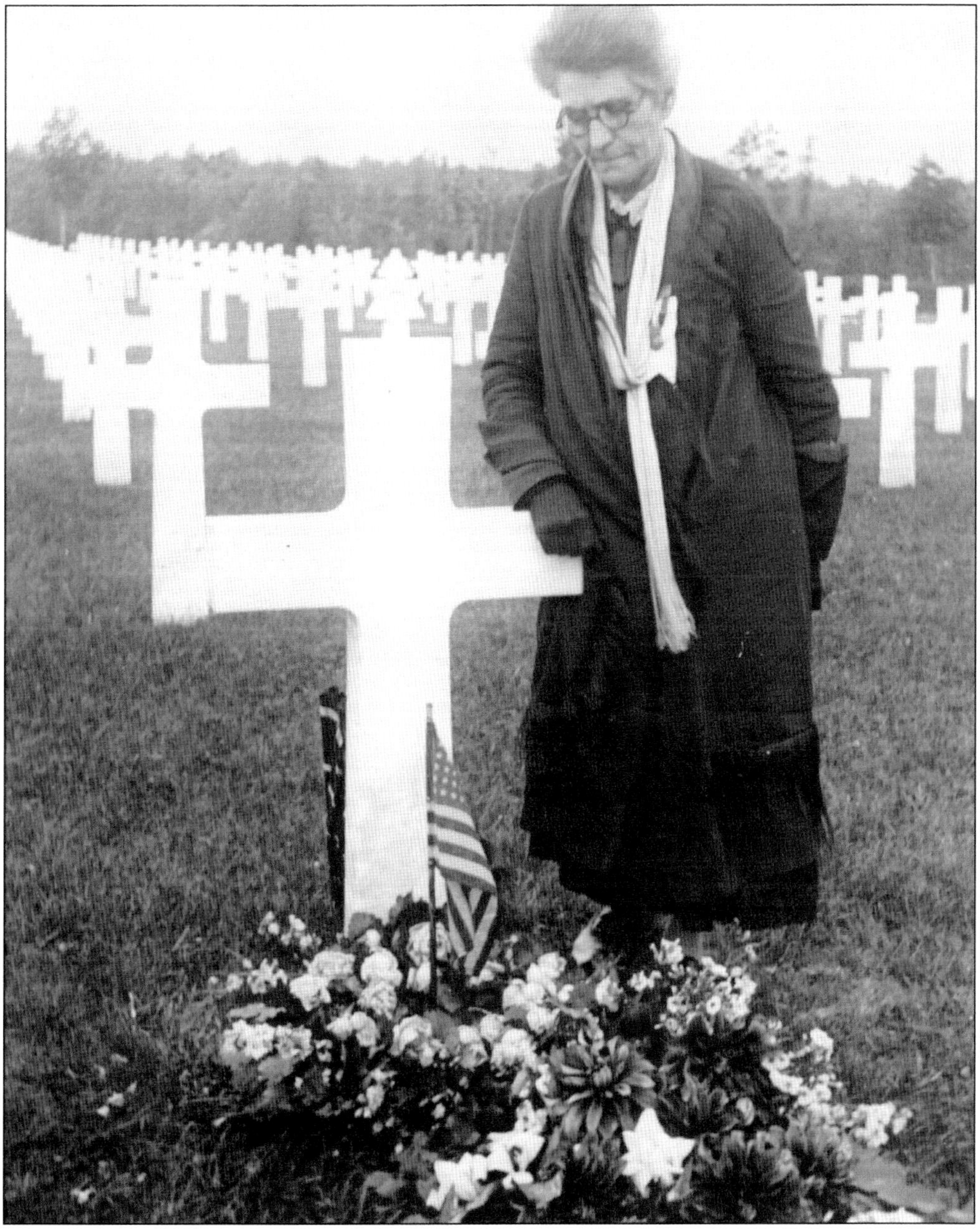

Carrie Vickery, originally from Wyoming, was a Gold Star Mother in the Laurel American Legion Auxiliary, a title earned by visiting the grave of her son, an American soldier who was killed and buried in France during World War I. (Courtesy of the Laurel Public Library.)

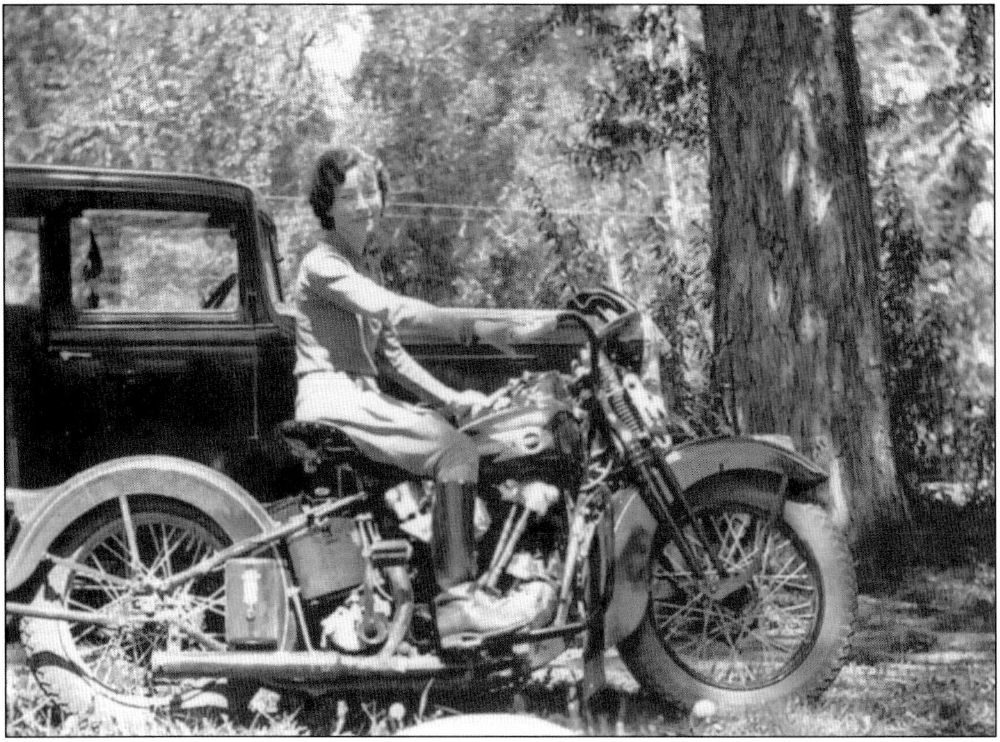

Isabel Erb sits astride her husband's motorcycle while on a weekend outing. Myron, her husband, was an avid motorcyclist who regularly competed in the Billings Motorcycle Club's hill climb. (Both, courtesy of Allison Nys.)

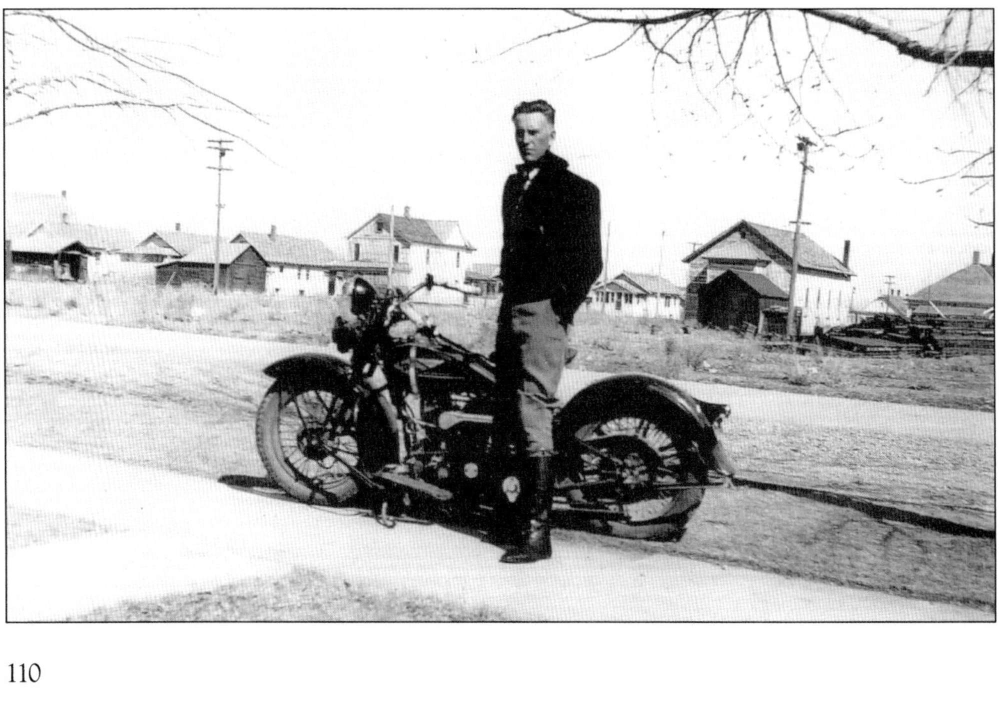

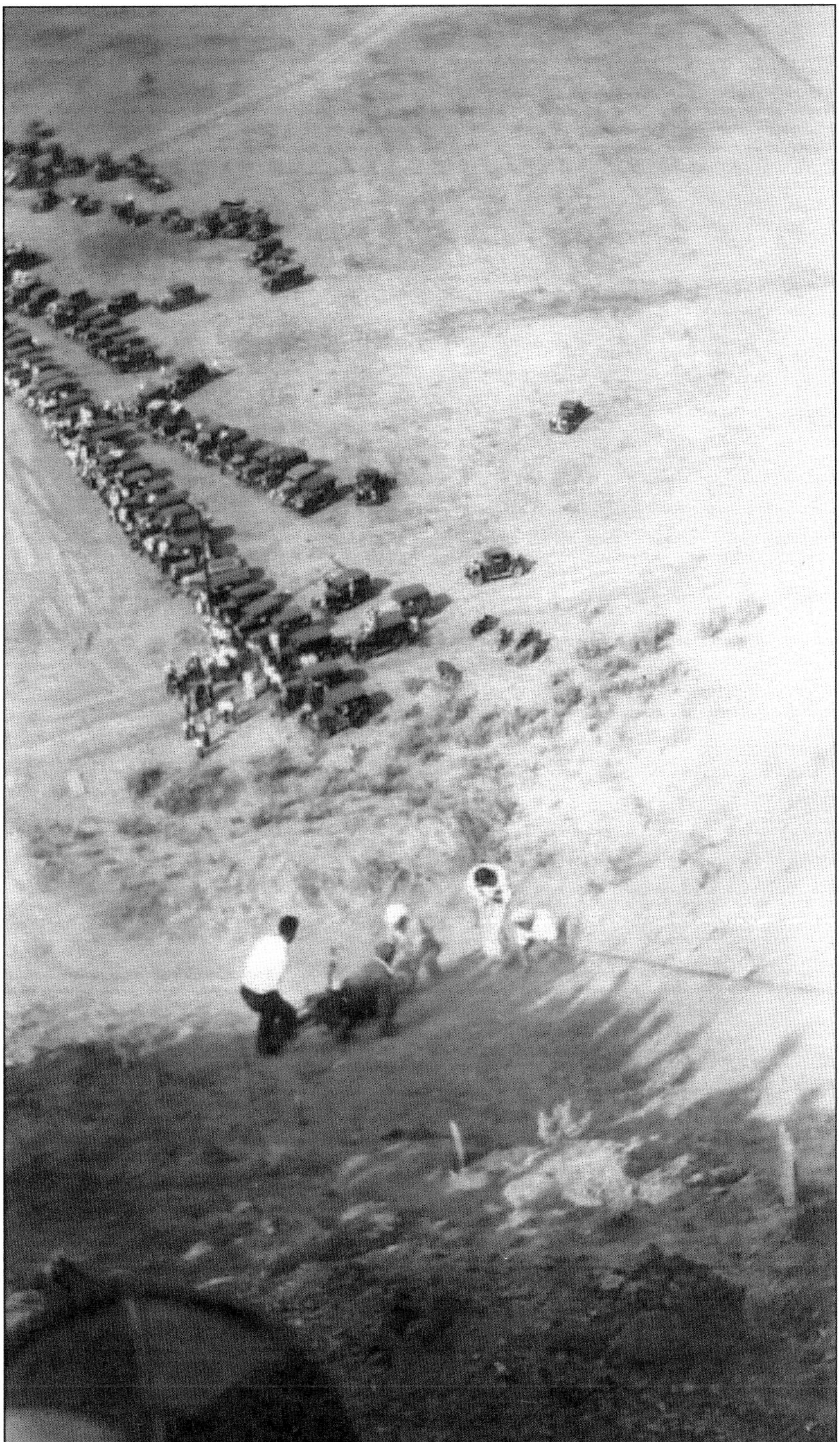

Myron Erb watches from above as a hill climb competitor crashes while attempting a run up the South Hill near Billings. (Courtesy of Allison Nys.)

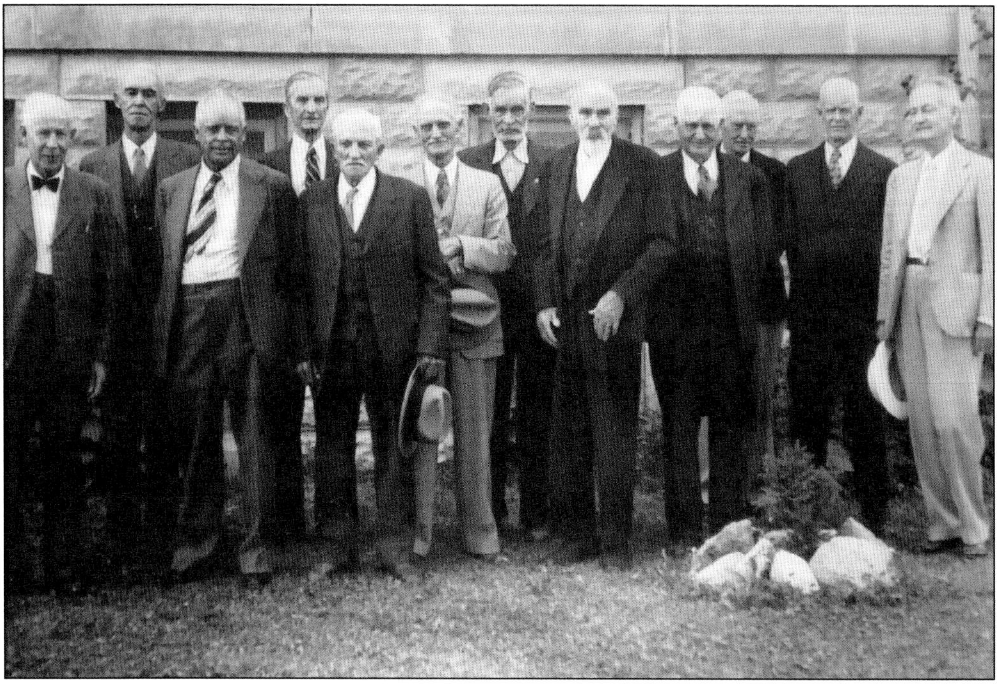

Several prominent men of the area gathered to reminisce at the Laurel Methodist Church in 1938. From left to right are Edwin Fenton, Thomas Armitage, Lucius Nutting, I.D. (Ignatius) O'Donnell, John Coombs, T.L. (Theodore) Wilkins, George Danford, Charles Rugg, Ben Lamb, Owen Young, Melvin Shay, and George Hays. (Photograph by Harold Van Nice; courtesy of Gerald Shay.)

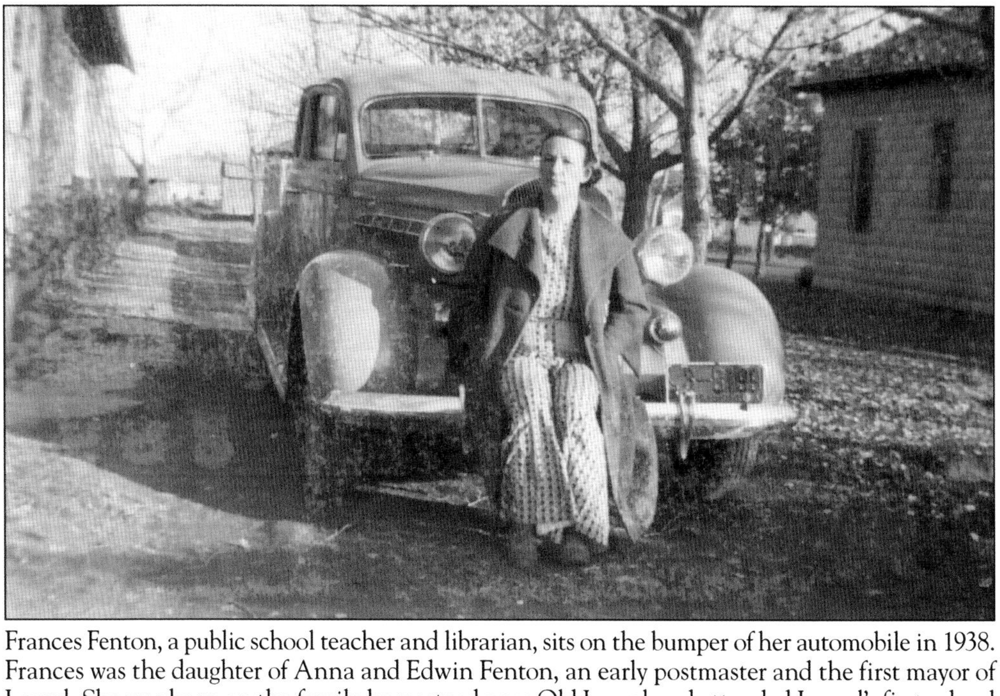

Frances Fenton, a public school teacher and librarian, sits on the bumper of her automobile in 1938. Frances was the daughter of Anna and Edwin Fenton, an early postmaster and the first mayor of Laurel. She was born on the family homestead near Old Laurel and attended Laurel's first school before the community moved to the new townsite. (Courtesy of the Laurel Public Library.)

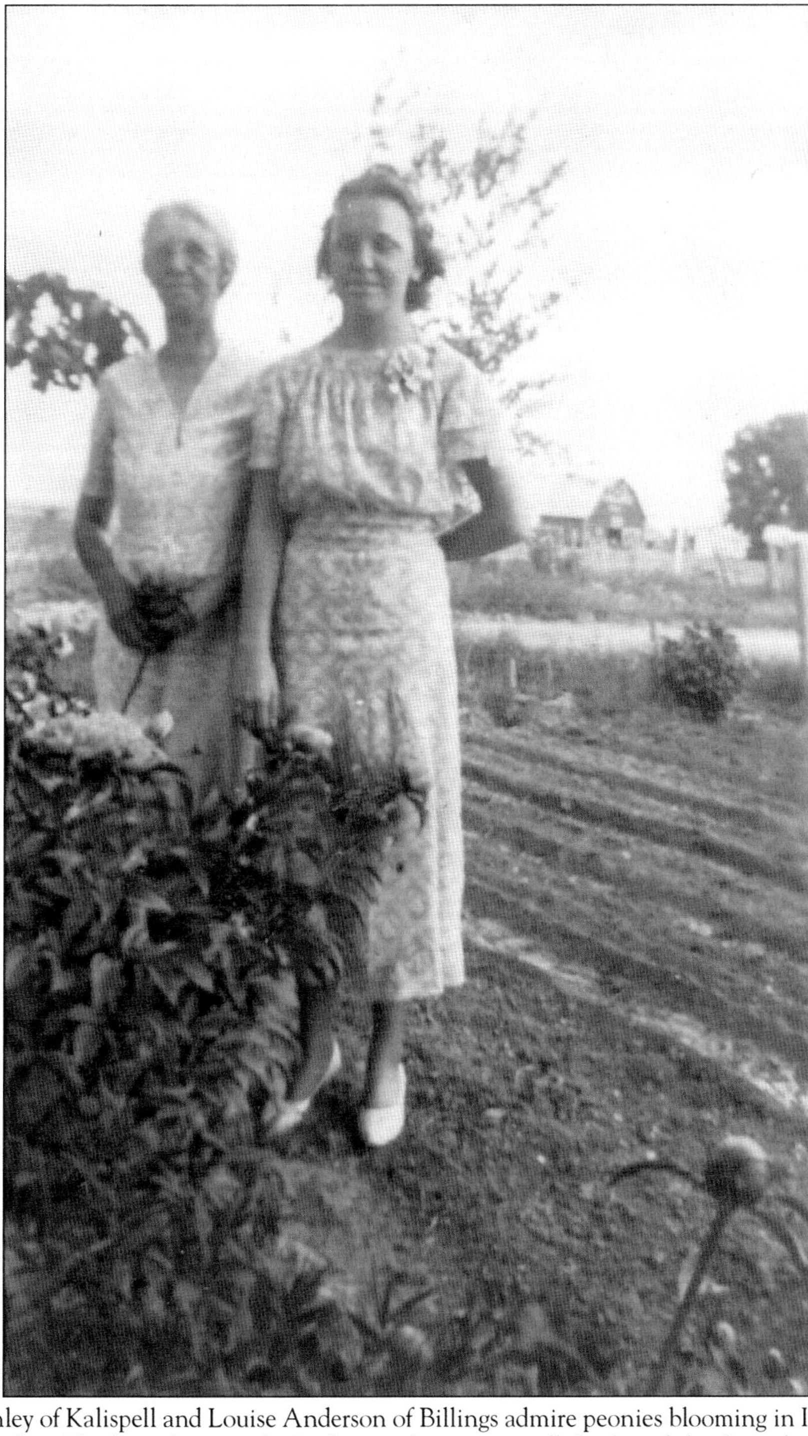

Edna Finley of Kalispell and Louise Anderson of Billings admire peonies blooming in Iris Shay's flower garden. The horse barn in the background was reportedly built with lumber salvaged from a former dormitory at Father Shevlin's orphanage. After the Shays mechanized their farm in the 1940s, Iris's sons converted the hayloft into a basketball court so that they and their friends from neighboring farms could play ball year-round. (Courtesy of Gerald Shay.)

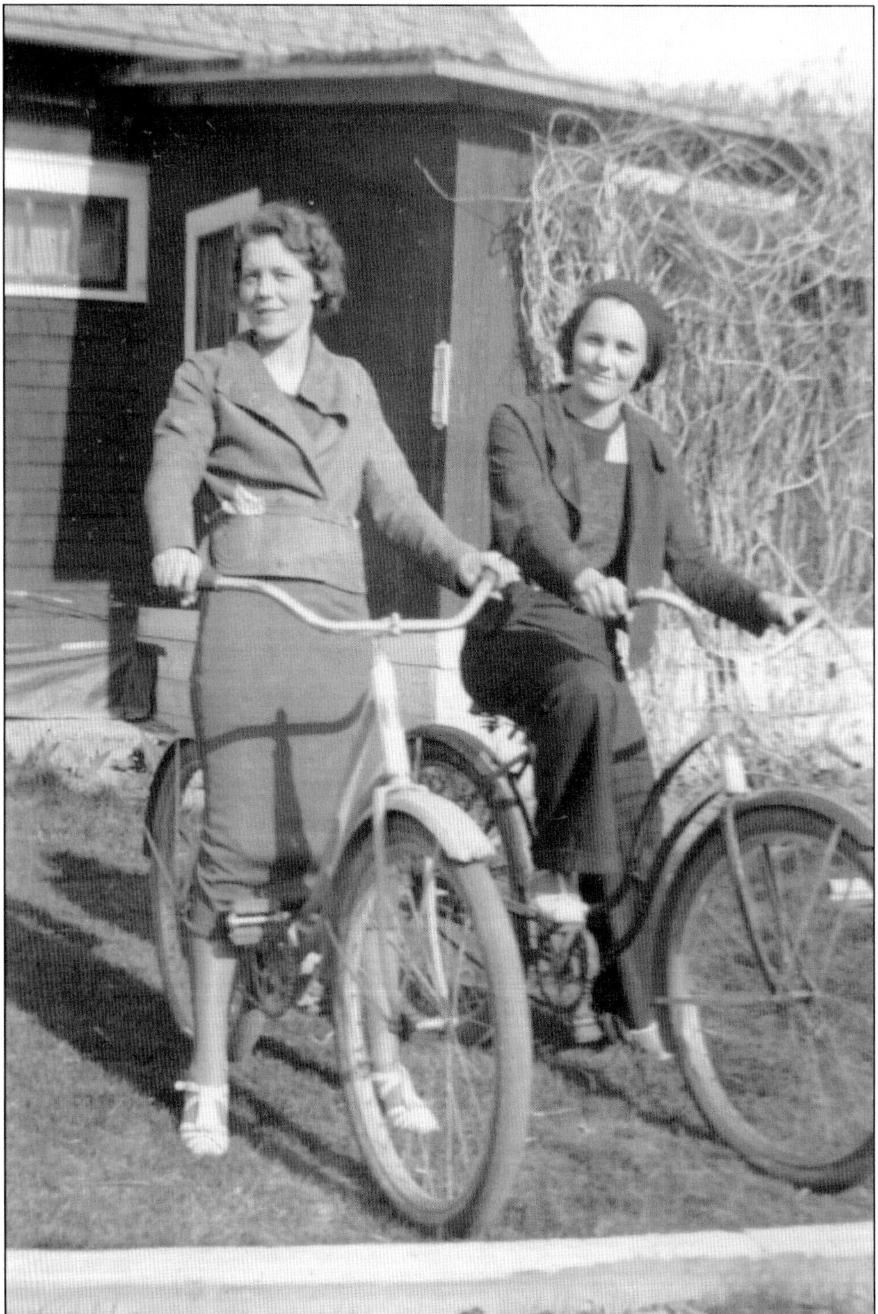

Rachel Scheidecker, left, and Frances Beslanwitch pause for a photograph on their bicycles in 1937. Rachel, the outgoing president of the American Legion Auxiliary, passed the torch of service to Frances, the newly elected president, that year. Both women were dedicated members of the American Legion Auxiliary, an organization committed to honoring veterans. Local women organized projects to assist with wartime Red Cross and USO efforts and promoted Victory gardens. They also cared for hospitalized and disabled veterans and sold paper poppies to fund community services. (Courtesy of the Laurel Public Library.)

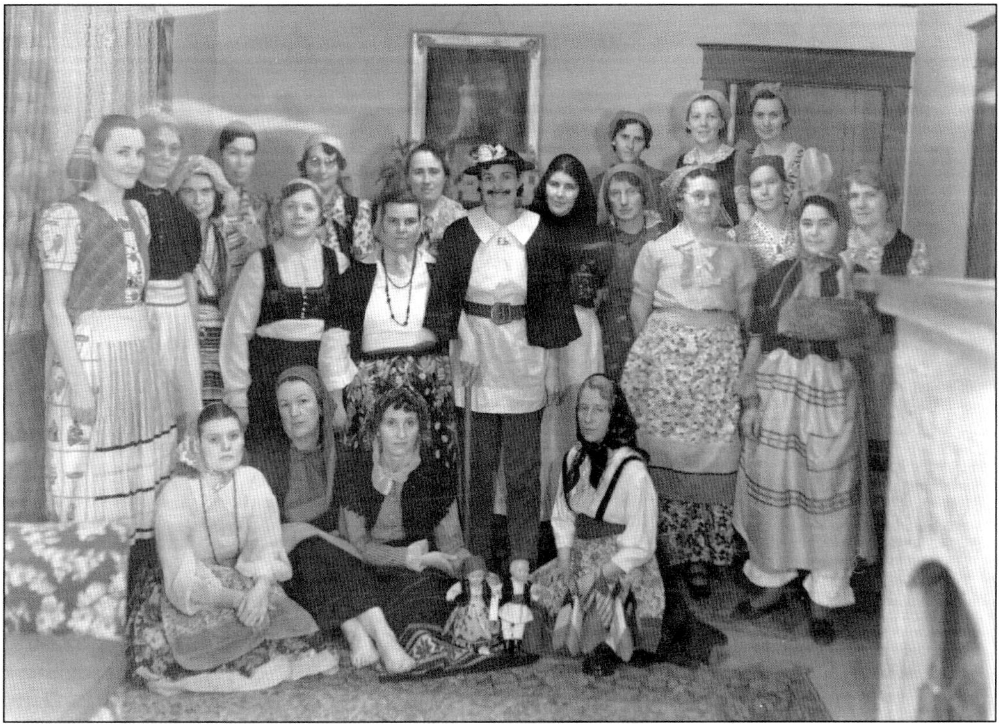

Ladies of the American Legion Auxiliary donned costumes for a Romanian-themed tea party at president Jennie Starkey's home in 1939. At right, a group of young musicians entertain the guests. (Both, courtesy of the Laurel Public Library.)

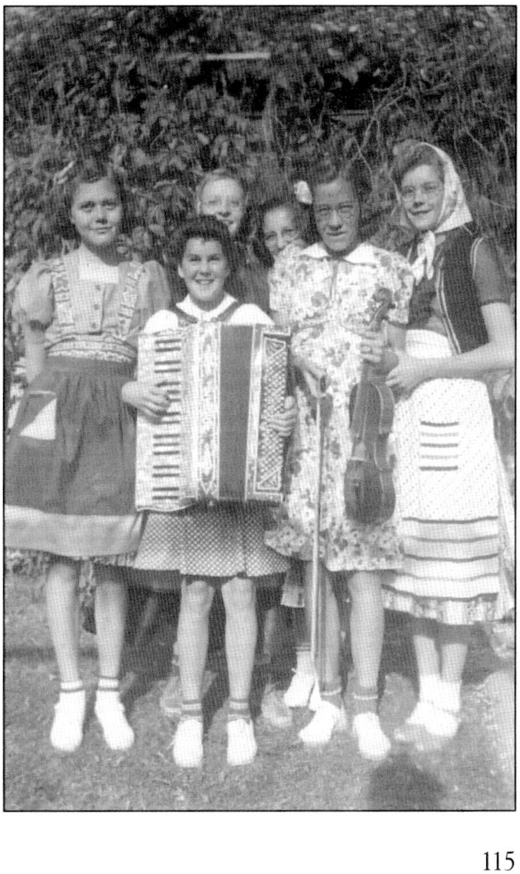

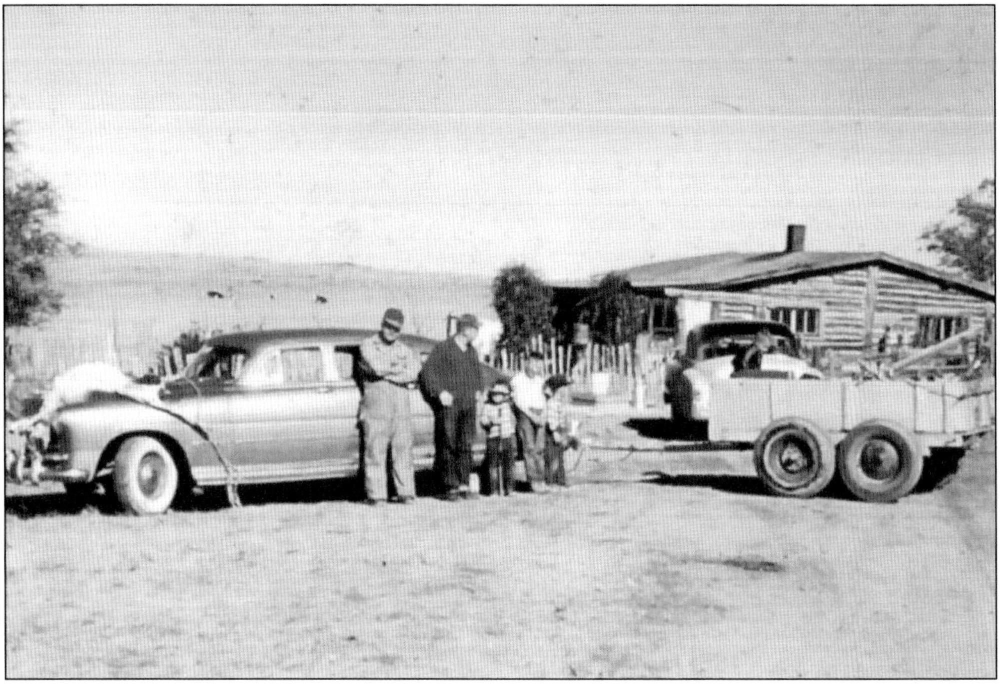

A deer is strapped to the hood of Karl George's car after a successful hunt near Laurel. (Courtesy of Vance George.)

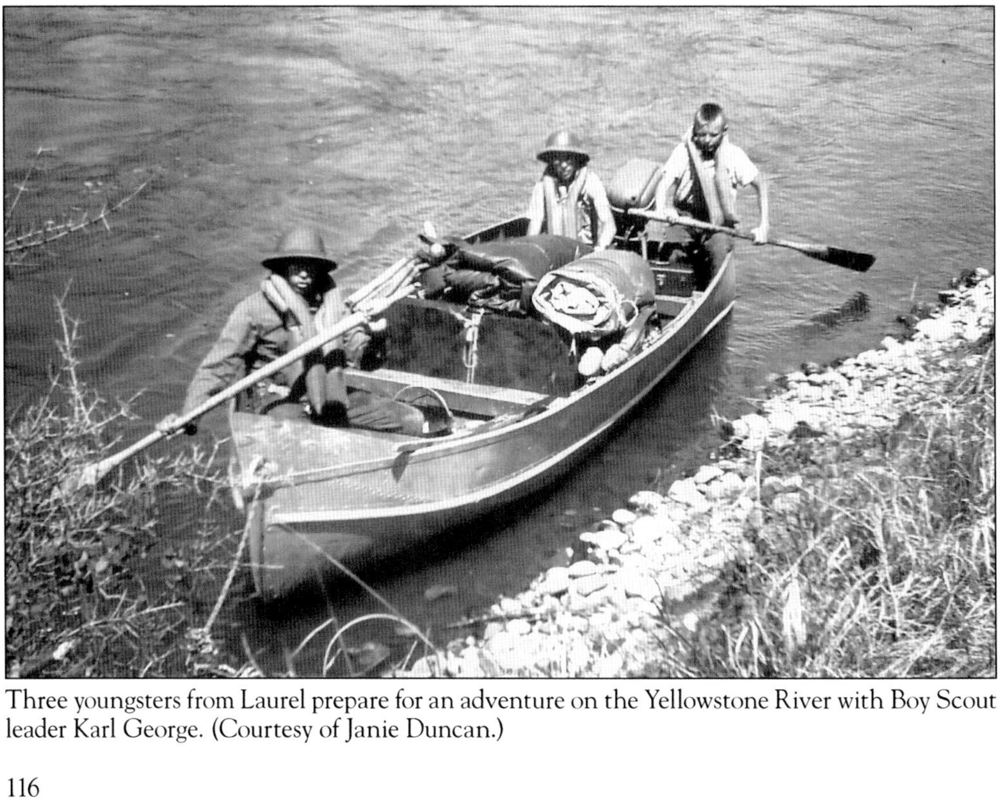

Three youngsters from Laurel prepare for an adventure on the Yellowstone River with Boy Scout leader Karl George. (Courtesy of Janie Duncan.)

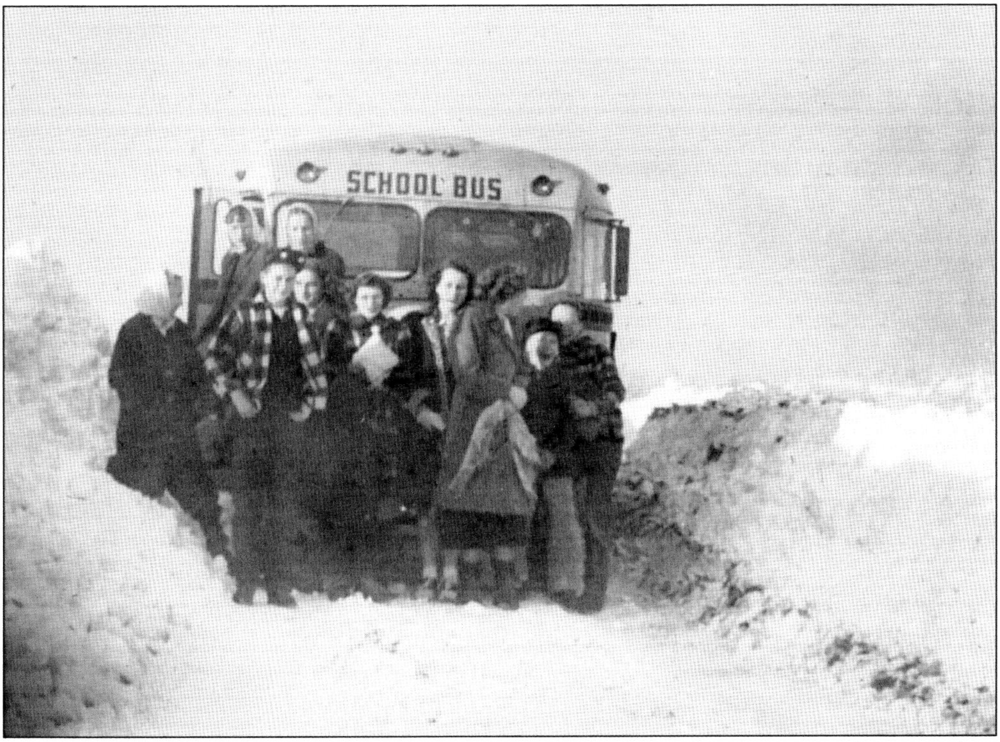

A bus driver captures the excitement of school children after a heavy snow around 1945. Robert and Maxine Boyd, both wearing plaid, stand next to each other in front of the bus. (Courtesy of Maxine Allman.)

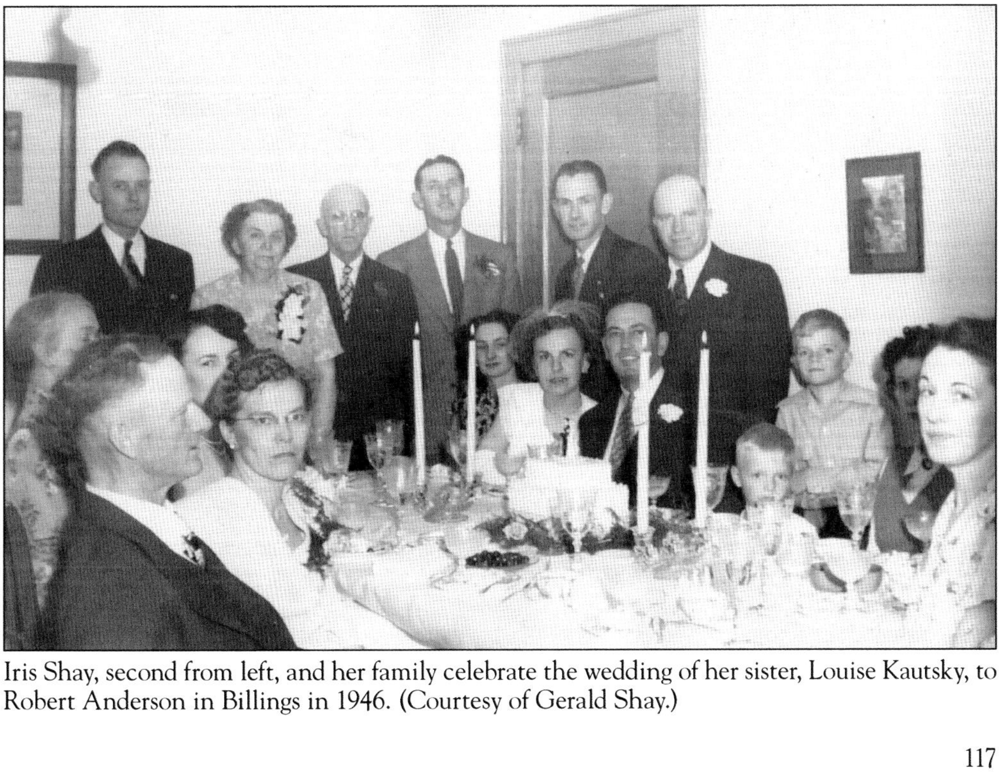
Iris Shay, second from left, and her family celebrate the wedding of her sister, Louise Kautsky, to Robert Anderson in Billings in 1946. (Courtesy of Gerald Shay.)

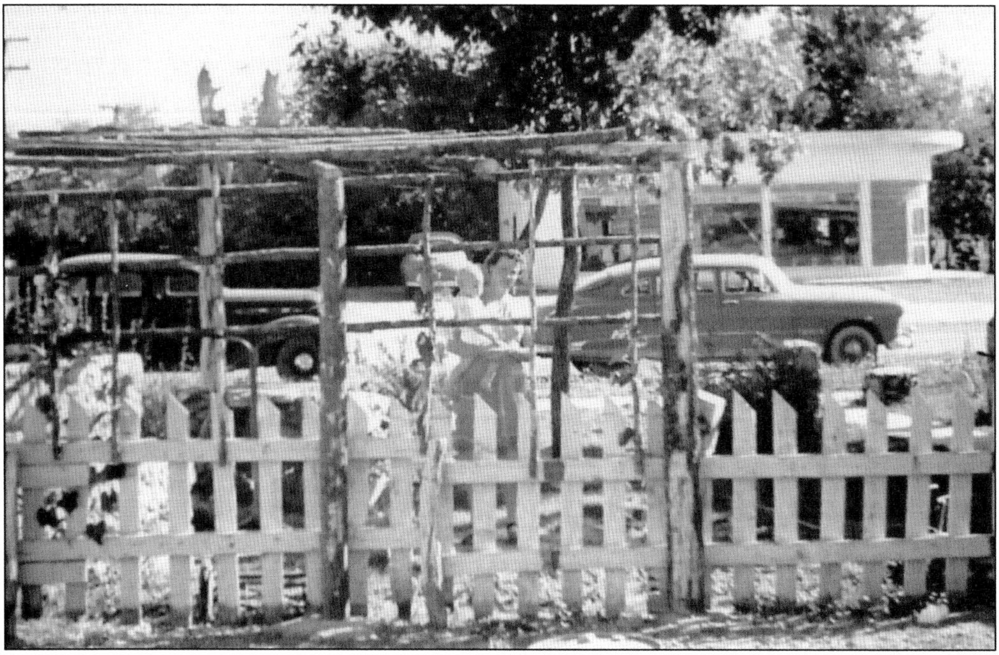

Karl George photographed his wife, Hallie George, through the grape arbor outside their home in the early 1950s. Hallie, who is holding their infant daughter Janie, was a longtime member of the Laurel Garden Club. Karl owned George's Photo Lab and Studio. He also belonged to the Laurel Camera Club, a group that took turns giving home slide shows of their travel adventures. (Courtesy of Janie Duncan.)

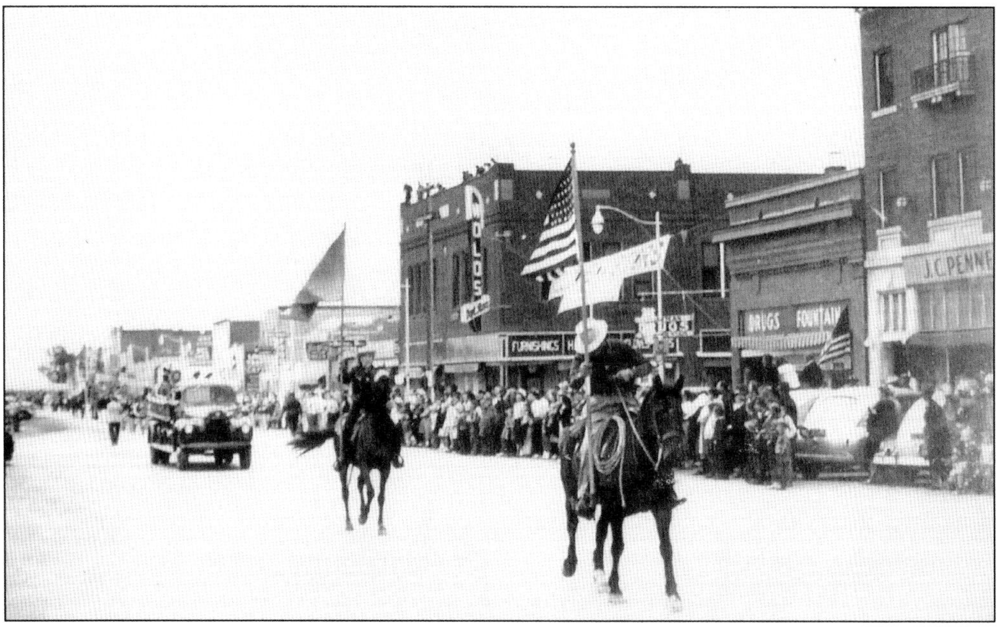

A mounted flag bearer leads the Fourth of July parade down Main Street in the 1940s. The Independence Day parade and firework show have long been an annual tradition in the Laurel community. Laurel Saddle Club riders have regularly participated in the festivities since the club organized in 1945. (Courtesy of the Laurel Museum.)

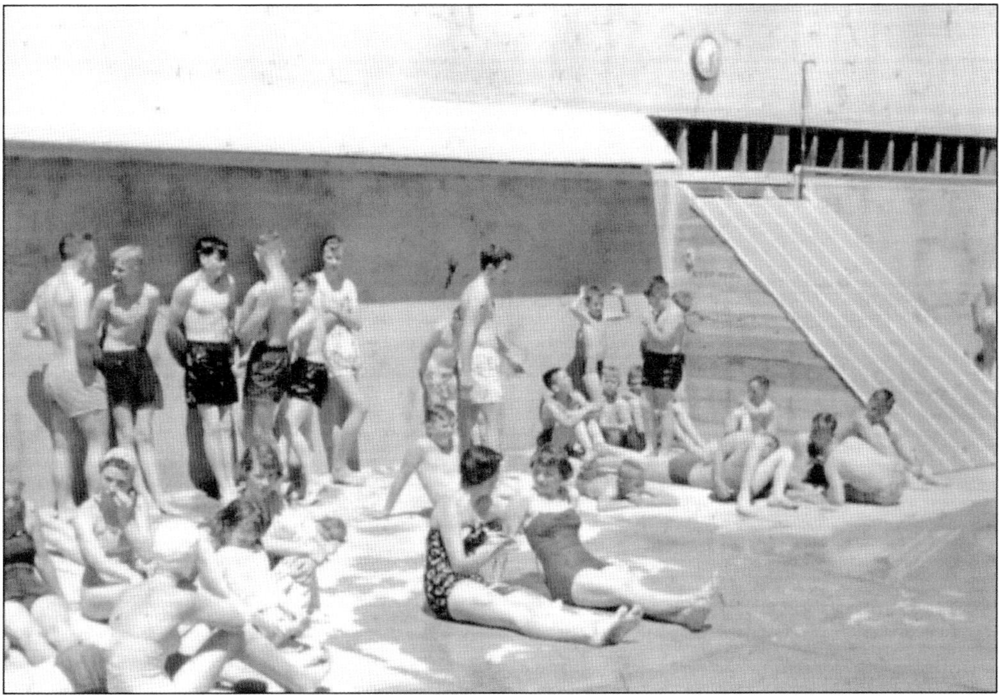

Laurel youth spend a summer afternoon at the city pool. A bequest from Ruth Nutting, a local school teacher and postmistress, funded construction of the pool in 1949 in what is now known as Thomson Park. (Courtesy of Vance George.)

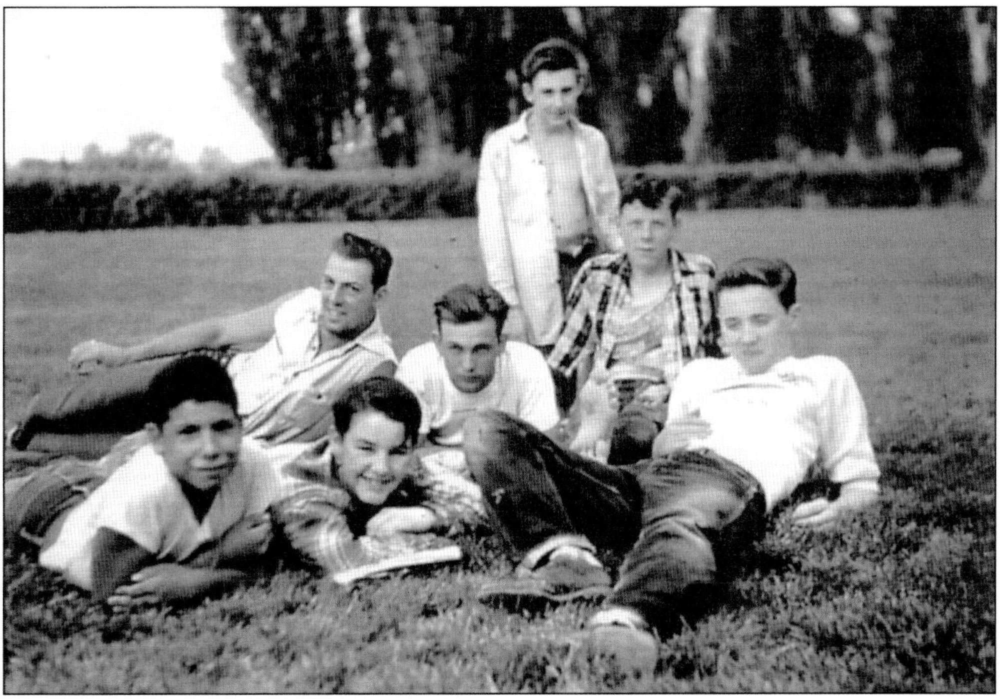

Friends of Eugene George lounge in the city park in the 1950s. (Courtesy of Vance George.)

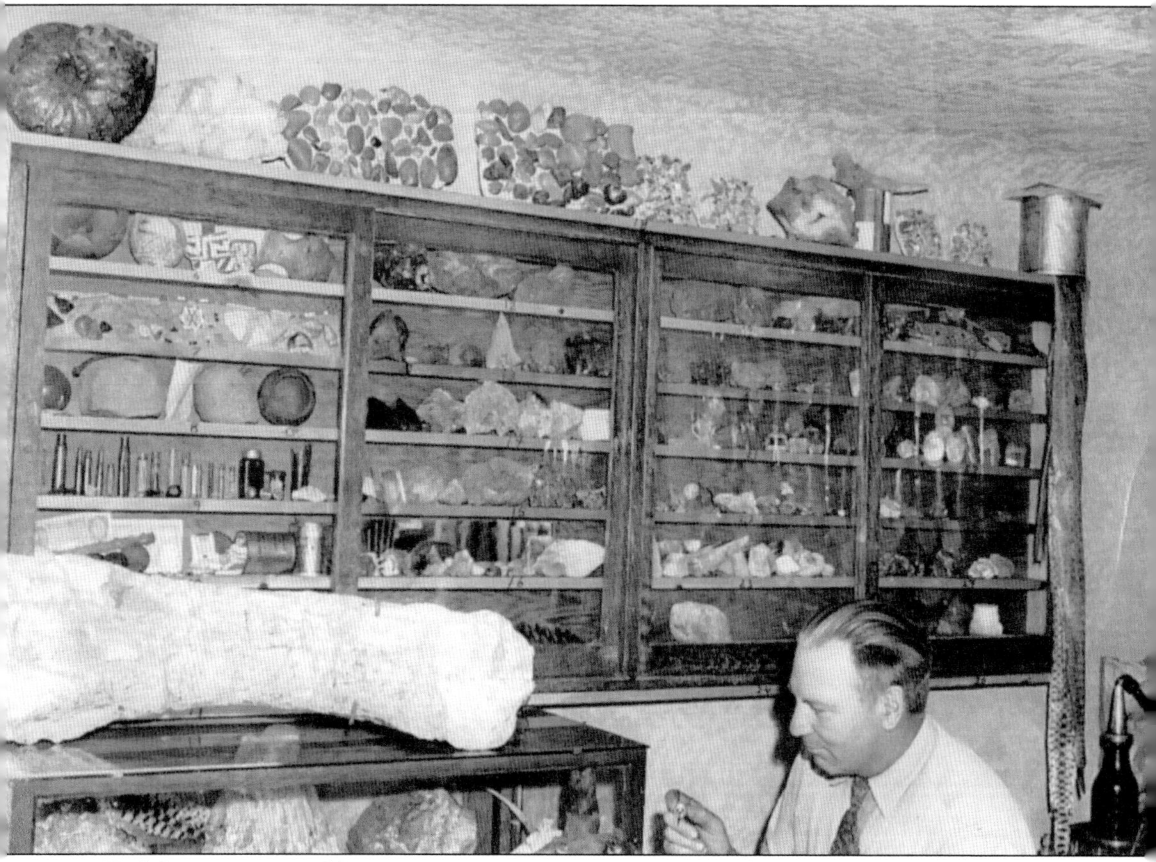

Karl George, owner of George's Tower Service Station, amassed an impressive collection of rocks and fossils that he preserved in a private museum at the office in his gas station. He discovered a 150-million-year-old Stegosaurus femur in 1938 in northern Wyoming, a find featured on National Geographic's *America's Lost Treasures* in 2012. Karl also discovered half of a large fossilized sea snail, seen on top of the shelf, on one of his rock hunting outings. In an unlikely turn of events, he met another rock hound with the missing half years later. Karl traded a third of his collection for the ammonite piece in 1943 and drove the restored fossil, wrapped in blankets, across the country to the Smithsonian Institution where he was told that it was the sixth largest fossil of its kind in the world. (Courtesy of Janie Duncan.)

Six

FAMOUS FACES AND LITTLE-KNOWN PLACES

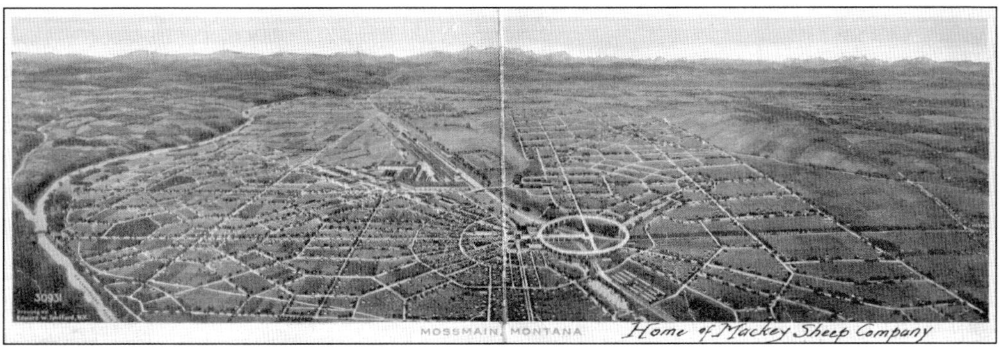

Billings entrepreneur Preston Boyd Moss envisioned developing a utopian garden city, called Mossmain, two miles east of Laurel at the junction of the Northern Pacific and Great Northern Railroads. He commissioned world-renowned architect Walter Burley Griffin in 1914 to design Mossmain with parks, community gardens, and small, irrigated farm tracts fanning out from the city center. Mossmain failed to attract investors, and its development was derailed by a statewide economic slump following World War I. Pictured is a promotional sketch of Mossmain, drawn by New York artist Edward W. Spofford. (Courtesy of the Western Heritage Center.)

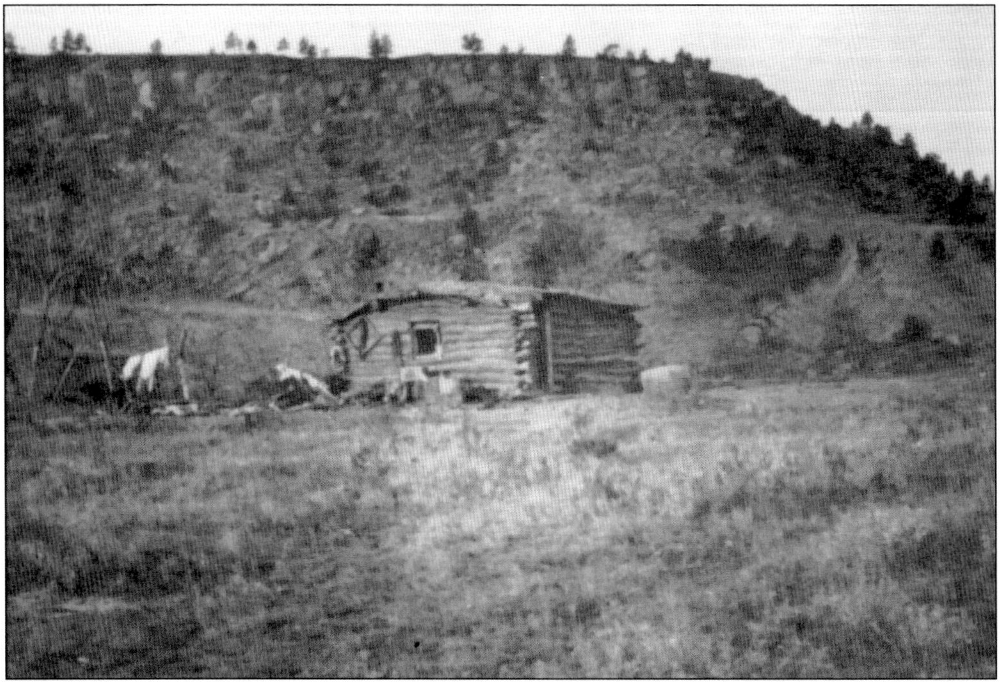

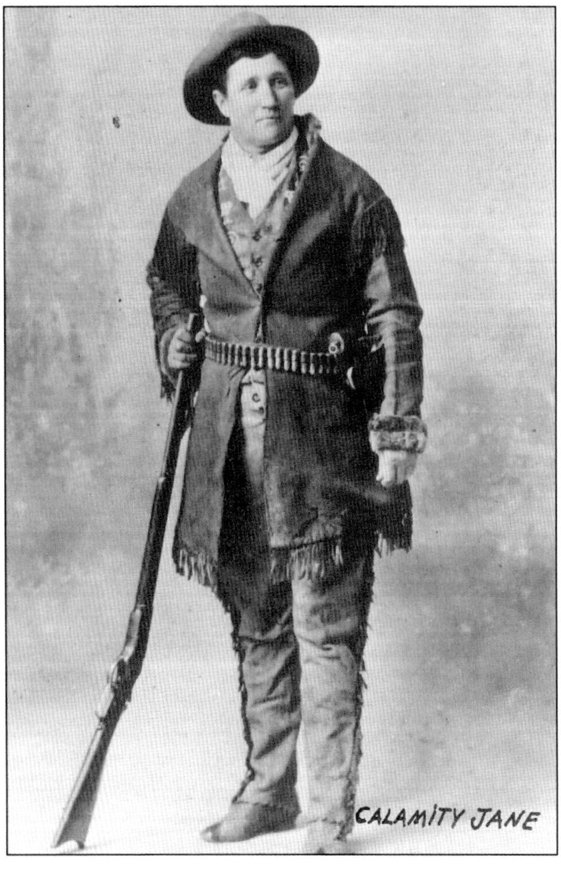

At Canyon Creek once stood Calamity Jane's rustic cabin and corrals. The legendary frontierswoman was known for her rough-riding, pistol-toting, whiskey-swilling ways in the mining camps and railroad towns of Montana and the Dakotas. She settled north of Laurel at Canyon Creek in 1882 and lived there off and on for nearly two decades. (Courtesy of the Western Heritage Center.)

Local lore offers an earthier version of Calamity Jane's life than the tales of her exploits as a Pony Express rider and Army scout, fueled by dime novels and a short spell in Buffalo Bill's Wild West Show. Locals knew her as a hardworking wife and mother who broke horses, cut and sold fence posts, and cooked for travelers at the Canyon Creek stage stop. (Courtesy of the Billings Public Library.)

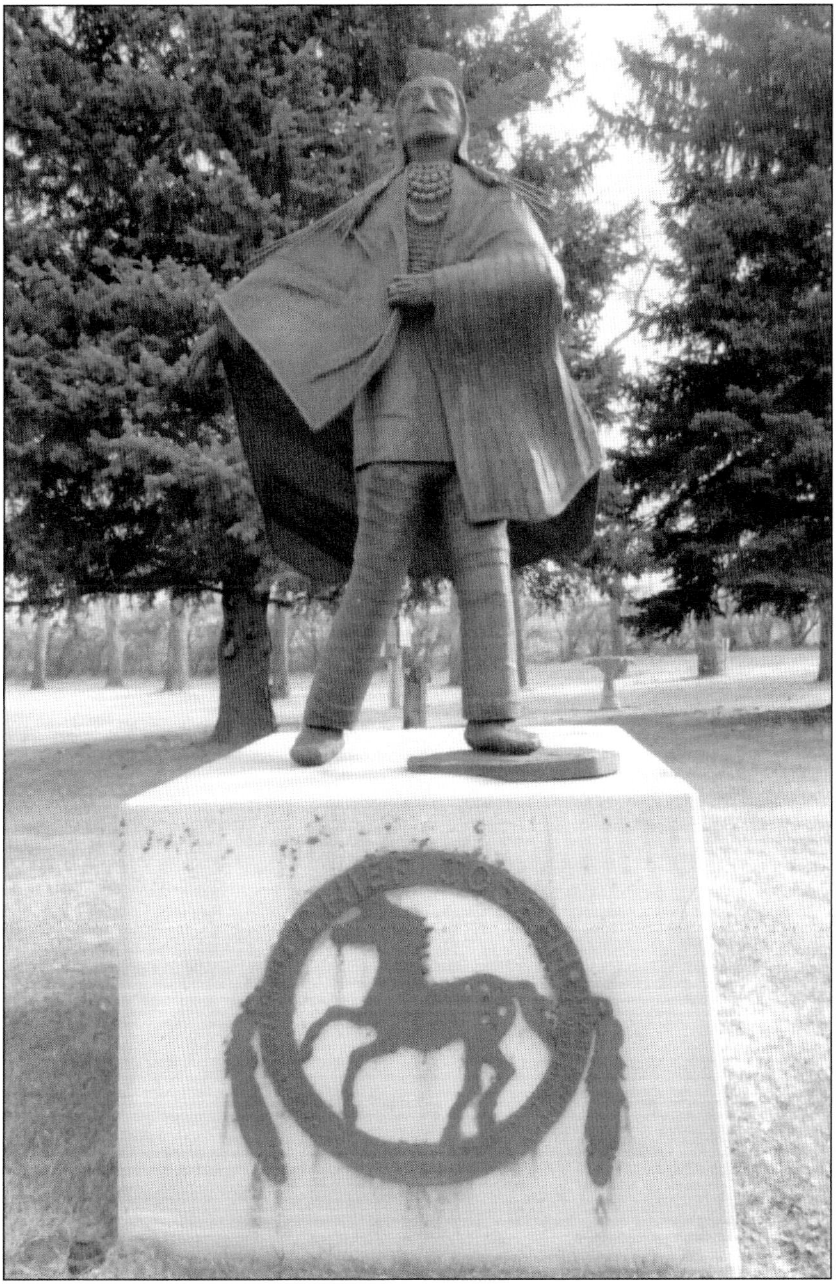

The Indian Wars of the late 1800s left an indelible mark on the history of the Yellowstone River Valley. Canyon Creek, seven miles north of Laurel, was the site of a skirmish between the Nez Perce Indians and the 7th Cavalry on September 13, 1877. The conflict began in June of that year when five chiefs, among them famed Chief Joseph, fled with their people for Canada in defiance of a military order to remove the Nez Perce from their homeland in northeast Oregon to a reservation in Idaho. The 1,170-mile trek took them from Oregon to Montana's Big Hole Valley, south through Yellowstone Park, and north again to the Bear Paw Mountains where, on October 5, the battered and weary band surrendered to Col. Nelson Miles. (Photograph by Lilly Kooistra-Manning.)

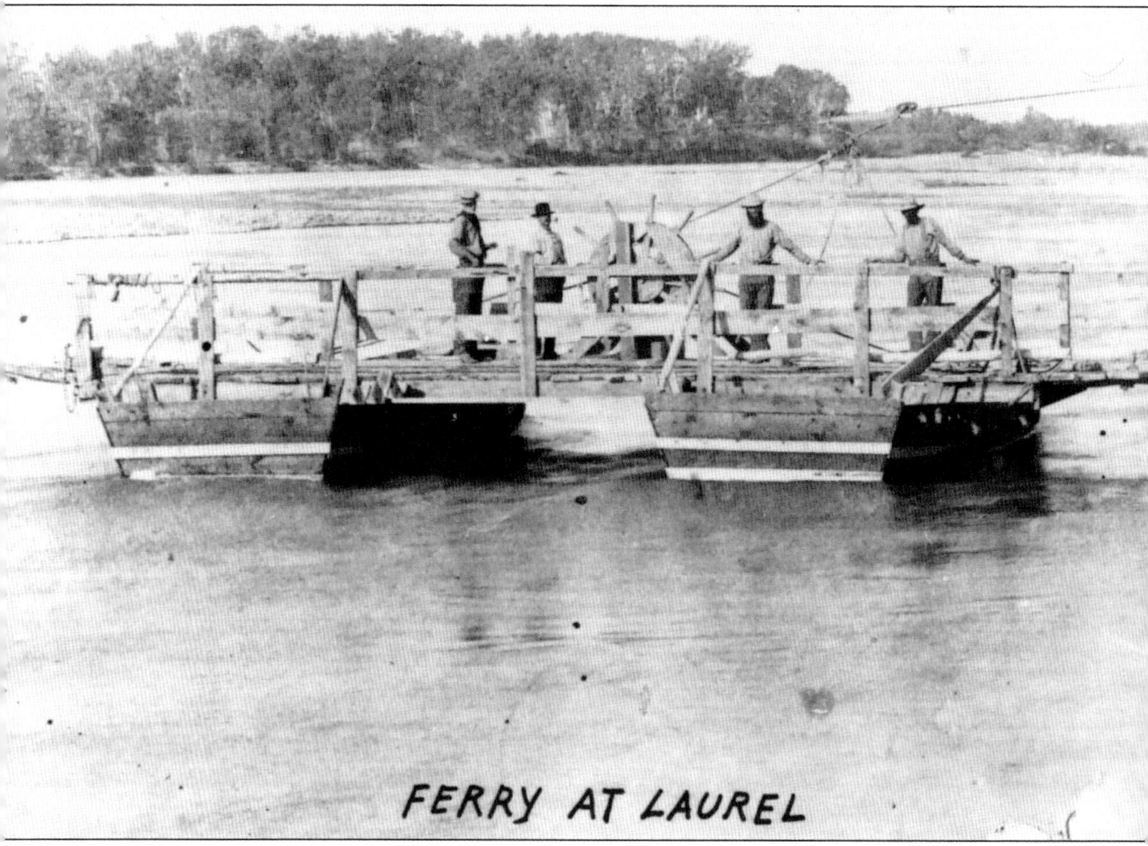

O.C. Bundy's ferry made headlines in 1888 when Undersheriff Charles Reed nabbed Teton Jackson, a notorious horse thief and murderer, and his accomplice with 58 stolen horses near the ferry landing. The accomplice, released shortly after his arrest, was shot in the head during a scuffle with Deputy Jack Hurley while trying to retrieve some of the stolen horses. Authorities remanded Teton Jackson to Idaho, where he had escaped prison two years before. (Courtesy of the Western Heritage Center.)

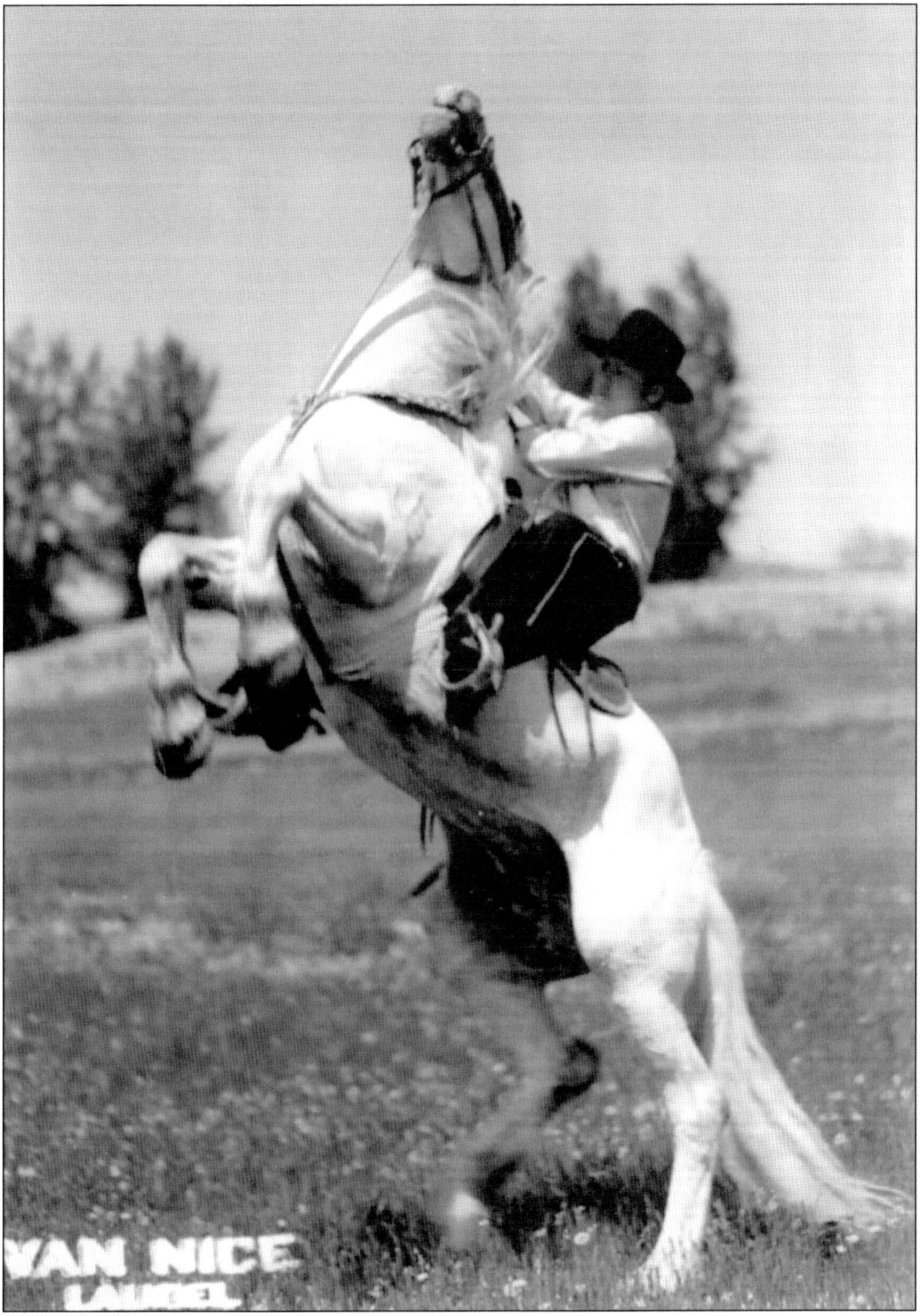

Elroy Gilles became a national sensation at age 18 when he set off from Laurel on horseback for the 1940 World's Fair in New York. He financed the 121-day, 2,300-mile trip by selling autographed postcards of himself clad in classic cowboy attire astride Shamrock, his rearing white Arabian steed. (Photograph by Harold Van Nice; courtesy of T.J. Gilles.)

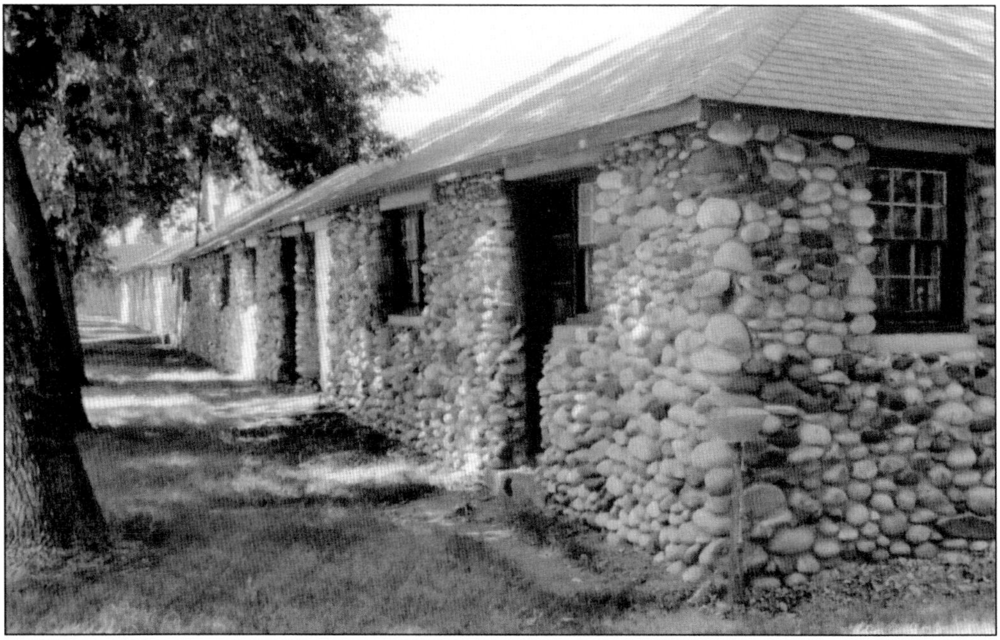

A shortage of farmworkers during World War II prompted the American government to hire out German and Italian prisoners-of-war as farm laborers. Temporary work camps were set up throughout the country, including one at Riverside Park in Laurel. Cobblestone buildings, constructed by the Civilian Conservation Corps in the 1930s and used by the Laurel Rifle Club and Boy Scouts before the war, were converted into prison barracks. (Photograph by Ann Kooistra-Manning.)

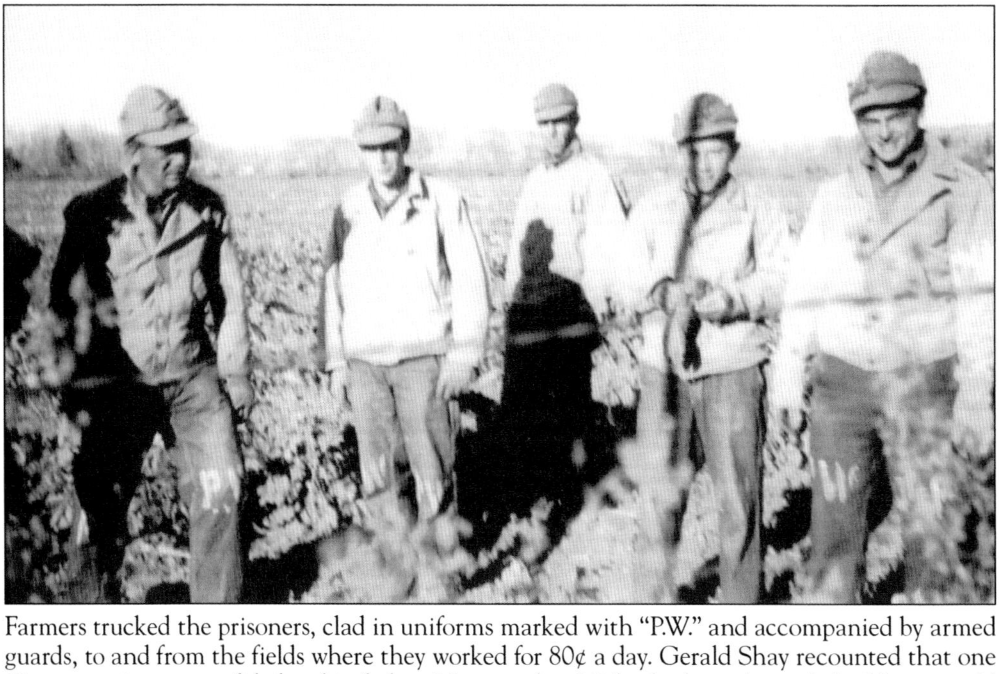

Farmers trucked the prisoners, clad in uniforms marked with "P.W." and accompanied by armed guards, to and from the fields where they worked for 80¢ a day. Gerald Shay recounted that one German prisoner confided to his father, Vinton, that Hitler had proclaimed the Nazis would march across America, but he never expected to do it on his hands and knees, thinning sugar beets. (Courtesy of Dorothy Sitzman.)

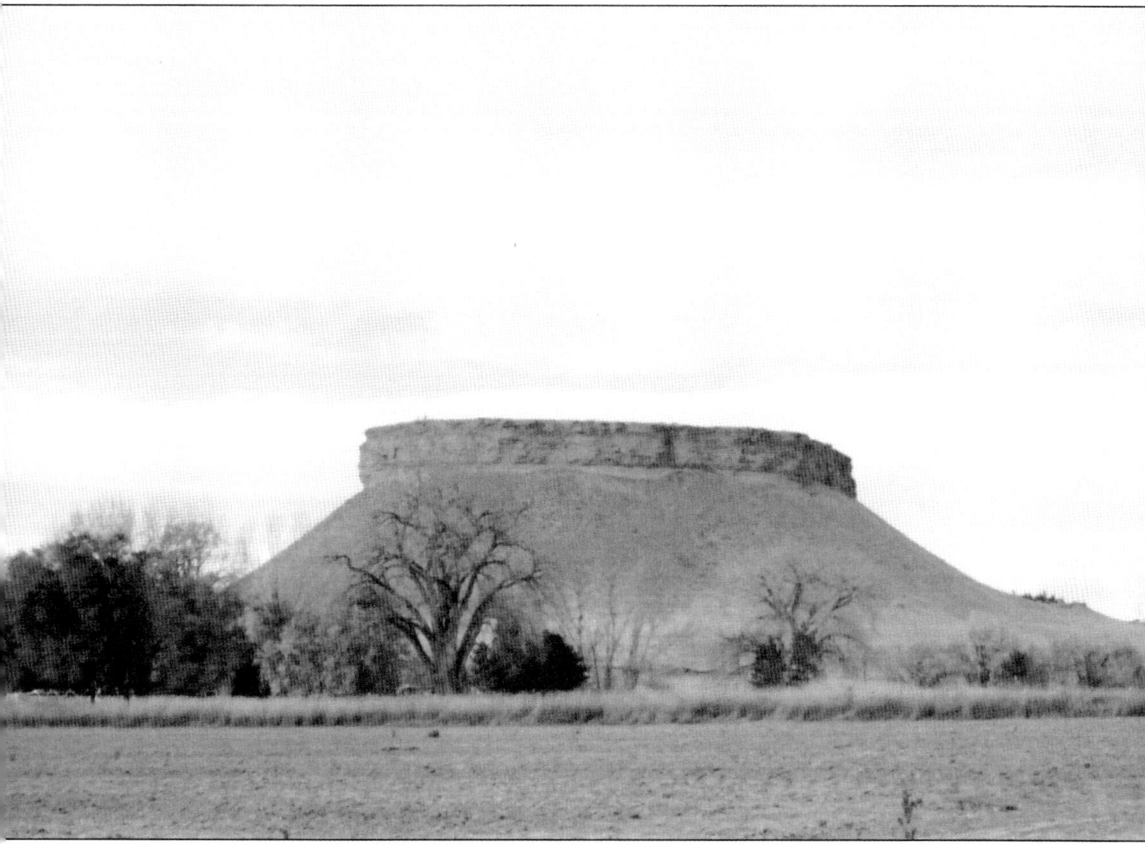

Square Butte is an imposing landmark that rises from the prairie about four miles west of Laurel. The historical Native American vantage point gained notoriety in 1925 when the Ku Klux Klan staged a rally at the butte and lit up the night sky with a burning cross. Two years later, the *Laurel Outlook* reported that a large group of hooded Klansmen, who had been seen elsewhere in Montana trying to garner support, appeared at the Methodist church during Reverend Shively's evening service. The Klansmen left before the service ended, and the reverend took the opportunity to deliver a sermon on patriotism and worship tempered by conscience. In 1953, the Laurel Methodist Church erected a large cross atop the sandstone butte, which local residents light at Christmas and Easter. (Photograph by Lilly Kooistra-Manning.)